*From Politics to Profit:
The Commercialization of Canadian
Newspapers, 1890–1920*

Describing a decisive period in the evolution of mass communication in Canada, Minko Sotiron documents the development of the Canadian newspaper from a political mouthpiece in the nineteenth century to a profit-driven industry in the twentieth.

Sotiron describes how, in their drive to maximize profits, publishers abandoned partisan politics and adopted sensationalistic journalism to build audiences for advertisers. He analyses the changes newspapers underwent in both content and appearance as the number of "fluff" pieces increased and hard news stories decreased, headlines became larger, prose became simpler, and illustrations and photographs became more abundant.

From Politics to Profit highlights the increasingly powerful role of the press barons – Lord Atholstan, John Ross Robertson, Joseph Atkinson, Walter Nichol, Clifford Sifton, and the Southam family. Sotiron provides a case study of the first Canadian newspaper chain, which formed the basis for modern mass communication empires, and shows how the Southams contributed to the disappearance of independent newspapers in Canada.

MINKO SOTIRON is professor of history, John Abbott College.

From Politics to Profit

The Commercialization of Canadian Daily Newspapers, 1890–1920

MINKO SOTIRON

McGill-Queen's University Press
Montreal & Kingston · London · Ithaca

© McGill-Queen's University Press 1997
ISBN 0-7735-1875-2 (cloth)
ISBN 0-7735-3063-0 (paper)

Legal deposit first quarter 1997
Bibliothèque nationale du Québec

Printed in Canada on acid-free paper
First paperback edition 2005

McGill-Queen's University Press acknowledges the support of the Canada Council for the Arts for our publishing program. We also acknowledge the financial support of the Government of Canada through the Book Publishing Industry Development Program (BPIDP) for our publishing activities.

Canadian Cataloguing in Publication Data

Sotiron, Minko, 1945–
  From politics to profits: the commercialization of
Canadian daily newspapers, 1890–1920
  Includes bibliographical references and index.
  ISBN 0-7735-1875-2 (bnd)
  ISBN 0-7735-3063-0 (pbk)
  1. Canadian newspapers – History. 2. Journalism –
Canada – History. I. Title.
  III. Forum des fédérations
  PN4908.S68 1997   071'.1'09   C96-900872-4

Typeset in New Baskerville 10/12
by Chris McDonell, Hawkline Graphics.

*To my mother, Ehrentraut Sotiron,
who always believed in me*

Contents

Acknowledgments ix

Introduction 3

1 Public Myth and Private Reality 10

2 Big Business 23

3 Publisher Power and the Rise of the Business Manager 39

4 It Pays to Advertise 52

5 Competition and Collusion 70

6 Concentration 93

7 Patronage and Independence 106

8 Joining the Élite 125

9 Interest Politics 136

Conclusion 156

Notes 163

Bibliography 193

Index 211

Acknowledgments

I wish to thank my wife Suzanne Marcotte for her unfailing support and help in completing this work. For their constructive criticism of the original research, I wish to express my gratitude to Professors Mary Vipond, Graham Carr, and Enn Raudsepp. I am grateful to my two children, Véronique and Jean-Michel, for cheerfully putting up with their distracted father.

From Politics to Profit

Introduction

In 1970 the Senate Special Committee on the Mass Media (the Davey Committee) warned that ownership of daily newspapers was becoming concentrated in fewer and fewer hands. Ten years later another federal inquiry, the Royal Commission on Newspapers (the Kent Commission), confirmed the Davey Committee's observations when it concluded that "concentration engulfs Canadian daily newspaper publishing." Both bodies cautioned that concentration of newspaper ownership led to a decrease in the variety of news and views in the daily publications and thus threatened the public's right to freedom of expression, which they equated with freedom of the press.

Canada was not alone in its concern. The United States and the United Kingdom also established special commissions to investigate the effect of concentration of newspaper ownership on freedom of the press. The issue was, and is, important because freedom of the press is widely considered to be a fundamental civil liberty. Newspapers, many believe, have a social responsibility that makes them unlike other commercial undertakings. In the words of the Kent Commission, "freedom of the press is not a property right of owners. It is a right of the people. It is part of their right to inform themselves."[1]

Yet this right to inform themselves was threatened by what the Davey Committee observed was the newspapers' "apparently irresistible tendency" to merge into larger and larger economic units. The Kent Commission alluded to a "rationalization" of Canadian newspaper ownership that had promoted the "establishment of one-newspaper markets during the past 100 years."[2] Since these reports were issued, the situation has grown worse. Today there are no independent daily newspapers in Canada; all are controlled by chains or conglomerates.

A century ago the Canadian newspaper world was competitive and diverse. Newspapers proliferated during the latter half of the nineteenth century: most cities, and even some smaller centres, had two, if not more. Toronto, with approximately 182,000 residents in 1892, had seven daily newspapers, reflecting every political stripe. What has happened during the last hundred years to reduce the flourishing newspaper markets of the late Victorian era to one-newspaper, chain-controlled towns? How did the Canadian daily press become so concentrated? Who was responsible for the changes in the newspaper business? The answers lie in the period from 1890 to 1920, when among other things, a rapidly expanding urban population, increased literacy, the economic boom of the Laurier era, and a growing national market for consumer goods contributed to the profitability of new newspaper ventures. This period in Canadian history marked the transition from the politically oriented newspaper of the nineteenth century to the corporate entity of the twentieth.

One reason newspapers abounded in the 1890s was that they were so easy to start: all that was needed, according to Manitoba *Free Press* editor J.W. Dafoe, was a "handful of type, a printer and a 'slashing' writer."[3] The last was essential because the editorial page, the backbone of the nineteenth-century newspaper, needed a skilled writer who could stir up controversy and attack the newspaper's political enemies. The nineteenth century had a long tradition of aspiring politicians, from George Brown to Wilfrid Laurier, who used the editorial page to gain entry into Parliament and acquire political influence. Publishers tended to be editors first and entrepreneurs second. For the most part they managed small, financially unstable enterprises that acted as spokesmen for, and were largely dependent on, the support of a particular political party. In 1883 the Montreal *Gazette*'s Thomas White said that "no man has made a fortune of newspaper enterprise in this country, while a great deal of money has been sunk in the attempt to maintain it."[4] By the 1920s, however, that had changed as financial considerations, not political ones, came to dominate the newspaper business.

In contrast to the capital-intensive nature of newspaper publishing in the twentieth century, nineteenth-century newspapers, as Dafoe's remarks showed, required no large capital expenditures. For most of the nineteenth century the layout and content of Canadian newspapers resembled that of the four-page Toronto *Globe* in 1844. Page one usually offered lengthy non-political articles lifted from the British and American press and, when the British and Canadian parliaments were in session, dense, almost verbatim reports of the debates. Page two, the most important page, contained the editorials. Page three presented "commercial intelligence," snippets from the foreign press. The advertisements were found on page four. By 1865 not much had changed, except that there were more advertisements and they were found on more pages.[5] Circulation figures for daily newspapers ranged from a few hundred to a few thousand. The only Canadian daily of some size and complexity was the Toronto *Globe*, which had a circulation of 20,200 in 1872.[6] It was only at the end of the century that newspaper circulations rose dramatically, the leader in this regard being the Montreal *Star*, the first Canadian mass circulation penny daily, with 52,600 readers in 1899.[7]

Until the 1890s newspaper operations were usually modest even in the largest cities, and this was reflected in news coverage and in the number of people they employed. A commentator on the two Vancouver newspapers of the 1890s noted that "there was a lack of balance about them, a lack of variety and a lack of the features that are considered necessary to-day to attract and maintain reader interest. There was little world news in either of them, and the local news ran quite largely to politics with appallingly long reports of political meetings and sessions of the legislature and quite often of court proceedings, and City Council sessions."[8] In 1884, one account noted, most newspapers only needed "an editor and two or three other men."[9]

Ten years later much had changed according to the same source. The staff numbers had quadrupled: "To-day, instead of an editor there are at least five or six departments, which each require that many men or nearly so" because "the news supplied has more than quadrupled in volume, and to gather up and arrange the vast amount of matter, means a vast amount of money."[10] By 1900 there were more newspapers than there had been in 1890, and the number of pages in each had increased substantially. The Canadian newspaper world was responding to the nation's rapid industrialization. Publishers who were more entrepreneurial-minded came to the fore to found new newspapers or to take control of newspapers from the politicians. There was money to be made in a successful newspaper, and profit became the guiding principle. Competition intensified for winning elections was now less important than gaining advertising revenues by pleasing audiences. This meant playing up the news by sensationalizing it. For the first time the typical newspaper was exciting to read: screaming headlines, breathless stories, the latest fiction, and features to interest every member of the family.

During World War I the number of newspapers in Canada began to decline. By the 1920s multiple ownership had increased and would continue to do so until the present day. What happened? The role of the publisher as entrepreneur is key to understanding the present state of concentration in news media. Advertising, in particular, played an important part in the metamorphosis of the newspaper from a nineteenth-century partisan organ to twentieth-century corporation. Vastly increased advertising revenues financed the industrial revolution in the press – faster and bigger presses, linotypes that speeded up typesetting, and photoengraving plants that made the newspapers more attractive – all of which allowed newspaper publishers to reach a mass audience to sell the goods of their advertisers. The result was that the capital needed to establish and maintain plants and machinery for newspaper publishing rose enormously.[11] The publisher was forced to commercialize the daily press in order to attract the wider readership necessary to attract the advertising revenues that were in turn necessary to pay for the new equipment and techniques. As a consequence, the political role of their publications was reduced: news as information was replaced by information as commodity.[12]

In their pursuit of profit, publishers initiated many important changes in the Canadian newspaper industry during the early twentieth century: the formation of the first newspaper chain, the rise to predominance of newspaper business offices, the weakening and gradual disappearance of press partisanship, an increase in commercial bias in news columns, and the spread of local and then industry-wide collusion to restrict competition. Like other captains of industry they adopted the latest business methods and tactics such as scientific management, double-entry accounting, and, in their relations with other newspapers, predatory expansionism. Commercialization resulted in concentration and monopoly and the eventual integration of the newspaper world into the world of Canadian business.[13]

The corporatization of the Canadian press was already apparent in the 1890s, as publishers sought to dominate local markets. Between 1890 and 1920, the newspaper industry underwent a competitive shake-out. Like their American counterparts, Canadian publishers attempted to rationalize their holdings and eliminate competition by employing collusive strategies.[14] Until World War I the drive towards monopoly at first concentrated on price cutting and combinations to restrain competition. During the war the purchase and amalgamation of competitors became the preferred strategy. Publishers waged aggressive campaigns to rid their communities of rival newspapers, and although the methods used varied from place to place, the result was everywhere the same – significantly fewer newspapers in every city in Canada by 1921. By the

1920s, as Paul Rutherford concluded, the "rationalization" of the press occurred and "signalled the close of the heyday of entrepreneurship."[15] It all fit Michael Bliss's depiction of free enterprise at the time as "ruthlessly destructive," so that "in the long run only the fittest survived."[16]

During their transformation into businesses Canadian newspapers underwent a dramatic change in appearance and content similar to those Michael Schudson has described in American newspapers.[17] A significant change in the relationship between advertisers and the newspapers after the 1880s was signalled by the sensationalistic and more strikingly designed newspapers. Changes in content and appearance were also linked to the growth of the department stores and the development of brand names and national trademarks, all of which accelerated the demand for newspaper space. Advertising and the related drive towards circulation growth and self-promotion became the chief engine of newspaper development.

Advertising not only paid for the new technology but gave wealth and power to those who controlled the press.[18] Canadian publishers, to use George Boyce's words, were increasingly "men of capital," unafraid to assert their new wealth and influence. The Canadian press acted as an extension of the political system, not as a check on Parliament and the executive. Newspapers served as vehicles of political influence and power and gave the publishers access to the political élite, whose decisions they wished to shape.[19]

This behaviour by Canadian newspaper entrepreneurs was not completely new; their predecessors had also used the press as a vehicle for gaining influence in government circles. The distinctive contribution of the commercially minded late Victorian and Edwardian publishers was that they reduced political content in their papers in order to increase sensationalist and entertainment content.

The publishers of the new popular press were an integral part of the wave of entrepreneurs who industrialized Canada in the latter nineteenth century.[20] The present study examines those publishers, who were independent, risk-taking economic agents whose innovations involved bringing economic resources together in new ways. Mid-Victorian publishers such as the *Globe*'s George Brown and the Montreal *Witness*'s John Dougall fit part of this pattern. But because of their preoccupation with non-business activities – Brown with politics and Dougal with moral-religious proselytizing – they do not conform to the later model of publisher-entrepreneur. Late nineteenth and early twentieth century publishers such as Joseph Atkinson, Treffle Berthiaume, Hugh Graham, John Ross Robertson, W.F. Maclean, Walter Nichol, P.D. Ross, Clifford Sifton and the

Southams represented the new breed of entrepreneur.[21] They believed in the superiority of modern business methods for dealing with social and political problems as well as purely economic concerns. Their pro-business stance also included a reaction against contemporary politicians, who were considered to be too concerned with personal gain and advantage, or with what was characterized as "partyism," and unable to solve society's problems.

How did publishers become successful businessmen and transform their publications into profitable corporations? How did the Southams, the Bassetts, the Whites, the McConnells, the Atkinsons, the Hindmarshes, the Siftons, and other Canadian newspaper families come to be so "well established in the Canadian upper classes," as John Porter put it in the 1960s.[22]

The situation had been otherwise before the 1890s. Newspaper publishers, on the whole, did not belong to the Canadian élite and were not wealthy. Indeed, newspaper work represented a kind of school in which lower-class young men could better themselves. However, newspapers became an increasingly popular investment in the later nineteenth century. Technical advances, improved communications, and urbanization opened up new market opportunities. As the industry grew in size, complexity followed and gave rise to specialization. The roles of proprietor, manager, and editor, formerly united in a single individual, became distinct. The emergence of joint-stock companies in the newspaper business, beginning with the creation of the Toronto *Empire* in 1895, accelerated specialization by forcing the publisher to devote more time to money matters than to editorial concerns. Specialized workers, from accountants to journalists with specific tasks, copy editors, city desk men, and so on, were needed. Successful publishers who had access to capital and delegated work well gained in social status and became part of the ruling élite.

By the end of World War I, according to Carlton McNaught, newspaper publishers had become businessmen "first and foremost."[23] This study will describe the process by which publishers created family dynasties and newspaper organizations that ranked with the most powerful firms in Canada. Surprisingly, even though American commentators in the 1920s were already noting that commercialization had led to newspaper concentration and the "disappearing daily,"[24] the corporative transformation of the newspaper has not received extensive scholarly attention in the United States.[25] In Canada, although there had been discussion of increasing press concentration in the 1920s, there had been only one serious look at the problem before the 1970s. In 1940 Carlton McNaught had commented on the trend towards narrowing of control through the elimination of weaker units and a standardization of methods and product.[26] Until recently, most of the literature has consisted of anecdotal, self-serving, "those were the days" reminiscences by prominent newsmen,[27] or general accounts and biographies written by journalists that, not surprisingly, lack systematic research and sources.[28] A handful of masters' and doctoral studies have focused on the political ideas of prominent newsmen rather than on the journalist and the newspaper within an integrated socio-economic and political framework.[29] The crucial period from 1890 to 1920, especially the significance of advertising, has not been adequately studied.[30]

This book explores the fundamental role of the publisher in changing the Canadian daily newspaper from a political-party mouthpiece in the late nineteenth century into a modern profit-seeking corporation. Chapter 1 explores the origins of the public's idea of the newspaper as public utility versus the publishers' concern with profit, thus providing the historical background to the Davey and Kent inquiries. The next two chapters describe the growth of the newspaper as big business and show how the business manager usurped the power of the editor. The primary role of advertising in financing newspaper operations is detailed in chapter 4. Chapters 5 and 6 examine how intense competition between the dailies led to their collusion and concentration. Chapter 7 analyses the weakening of traditional political patronage for the newspaper and shows how publishers engineered the political independence of their organs. The last two chapters analyze the significance and consequences of the higher social status and greater political influence of publishers.

1 Public Myth and Private Reality

By the end of the nineteenth century the commercialization of Canada's English-language press had spread from Montreal and Toronto to other cities. This caused a growing difference of opinion between the public, which believed that the press's role was to educate and to guard society's freedoms, and the publishers, who thought that the prime purpose of newspapers was to make money by attracting more readers and thus more advertisers. Publishers increased their readership by making newspapers more sensational and by adding women's, sports, and entertainment features, which resulted in a dilution of the press's educative function. The public held on to the nineteenth-century reality of the press as political advocate and champion of a better society, while the publishers believed in the twentieth-century reality of newspapers as enterprises driven by business considerations.

The concept of the press as a servant of the public interest had begun to appear in the 1860s and blossomed under the "civic populism" movement of the late Victorian era. In this period, newsmen and others increasingly assigned the newspaper altruistic roles for the benefit of the public. Indeed, it was claimed that the formation of the Canadian Publishers' Association (CPA) in 1859 was "to promote the influence of the press as a factor in the welfare of the State."[1]

The idea of the newspaper as public educator grew in popularity in Canada during the latter part of the nineteenth century. In 1876 the London *Advertiser*'s William Cameron spoke to a CPA convention about the newspaper's "power to educate."[2] The concept of the newspaper as teacher also became intertwined with the concept of the press as public defender. In 1880, for example, A.J. Matheson of the Perth *Expositor* described the recently assassinated George

Brown as a believer "in the newspaper as a public educator and as a power to defend the rights and privileges of the people."[3] The popular belief in the press's responsibility to educate the public stemmed from the partisan nature of nineteenth-century Canadian newspapers. "Responsible government" was the nineteenth-century editor's greatest concern. An emphasis on the editorial role of newspapers and on their function as a public record of legislative proceedings contributed to the idea of the press as a "public utility" to educate the people. Joseph Howe's libel trial, in which he successfully played the role of defender of the public interest against the depredations of Family Compact favouritism, and William Lyon Mackenzie's adoption of a similar stance in Ontario helped to further the notion of the press as a "Fourth Estate." Thus, the idea arose that the press had a public responsibility and was more than a mere commercial enterprise.

By the 1890s, however, this vision of the educative function of the press was threatened. Contemporary observers were concerned that the growing emphasis on boosting circulation and the increasing dependence on advertising signalled an increase in sensationalism, trivial news, and entertainment at the expense of editorial opinion, social analysis, and serious commentary. Others believed that the decline in importance of the editorial indicated that the newspaper was losing its power to do good and its educative purpose. They pointed to the famous dictum of celebrated *Manchester Guardian* editor C.P. Scott: "A newspaper has two sides to it. It is a business like any other, and has to pay in the material sense in order to live. But it is more than a business; it is an institution; it reflects and influences the whole community ... its primary office is the gathering of news. At the peril of its soul, it must see that the supply is not tainted."[4] Mindful of this danger, Toronto *Globe* business manager J.F. Mackay noted in 1903 that the "press as presently constituted is a commercial venture," which meant it was "weakening in its social role" as the watchdog of the public interest. Its increasing dependence on advertising, he warned, was leading to a fear of taking "strong stands," which in turn would lessen its social influence. Mackay contended that "so soon as the newspaper has become entirely commercialized so soon will the press have fallen from its high estate."[5]

Indeed, some feared that the newspaper industry was falling under the sway of the huge trusts and corporations that dominated other industries. A.H.U. Colquhoun warned in 1902 that the "danger is not imaginary" of a "newspaper trust which might be organized by persons with large selfish ends to serve in gaining the ear of the public."[6] Echoing these fears in 1905, Goldwin Smith expressed concern about the changing nature of the press: "Is it succumbing to the omnipotence of wealth? Is the Tribune of the people becoming the slave of the millionaire?"[7]

The daily press itself addressed this issue. In a story headlined "Does Capital Threaten Liberty of the Press?" the Toronto *Star* commented on the public's fear that newspapers had come under the influence of monopolistic business concerns. According to the *Star*, people believed that this state of affairs was leading to conflicts of interest, and that newspapers now were being run like any other commercial enterprise. The newspapers' "sole object [was] ... making money for the proprietors," who in turn depended on the advertisers for the greater proportion of their revenues. Although the *Star* dismissed public fears of a corporative threat to press freedom as a "bugaboo," it admitted that there were grounds for suspicion, especially since newspapers had become assets of immense value. If a newspaper came onto the market, the *Star* noted, "it [was] impossible on account of the magnitude of the enterprise for anyone but a millionaire or a company of men with large means to become the purchaser." The *Star* added that "the day of the editor-proprietor, running a paper solely for the opportunity of expressing his own opinions" was gone. "A man may be willing sometimes to pay a lot to see his composition in print, but he is not likely to pay two or three hundred thousand dollars for it."[8]

The *Star* put its finger on the dramatic transformation of the daily newspaper from a small undertaking, published more for political influence than commercial gain, to a valuable property operated for profit. As newspapers everywhere grew in size and value between 1890 and 1920, publishers adopted business methods and goals, first to encourage the newspaper's growth and to protect the successful newspaper's competitive edge, and then to sustain the owner's increasingly valuable financial interest in the enterprise.

A parliamentary exchange in 1898 between Sir Charles Tupper and John Ross Robertson, founder of the Toronto *Telegram* and a pioneer of the popular and commercial press, illustrated the significant gap between the public understanding of the press's primary role and that of the publishers. Tupper, a supporter of the press, argued in favour of the subsidies that substantially reduced newspaper postal rates, which Postmaster General William Mulock was attempting to cancel. Speaking against the subsidies, Robertson dismissed the idea of the newspaper as public educator and pointed out that a "newspaper is published to make money, and its educational influence is merely an incident in the business of making money."[9] Another newsman, Robson Black, described the twentieth-century reality of newspapers in even blunter terms. Arguing in 1909 against the view that the newspaper was an "educational force," he concluded that the newspaper was a "commercial enterprise, pure and simply, to make money, or help some man or party to political or other preferment. This is borne out by the fact that the greatest newspapers on the continent claim to be nothing else than large corporations to give the public something they desire in return for the dear public's money."[10]

Despite these pragmatic views, the idea of the newspaper as educator grew during the twentieth century. Several contributors to the 1901 collection of essays on *Journalism and the University* emphasized the newspaper's educational function.[11] Joseph Flavelle bought the Toronto *News* in 1902 because he believed in the "service" the newspaper would render to the "administration of public affairs."[12] The newly purchased *News* proclaimed that its "province" was to educate the public. On this account, said the *Canadian Printer and Publisher* (*CPP*), Flavelle should be considered a public benefactor, because "Mr Flavelle has made a great deal of money, far more than a man of his quiet but liberal tastes can ever use. He might have endowed universities or established free libraries, but he has adopted the far more practical policy of educating the people. He endows newspapers; good newspapers are the universities of the people."[13]

The two most prominent Canadian editors of the time, J.W. Dafoe and J.S. Willison, certainly believed that it was their mission to educate the people and improve society. Willison considered the press "necessarily and legitimately an agitator, very often a voice crying in the wilderness always, if it performs its true functions, seeking to better social and material conditions." Furthermore, "it is the business of the journalist to develop public opinion, to liberalize and energize the social and industrial forces, to utter the voice of the people."[14]

Non-journalists also shared these views. Addressing the Toronto Press Club in 1904, Canon Cody said that the pulpit and the press "were co-workers for the good of man,"[15] and in 1910 the mayor of Truro, Nova Scotia, called newspapermen "gladiatorial educators, in whose hands rest largely the responsibility of the making of good or bad governments."[16]

The press's view of itself as a kind of public utility persisted after World War I. In 1922 the Ottawa *Journal*'s P.D. Ross stated that the newspaper's function was "to guide and mould public opinion" and "to support all good causes ... and fight wrongs or rank injustice."[17] Celebrating its ninetieth anniversary on 5 March 1934, the Toronto *Globe* trumpeted its tradition of championing public rights and "honesty in administration" and of waging "war against privilege and corruption."[18]

Despite the rhetoric, however, early twentieth-century press commentators acknowledged that there was a conflict between the economic realities of the newspaper as business and the public's belief that the press was an instrument of social reform. As early as 1896, J.S. Brierley, publisher of the Montreal *Herald*, wondered why the newspaper owner, who had invested money in a business enterprise, should be "a guardian of the public peace" or a "moral policeman, governed by the Sermon of the Mount?" Indeed, he asked, "what right has the public to demand that their business shall be conducted with a view to the interests of the state?"[19]

It is significant that the men who discussed the inevitable contradiction between public and industry perceptions of the press's function were those who either owned a newspaper or were involved with the management of one. The Toronto *Star*'s Joseph Atkinson astutely observed that the public laid stress on the educational side of the press, while "the commercial is left entirely out of sight, as though there was nothing to be done but for the editors to write instructive articles which would be eagerly bought by the public." Atkinson underlined the economic reality of newspaper publishing, since "this everlasting question of subsistence lies at the root of journalism." He admitted, however, that a newspaper may be so far "governed by the question of profits that it may become a trading concern without other aims than dividends. Or a newspaper may make mere circulation its god, sacrificing everything to boast of figures."[20]

Atkinson's managing editor, John R. Bone, considered that commercialism posed the greatest danger to freedom of the press, and that advertising was the spearhead of this danger. "'I will take my advertisement out' is a threat which confronts the editor almost every day he picks up his pen. The threat does not need to be spoken, the editor knows it is there. It takes courage to disregard it."[21] J.S. Willison likewise warned of the "growing power of corporations and the influence of great aggregations of capital in a few hands." This state of affairs presented a "real danger" to the press, which had no "mission in the world except as the articulate voice of the plain unorganized and unsubsidized people."[22]

These fears of a growing commercialization of the press were not illusory. Beginning in the 1890s publishers and their business managers reduced the role of the editorial page and decreased the amount of political coverage and social commentary in their newspapers. More space was devoted to news and entertainment. The amount of sensational and trivial material, such as "human interest" stories, increased. By 1917 Manitoba *Free Press* editor John Dafoe disapprovingly noted that "publishers had dropped into the notion that editorial opinion was a sort of luxury, perhaps a useless luxury in the paper. They looked doubtingly at the editorial page, begrudging the space given to mere opinion, and figuring out how many comic features or other 'real' circulation builders they could accommodate in that space."[23]

The decline, in the 1880s, of the editorial page in the more popular big-city dailies such as the *Star* in Montreal and the *Telegram, News,* and *World* in Toronto presaged an industry-wide diminution of its importance in the twentieth century. By 1898 many papers had abandoned the practice of printing verbatim accounts of parliamentary debates, another sign of the shift away from an ethos of public service towards an emphasis on entertainment and profitability. The Toronto *Star* commented in 1905 that "the debates of the House ... have become a comparatively unimportant news feature."[24]

The declining importance of the editorial page perhaps explains why Hugh Graham of the Montreal *Star* toyed at one time with the idea of getting rid of his newspaper's editorial page.[25] F.A. Acland, the Toronto *Globe*'s business manager, figured that in the 1890s the paper could have doubled its profits without its editorial columns.[26] In 1909 an eastern daily dropped its editorial page because its management believed that the public was more interested in a "straight, unvarnished news service than in the opinion of the editors on the issues of the day."[27] At the CPA's convention in the same year, a sign of the lessening importance of the editorial pages was that the association actually took up the question whether the editorial page was necessary.[28]

Even such resolutely partisan newspapers as the Winnipeg *Free Press* began to de-emphasize the editorial page in favour of increased news coverage. In 1904, for example, editor Dafoe added commentary on international events to his editorial pages, which formerly had included only expressions of political partisanship and anti-imperial rhetoric. When publisher Clifford Sifton resigned from the federal cabinet the next year, the *Free Press* began to move even more determinedly away from political polemic and hard news.[29]

Stewart Lyon, the Toronto *Globe*'s managing editor, remarked on a similar trend in the newspapers of his city. He compared a week of editorial pages from 1889 with others from 1916 in both the *Globe* and its archrival Tory daily the *Mail* (later amalgamated with the *Empire*). In 1889 the *Globe* contained twenty-one articles on politics and public affairs. This number fell to eight in 1916, another six articles addressed religious subjects, and one covered miscellaneous affairs. In 1916 the *Globe* ran ten articles on the war and another twelve on a variety of non-political issues. The trend at the *Mail* was roughly similar. In 1889 it published fifteen political articles, one on a religious subject, and four on other subjects. In 1916 the *Globe* had ten articles on the war and twelve on miscellaneous subjects. Lyon concluded that the "opinion-making side" had declined between 1889 and 1916 because readers were no longer interested in the views of newspaper editors.[30] Lyon realized that newspaper readers had become more interested in features such as the comics, advice columns, sensational crime stories, and human interest stories than in news columns that preached and enlightened.

The decline of the editorial page was tied to the rising costs of operating a newspaper, which compelled publishers to attempt to increase readership by resorting to more aggressive promotional strategies. In the process, the way the news was deployed changed. Before the 1890s most newspapers, perhaps with the exception of such pioneers of the popular press as Toronto's *Telegram* and *World* and the Montreal *Star*, emphasized the informational aspects of news. News reports may have been politically biased, but their main purpose was either to persuade or to inform. A newspaper's physical appearance was not important. The news was generally set in a small, crabbed typeface and crammed onto the pages with little regard for graphic organization. Newspapers were meant to be read and studied, not to attract the attention of large numbers of readers.

By the 1890s, however, news was being transformed from a source of information into a commodity that could be sold to a larger readership, which in turn would attract more advertising revenue. *Saturday Night*'s E.E. Sheppard observed in 1893 that the publisher's role was not to be a "moulder of public opinion" but "to make the paper pay and to mould it in such a way as to make the most money out of it."[31] More and more this meant that the news had to be enticingly written and attractively presented. As Michael Schudson observes, newspapers increasingly had to advertise their product – the news – and this led to self-promotion and sensationalism. All aspects of newspaper policy and design were affected (with the exception of basic news-gathering routines). Newspapers were now designed to attract the eye and pocket-change of readers.[32] The new strategy of self-promotion included extensive and sensational coverage of local affairs and crime, scandal, natural disasters, and war; vigorous touting of the newspaper's circulation status, advertising gains, and news-gathering prowess; self-advertisement of special and exclusive features and correspondence (for example, the Montreal *Star* promoted its correspondent during the Boer War in South Africa on its front pages); an end to front-page advertising; greater use of illustrations and white space; and the addition of bolder, blacker, multi-column headlines. Newspapers discarded the traditional way of telling a news story, which presented events in chronological order and ended with a dramatic conclusion. Instead, they adopted the new inverted pyramid style that led off with a reference to the most important aspect of the event in question.

To sell newspapers the news had to be attractively displayed. Successful newspapers increasingly used photographs and design changes to make the news easier to read and thus more saleable. Information was packaged like merchandise in department store display cases with local news separate from provincial, national, and international news, and sports separate from business or women's news. Getting the news out as speedily as possible became the order of the day. Less and less emphasis was placed on the context of news; newspapers strove more often to highlight the spectacular and the unusual than to explain the significant.[33]

Based on a random sample of Canadian daily newspapers from 1890, 1895, 1898, 1899, 1900, 1902, 1904, and 1905, it is clear that the changes in content and layout that gave rise to today's omnibus newspaper (serving as wide a readership as possible) occurred, in the main, between 1895 and 1905. In 1890 most of the newspapers in the sample were not organized around separate sections confined to specific areas of interest, such as news or sports. News stories and other items were scattered throughout the newspaper. Small-size type filled the page and was organized into ruled columns broken only by short, neutral heads. Rarely, if ever, were the newspapers enlivened by illustrations. With the exception of the *Telegram* and *World* in Toronto and the *Star* in Montreal, newspaper content was dominated by political news, verbatim reports of parliamentary debates, dry commercial information and accounts of events in foreign places.[34]

By 1905, however, the newspapers had undergone significant change. Their front pages were mostly ad-free. The newspapers employed streamer headlines that crossed columns; they were often stacked with vivid, descriptive headlines and they used illustrations and photographs to dramatize the news stories. The papers were organized into separate sections devoted to finance, sports, drama, literature and entertainment, women's concerns, and other areas.

The Canadian newspapers of 1905 resembled those of the United States. Indeed, in the 1890s Canadian publishers had only to look across the border to see that visually exciting newspapers meant increased profit. They were aware of Joseph Pulitzer's innovative journalistic methods of the 1880s, and of how his turn-of-the-century circulation war with William Randolph Hearst had led to spectacular circulation gains for Pulitzer's *World*. Canadian publishers and editors, despite their occasional denunciations of sensationalism and "yellow journalism," were clearly influenced by developments in the American newspaper industry. Their trade journals regularly reprinted articles from American trade journals such as *Editor and Publisher* and *Newspaperdom*. In addition, Canadians attended American newspaper conventions and belonged to American associations.[35] In the early twentieth century newsman Orlo Miller observed that more and more American methods were being adopted, both in the writing of news and its display tradition, following the lead of the big New York dailies.[36] A typical piece of American advice from 1902 recommended the use of methods that would "make a paying paper." It suggested the inclusion of an index and news summaries, the publication of bulletins, the subdivision of the paper into departments, and a list summing up all advertised bargains.[37]

With readership, rather than partisanship, becoming progressively more important, newspapers had to be made more appealing to readers. Front-page news began to be presented in a more dramatic fashion and more weight was given to local events. Greater attention was paid to the importance of the front page as an advertising window for the newspaper. As well, placement of the news became important, as John Dafoe argued in his 1895 piece "Where the Best News Should Be." Dafoe criticized the old-fashioned habit of putting abbreviated telegraph reports on the front page and relegating sensational but local news to the inside pages. His advice was: "First page for the best news ... the best news is that which will interest the greatest proportion of readers. That is the modern, sensible plan. Four times out of five the best news, under this rule, will be local news."[38]

More and more newspapers removed advertisements from the front page, which shows that publishers had become aware that front-page news lured customers. The editor of Gaven, Saskatchewan's *Prairie News* called the front page "the display window of his store of news, [which] must be well filled with good samples." He added that "the front page of a local newspaper is the parade to the circus. Interest is created. Those who have the money follow, place their money on the ticket counter, and pass inside."[39] Similarly, the Toronto *Globe*'s business manager J.F. Mackay called for "better make-up on the front page so as to better promote circulation."[40]

Despite some assertions to the contrary by newspapermen of the time, yellow journalism in Canada was widespread because it made money for the newspapers. In 1894 the Montreal *Herald*'s new evening edition was condemned for its sensationalism, although one critic realized "that this is the kind of news that takes with the masses."[41] John Cameron, editor of the Toronto *Globe* from 1882 to 1890, recognized that yellow journalism did exist in Canada. He mentioned the existence of "flaring headlines, out of proportion of the matter following." He cited the "coarse caricatures" and the "too large space given to murders and other crimes, often with details that simply pointed out to everybody how crime could be committed." Other hallmarks of yellow journalism in Canada included "the tearing open of private wounds of families for sensational ends, and the unfair appeals to mere demagogic prejudice."[42]

For some newspapers, especially those facing strong competition, the temptation to sensationalize must have been irresistible. Quality newspapers such as the Montreal *Gazette* and the Toronto *Globe*, whose financial status was secure, remained aloof from sensationalism. But newspapers in desperate circumstances, such as the Montreal *Herald* in the mid-1890s and the Toronto *Star* at the end of the century – when the new owners fought for survival in a crowded and extremely competitive market – had little choice but to sensationalize the news.[43] The Halifax *Herald* was a case in point. Locked in a circulation standoff with its rival, the Halifax *Chronicle*, it lost the financial advantage of federal patronage after the Laurier election victory of 1896. To boost circulation, publisher William Dennis adopted modern business methods and shifted the news focus towards local news, with an emphasis on crime, scandal, and fires.[44]

Sensational accounts of events increased, and more newspapers adopted the practice. In 1894 the Toronto grand jury denounced the Toronto press's extensive and descriptive coverage of several trials involving assaults on women and girls.[45] The Montreal papers' coverage of the murder of a young girl in 1906 was deemed so sordid, according to one commentator, that "the dailies were hardly fit to be picked up with a pair of tongs."[46] The Vancouver *Province*, while denying charges by its rival, the Vancouver *World*, that it was "yellow," ran lurid stories of murders and other mayhem and was fond of references to the alleged depredations of "wily Mongolians" or "slit-eyed Chinks."[47] It took the Boer War, however, to bring to full flower all the eye-grabbing, attention-getting tactics of yellow journalism – the bold streamer headlines, the loud promotion of special war coverage.[48]

Critics realized that sensationalism weakened the public utility function of the newspaper. The *Canadian Printer and Publisher* ran an editorial on the difficulties of managing a newspaper "like a

Methodist prayer meeting" in an era of yellow journalism. But, it argued, sensationalism had to be resisted if newspapers were to continue to act as public educators.[49]

Fears that newspapers were retreating from their public responsibilities prompted concerned citizens – educational reformers, women's groups and the clergy – to protest the introduction of comics strips. When the London *Free Press* began carrying "The Yellow Kid," the famous weekly coloured comic strip, the newspaper drew a barrage of public criticism. The *Free Press* was called a "corrupter of the young" and the furore reached such heights that the newspaper was forced to suspend the feature. It was some years before the *Free Press* again offered its readers a comic strip, and this time it chose the far less controversial "Buster Brown."[50] In Ottawa the Women Teachers Association asked the city newspapers not to publish comic strips because, the teachers said, they failed to teach accuracy in drawing, politeness, or deportment. But the Ottawa *Journal*'s P.D. Ross was unmoved; the comics would stay.[51] No publisher could ignore the importance of comic strips in attracting readers. The *Gazette*'s R.S. White made this clear when he complained about how "degrading" it was to be forced to rely on those "frightful monstrosities" to increase circulation.[52] W.J. Darby, the Toronto *Mail and Empire*'s circulation manager, concluded that the comic strips would be valuable "so long as advertisers make the circulation of a paper ... the sole standard of the newspaper's merit as an advertising medium."[53]

The success of publisher Joseph Atkinson's Toronto *Star* was attributed by his long-time employee J.H. Cranston to his understanding of the publisher's view that what the average Canadian wanted in a paper was not "instruction in the more serious aspects of the news, but entertainment and amusement. And since his objective was a large circulation, he must seek the tastes and preference of this wider audience. He must win favour in every section of the community large enough to provide a sizeable body of readers."[54]

In Canada, the *Star* led the way in rejecting the florid, embroidered style characteristic of nineteenth-century newspapers with their heavy emphasis on partisan editorializing. By the early years of the first decade of the twentieth century the *Star* had adopted the streamlined style and more "objective" approach to the news that present-day readers are familiar with. In 1905 the *Star*'s advice to its reporters was "Boil it down."[55] Other newspapers followed suit. Gone were the homespun moralizing and leisurely style where the reporter ended with a dramatic conclusion. Triple-decker narrative-style headlines were abandoned for shorter, more sensational headlines that set forth only the highlights of a story.

Some people gave wire services the credit for inventing the inverted pyramid style, because the expense and constraints of the telegraph demanded brevity. But according to the Toronto *Star*'s sports editor W.A. Hewitt, who around the turn of the century was the first to use the inverted pyramid style in Canada, the reason for its use really lay in the overriding needs of advertising. Because Hewett never knew how much space an advertisement would require, he instructed his reporters to "tell the result of the contest in your first paragraph, then if your report has to be cut for an advertisement, the readers will at least know who played, where, and who won, and the score."[56]

By the start of twentieth century, partisan shrillness and heavy doses of political news began to give way to "human interest" news stories and other features designed to turn as many family members as possible into devoted newspaper readers. It became plain that success rested on the publisher's ability to shift the newspaper's emphasis from political news and advocacy to entertainment. The contrasting fortunes of the Toronto *Star* and its rival, the Toronto *News*, certainly demonstrated this. While both were taken over by new owners at roughly the same time (the *Star* in 1899 and the *News* in 1902), their subsequent histories could not have been more different. While the *Star* became the Canadian newspaper success story of the twentieth century, the *News*, despite vast amounts of investor money, remained in the red until it was closed down in 1920.

In 1906 Charles Clarke, an ex-Toronto *Telegram* newsman working for Hearst's New York *Journal*, wrote to the *News*'s publisher, Joseph Flavelle, pinpointing the reasons for the *News*'s lack of success and suggesting that it could solve its problems by adopting Hearst's journalistic methods. He categorized editor J.S. Willison as "helplessly a pupil of the old Toronto school," whose editorials were "picayune, hair-splitting, temporizing" and "replete with classical allusions comprehensible to no one but a university man." What was needed, Clarke advised, was to give readers "something in short sentences, and short words, with a bunch of ideas, instead of a hazy idea spread out to fill so much space with no regard to the value of space. It is far better to bring out an edition of your paper without an editorial than to inflict a fixed quantity of drivel on your readers every week." Clarke also suggested focusing on Toronto news rather than British stories, since "Toronto is big enough to furnish the story that leads the paper every edition, except in case of very important outside happenings." He concluded that Willison did not understand how to present news to modern readers. "The comparative value of news is a sealed book to him. He goes on the old-fashioned English plan that a good editorial column (in his eyes) is all that is needed, and is ignorant of the fact that proper display of news attracts the people, and that circulation comes from giving the news, first, last and all the time."[57]

Flavelle's response provides an interesting contrast between the new journalism of profit and the old journalism of political advocacy. He confessed to being "old-fashioned enough to believe that a newspaper proprietor has some other duty to the public than to make money, and some other responsibility to society than seeking to inflame prejudice and passion."[58]

Flavelle represented the waning reality of the publisher as educator and moral instructor. The need for profit had become paramount and the way to achieve it was through the adoption of sensationalistic news coverage and the introduction of entertainment features such as the comic strips. Publishers became more interested in building their newspapers into big businesses. The next chapter will show how publishers learned to employ managerial and other business methods in order to survive in an increasingly competitive newspaper world.

2 Big Business

The growing independence of publishers and their quest for wider audiences during the 1890s signalled the changing reality of newspaper publishing. Newspaper publishers were confronted with crowded markets and increasing readership saturation – that is, lack of new readers – in addition to rising expenses for presses, typesetting equipment, and bigger staffs for the rapidly expanding dailies in Canada's largest cities. All this dramatically increased the start-up and operating costs of newspaper operations. Because the political world could no longer provide adequate financial support, the more entrepreneurial publishers turned to the business world for assistance. At the same time, a growing number of businessmen entered the newspaper world by buying or investing in newspapers as part of their larger entrepreneurial activities.

In the three decades leading up to 1920, entrepreneurs discovered that creating new daily newspapers was gradually becoming more difficult because of two factors that limited growth in a steadily rising number of cities: readership was no longer increasing, and the maximum number of dailies had been reached. From 1899 to 1911 the number of dailies rose and newspaper consumption increased significantly. But by 1921 this was no longer the case. Restrictive newspaper marketplaces were first evident in English-speaking Montreal and in Toronto in the late 1880s, and in the smaller cities by the 1890s, so that by 1900 there was no room for new dailies in "cluttered" Halifax, Quebec City, English-speaking Montreal, Ottawa, Toronto, Hamilton, London, or Winnipeg. The market limit for the number of dailies seemed to be three for middle-sized and smaller cities before World War I and two after the war. Only the largest cities – Montreal, Toronto, Vancouver, and, for a short time, Saint John – were able to support more than three dailies for a decade or more. Montreal supported four English-language dailies from 1869 to 1917, while Toronto supported six from 1869 to 1921 (seven Toronto newspapers in the early 1890s quickly proved to be unsustainable). By 1911 Vancouver had four daily publications up from the three it had enjoyed since the late 1890s. Cities such as Hamilton, Ottawa, Calgary, Winnipeg, Edmonton, London, and Halifax never went beyond the threshold of three, and even before World War I economic conditions had caused a reduction to two newspapers in several cities – London, Kingston, and Brantford, for example – and to one in Windsor. The constrained economic circumstances of the war years and the weakening of the ties between newspapers and political parties caused the number of newspapers to decrease everywhere, so that by 1921 most cities had lost at least one daily; Toronto and Montreal lost two, while Calgary, Vancouver, and Winnipeg lost one each. In Canada overall, the number of dailies rose from 119 in 1899 to 143 in 1911 and then declined to 113 in 1921.[1]

Newspaper readership rose in the country as a whole during the first decade of the twentieth century. Circulation increased from .106 per person in 1899 to .186 in 1911. It then seemingly stabilized, for in 1921 readership stood at .183. The years 1899–1921 saw daily newspapers increase by 233 percent, but the following decade experienced an increase of only eighteen percent, which was less than the growth rate of the Canadian population. It is evident that many newspaper markets were experiencing saturation; indeed, by the 1890s and early 1900s, according to Thomas Walkom, a kind of "supersaturation" existed in several cities where the average number of newspapers purchased by each family exceeded two.[2] In Ottawa the rate was 2.6, showing that many families took two or more newspapers. This encouraged the existence of three newspapers, which kept overhead costs high and prompted newspapers to attempt to expand circulation to alleviate expenses. Jean de Bonville describes the same expansion in English-speaking Montreal, where consumption leaped from 1.2 newspapers per family in 1891 to 1.9 in 1901 and 2.6 in 1911.[3]

Crowded markets contributed to rising costs and increased competitive pressures. Newsmen at the time were aware of the situation. The merger of the *Mail* and the *Empire* in Toronto in 1895 came about in part because of the general feeling among journalists that three morning dailies were one too many for the city. Four years later J.H. Cranston described Toronto as being "oversupplied" with newspapers, a situation that became progressively worse.[4] Similarly, The tight newspaper market in Montreal killed off four French-language dailies and one English-language daily in the decade 1892–1902. In English-speaking Montreal only the *Star* enjoyed significant circulation growth between 1880 and 1900. The *Star*'s competitor, the *Herald*, was forced to switch to afternoon publication. This was a desperate attempt not only to escape the constrictions of a "too limited" morning market but also to take advantage of a hinterland market that could be supplied only by afternoon publication and better railway connections.[5]

Indeed, the "dollar daily" phenomenon, which saw big-city dailies expand beyond the local markets into the smaller city markets, was a response to market saturation. Such big-city dailies as the Toronto *Star*, the Toronto *Globe*, the Manitoba *Free Press*, and especially the Montreal *Star* increasingly relied on market expansion to sustain their prosperity. By 1913, for example, the Montreal *Star*, then the largest and most prosperous English-language daily in Canada, sent forty percent of its newspapers out of the city, some as far as the Maritimes. About thirty-eight percent of the Toronto *Star*'s circulation was distributed outside the city proper.[6]

By the 1890s the so-called "cheap" newspaper had come into being because unit production costs had dropped significantly. Newsprint cost $250 a ton in the 1870s, $138 a ton in the 1880s, and only $68 a ton in the 1890s. By 1913 the cost was $45 a ton. Production costs dropped even further following the widespread use of faster, more powerful presses, such as the web-fed rotary press. Less-expensive paper and speedier, more productive presses created economies of scale that resulted in reduced unit production costs.[7]

At the same time, though, start-up costs for the purchase of labour- and money-saving equipment grew enormously. In Britain the growing demand for cheap newspapers during the latter half of the nineteenth century led to the development of expensive new printing and typesetting technology and numerous innovations in graphic reproduction. The Canadian newspaper industry was similarly affected by technological innovation, especially in the 1890s.[8] New technologies created the need for costly investment in new machinery. Although the cost of printing the larger newspapers rose in the 1880s, it was only in the 1890s that costs really exploded with the widespread adoption of the linotype (introduced in 1892), the increased use of illustrations, and the establishment of stereotyping plants. The steadily climbing number of readers attracted by the variety of features in the more popular papers forced publishers to replace their printing presses with faster, bigger, and more expensive models. For instance, in 1892 the Toronto *News* excited comment with its purchase of an $18,000 press capable of running the twelve-page editions it was publishing more frequently to meet the needs of advertisers and a growing readership.[9] A few years later, in 1898, even a medium-sized daily such as the Montreal *Gazette* felt obliged to purchase a $30,000 press. By the first years of the twentieth century it was commonplace for newspapers to buy presses costing as much as $40,000. In some circumstances these purchases necessitated a move to larger premises, as in the case of the Manitoba *Free Press*.

The introduction of the linotype contributed significantly to the spiralling costs of newspaper production. The linotype ended the laborious process of setting type by hand through the mechanical slug-casting of type. A solid, continuous line of copy was cast by a single unit, a process that was speeded up by a keyboard device. The process was at least five to six times as fast as the former method of typesetting. Canadian publishers rushed to the invention when they learned, for instance, that in 1893 the Toronto *News* was saving one hundred dollars a week on composing-room costs.[10] That one machine could replace five workers was very tempting for publishers who wished to cut labour costs and increase production at the same time. Yet the capital required to buy a linotype was daunting, as P.D. Ross, publisher of the small and struggling Ottawa *Journal*, discovered in 1892. He opted for six typograph presses at $1,500 each, only to replace them with a $3,000 linotype several months later because the typographs were not dependable.[11] Press and linotype purchases were paid on time, so increased business, circulation, and advertising had to be drummed up to pay the monthly instalments. The Montreal *Star*, which was estimated to be worth $250,000 in 1895, spent $42,000 for fourteen linotypes in 1898.[12] To meet the enormous costs of the new machinery, publishers were compelled to look for ways to increase circulation and boost advertising revenues.[13]

Other innovations that aimed at attracting a wider readership also raised capital costs. Canadian publishers, like Joseph Pulitzer before them, discovered that the "cuts [illustrations] sold papers." Before the 1890s illustrations were rarely placed on the front page, but the obvious popularity of the cartoons of J.W. Bengough and Sam Hunter on the front pages of the Toronto *News* and the Toronto *World* soon showed other publishers that illustrations could play a key role in circulation success. Even the visually conservative Toronto *Telegram* was forced to introduce its own daily cartoon in 1893.[14]

The use of black-and-white illustrations in the 1890s and of colour photographs and colour illustrations in the early twentieth century was proof of their circulation-boosting powers, but the sophisticated machinery and skilled staff needed to support such innovations meant increased expenses for publishers.[15] Although colour strengthened the visual attractiveness of newspapers, and while the technology for its use had existed since the early 1890s, its cost was such throughout the decade that the dailies only offered it in their Christmas and other special illustrated issues. It wasn't until the turn of the century that they began to use colour in their weekday editions, and then mainly to showcase advertising. Indeed, Joseph Atkinson was forced to buy a colour attachment for his new printing press because Timothy Eaton, despite owning ten percent of the *Star*, refused to advertise in the newspaper unless it could print a red line above a proposed full-page advertisement (like the Wanamaker store advertisement in the Philadelphia *North American*).[16] Photographs first appeared in the 1890s but could only be used in special coated-paper illustration sections of the Saturday editions. The Toronto *Globe* pioneered the use of photographs in Canadian newspapers in 1892, followed by the *Mail* in 1893. By 1910, the benefits of photographs had become obvious, according to the Dunnville *Chronicle*'s W.A. Fry, who noted their power to increase circulation but also their costliness, since they required engraving plants.[17]

In addition to machinery, paper and labour required large financial outlays. Jean de Bonville estimates that paper represented 70 to 80 percent of a newspaper's expenses. At Quebec City's *Le Soleil*, for example, salaries accounted for 47 percent and paper for 25 percent of the costs of running the newspaper. At the Montreal *Witness* the figures were 47 percent and 19 percent in 1905, typical of the industry.[18] Although the cost of paper dropped significantly, overall expenditures on paper rose for the simple reason that the longer newspapers of the 1890s and the early twentieth century required more paper.

Dailies expanded from an average of four pages at the beginning of the 1890s to eight pages, twelve pages, and more in the early twentieth century. The introduction of the linotype allowed the Toronto dailies to expand their average size from five pages to ten pages in the years 1892–98. From 1891 to 1905 the average newspaper size in Canada increased fivefold.[19] The Montreal *Star* spent $40,000 on paper in 1900.[20] Even a small newspaper such as the Calgary *Herald* managed to spend roughly $23,000 on paper in 1909, when its total expenditures for the year amounted to $82,000.[21]

Labour costs were even higher. Figures ranged from 41.9 percent at the Toronto *Mail and Empire* (1903) to 57.3 percent at the Ottawa *Citizen* (1900). Several papers, the Hamilton *Spectator*, *Le Soleil*, and the Montreal *Witness*, averaged 47 percent in 1905.[22] Much of the increase in labour expenses resulted from the growth in reporter staffs. More aggressive and extensive news gathering, necessary for survival in times of intense competition, also escalated the cost of newspaper operations.

The costs associated with the drive towards extended news coverage as a way of attracting more readers proved especially heavy during the Boer War. By November 1899 the Canadian dailies had sent six correspondents to cover the war, and the number increased as the war dragged on. Toronto's *Mail* and *Globe*, the first Canadian newspapers to send correspondents to cover the Spanish-American War, discovered that spectacular first-hand reports from the front sold newspapers. But the South African war was costly to cover. Some newspapers, such as Montreal's *Herald* and *Star*, financed their own correspondents, while others formed syndicates to defray the expense of hiring correspondents.[23] Cheque-book journalism was practised with a liberal hand to induce soldiers to become correspondents. Joseph Atkinson was especially active in this regard. Some soldiers were paid as much as seven dollars a column by Atkinson and others.[24] The Toronto *Globe* estimated that it spent $12,000 to cover the war, while other dailies spent approximately $10,000 each.[25] The South African experience encouraged publishers to increase capital investment during the post-war period; for they realized that expanded coverage of spectacular events and more equipment such as telephones and photo-engraving facilities, which meant additional staff, resulted in higher circulation numbers, hence higher advertising rates.[26] The Toronto *News*, which was the fourth largest paper in Toronto in 1902, had a payroll of seventy-eight staff whose salaries amounted to $1,200 a week.[27] In 1899 the Toronto *Star* employed fifty-two staff; by 1905 the number had more than doubled.[28] The expansion of the Toronto *Telegram*'s staff was equally dramatic: its 79 employees in 1891 grew to 100 in 1901 and to 156 in 1908.[29]

Given the greater emphasis on local news and the addition of new features such as sections devoted to sports, women's issues, and entertainment, it is understandable that news staffs would grow in size and expense. As the amount of newspaper space allotted to the new features expanded in the unceasing quest for wider readership and greater circulation, more syndicated material was required. The experience of the Ottawa *Citizen*, a medium-sized daily, illustrates this trend. During one week in July 1907 it published seven special features at a cost of $19.50. Five years later, in October 1912, the cost of one week's worth of special features – eighteen in all – was $77.04.[30]

The *Citizen* also learned first-hand how these special features affected circulation. In November 1914, Harry and Wilson Southam discontinued all the newspaper's special features as a cost-saving measure. They calculated that the "war news was sufficiently absorbing to hold such of our clientele as took the Citizen for these particular features," but they were wrong. In 1914 their rival, the Ottawa *Journal,* spent vast amounts of money to augment its special features sections. By the next year, the *Citizen* had lost 3,000 of its 18,000 subscribers while the *Journal* had increased its readership from 12,000 to 15,000. Advertisers, moreover, told the Southams that they wanted to reach the sort of audience that was attracted by special features. Not surprisingly, the Southams soon restored the women's and children's features and the comics page.[31]

Other publishers also discovered the lucrative rewards of carrying special features. In 1910, when Joseph Atkinson introduced a weekend paper, the Toronto *Star Weekly,* to compete with the Toronto *Sunday World,* the idea was to produce an inexpensive, unpretentious journal without colour comics or lavish illustration. Public response was poor; readers just would not buy a poorly illustrated weekend paper without a comics section. Atkinson responded by pouring money into a new four-page picture section, printed using fine-screen half tones and coated stock to increase the quality of the images. This helped somewhat, but it was the addition of comic strips in 1913 that really made the difference. Within a short time after the introduction of the comic strips, circulation rose from 4,000 to 26,000. Further rises in circulation were attributed to higher-quality photographic reproduction and a new emphasis on humorous and entertaining material.[32]

Newspaper promotion also increased capital costs. The Montreal *Star'*s Hugh Graham and the Toronto *Telegram'*s John Ross Robertson pioneered various expensive but attention-getting gimmicks in the late nineteenth century. Graham paid for smallpox inoculations, built a statue to John A. Macdonald in Montreal's Dominion Square, and paid for life insurance policies for Canadian volunteers in the South African war. Robertson became famous for well-publicized promotional campaigns that included importing an expensive ambulance with the latest features from London and donating it to a Toronto hospital. On another occasion he erected a fifty-foot screen and oxyhydrogen lights to display election results.[33]

After the turn of the century, the number of self-promotional schemes multiplied as newspapers scrambled to attract advertisers. The Calgary *Herald*'s J.H. Woods admitted that the newspaper's sponsorship of a 1914 aviation exhibition was "an advertising stunt as far as the *Herald* is concerned and we have had to commit ourselves rather steeply in expenses to do it, but I do not think there will be any doubt of our working out even."[34]

Newspapers advertised themselves on billboards, the sides of streetcars, and boardings. The Calgary *Herald* even made a movie of its operations, *The Making of a Metropolitan Newspaper*, which ran in fifty-two moviehouses. The *Star* copied this tactic in 1919 with its film *The Making of a Great Newspaper*, which profiled the entire operation from the receipt of news bulletins by telegraph to the sale of newspapers in the streets by paper-toting newsboys.[35]

Fixed capital costs also rose as mechanical workers began to unionize and demand higher wages. By the 1890s printing and typesetting staff at all the Toronto newspapers were unionized, and by World War I the same was true of most big-city papers. The success of the eight-hour-day movement at the start of the twentieth century also led to increased costs.[36] The managing editor of the Toronto *News* expressed the frustration felt by management when he lamented that "it is not in our power to do other than pay these wages which, as far as I can see, are not based on any known standards recognized outside of unionization."[37]

With all the financial pressures faced by newspapers, it is not surprising that costs began to approach figures that were large for the time. In 1903, for example, the Manitoba *Free Press*, then a medium-sized paper with a circulation of 20,000, had incurred expenditures exceeding $200,000.[38] And the Montreal *Star*, which cost more than $1 million a year to run in 1913, was clearly a big business.[39]

The large sums required to start and, more importantly, to run a newspaper were rising beyond the means of most investors. In 1904, veteran newsman Avern Pardoe, commenting on the newspaper industry of the 1870s, remarked that "anyone with a sufficient fund of native brass and credit for a week's rent, paper and composition could start a daily paper." But in 1904, "a new competitor has to challenge comparison at once and at all points with existing papers." The newspaper must "spring into life Minerva-like, full grown and with hundreds and thousands of capital behind to sustain it while it makes a business for itself."[40]

Crowded markets and rising fixed-capital costs raised entry barriers to newcomers, first in the largest cities and then, in the early years of the twentieth century, in the smaller cities. As noted earlier, increased demand for cheaper newspapers led to much larger print runs and lower unit costs, which in turn fuelled substantial increases in editorial expenditures caused by the need to create or buy additional editorial content to fill the extra pages. Higher advertising revenues led to the same result. The cumulative effect of these changes was increased circulation, but they also ensured that new newspapers took longer to reach the break-even point. In

Canada the costs associated with special features, press agency fees, and payments to correspondents in other cities tripled between 1892 and 1906.[41] The days when someone could enter the Montreal market with $1,000, as Hugh Graham did in 1869, or enter the Toronto market with $10,000, as John Ross Robertson and W.F. Maclean did in 1876 and 1880, were long over. By the 1890s, starting a newspaper was extremely difficult without the backing of substantial amounts of capital. In fact, almost no new newspapers appeared during that decade, except in western Canada. To enter the market, would-be publishers had to buy an existing property. In the 1890s some city dailies were still available for a reasonable price. The Montreal *Herald* sold for $11,250 in 1892, the Ottawa *Citizen* for $15,000 in 1898, and the Toronto *Star* for $32,000 in 1899.[42] These were not bargain prices, however, as the three newspapers had the weakest circulations in their respective markets. They were also encumbered with debt and needed substantial outlays of capital to stay afloat. The *Herald*, for example, used up its initial capitalization of $90,000 and a further $50,000 between 1892 and 1895 and still lost $10,000 in 1895. As for the *Citizen*, it took the Southam family's extensive financial resources to keep the newspaper alive with a $50,000 investment in machinery. The *Citizen*'s principal owners denied themselves remuneration for the first year and a half after their 1898 purchase of the paper, and dividends were not declared until 1905.[43] In the case of the Toronto *Star*, an investment of $68,000 beyond the purchase price was needed before the newspaper first showed a profit in 1905.[44] The examples of the *Citizen* and the *Star*, both of which took more than five years to turn a profit after being sold despite large infusions of capital, are evidence of the restrictions on profitability that purchasers of newspaper businesses faced in the 1890s. The *Herald*, in fact, never made money for its new owners and required the patronage of the Laurier government to stay in business.[45]

It was in the early years of the twentieth century, however, that the prices for newspaper operations really soared. The Toronto *Star* was right in noting in 1905 that it would cost hundreds of thousands of dollars for someone to see his or her opinion in a daily editorial.[46] Joseph Flavelle, owner of a meat-packing empire, discovered this for himself when he paid $150,000 at the end of 1902 for the floundering Toronto *News*.[47] It cost him a further $250,000 over the next five years to keep the newspaper running until its financial haemorrhaging forced him to relinquish control in 1908.[48] But the price Flavelle paid for the *News* was a bargain compared to the reputed $500,000 that the Toronto *Mail and Empire* was worth in 1905.[49] Toronto *News* editor J.S. Willison claimed that it had cost from $75,000 to $100,000 to publish a newspaper in a large Canadian city in 1883; by 1913, however, the estimated cost was $750,000 to $1 million per year.[50] The Toronto *Star* exemplified the inflationary value of newspaper operations: in 1896 its market value was $20,750, but by 1905 its plant and building alone were valued at $400,000.[51] In 1912 the Tarte brothers refused an offer of $1.5 million for Montreal's *La Patrie*.[52] In 1913 the official value of the Toronto *Telegram* was set at $1,750,000, while Walter Nichol sold the Vancouver *Province* to the Southams for $2.5 million in 1923.[53] Clearly, as these amounts show, big-city daily newspapers had become substantial enterprises requiring significant amounts of capital to found and maintain.

The rise in the financial worth of daily newspapers was not confined to Toronto and Montreal but also affected the smaller urban centres. For Calgary, a city of 30,000, it was estimated in 1909 that the cost of starting a newspaper would range from $35,000 to $50,000, and in the same year prospective newspaper publishers in Halifax and Waterloo sought at least $100,000 for their ventures.[54] Harry and Wilson Southam paid $15,000 for the Ottawa *Citizen* in 1897, a newspaper that was valued at almost $200,000 seventeen years later.[55] The Vancouver *World* was not the largest newspaper in its city, yet it was valued at $400,000 in 1912.[56]

Often, the value of a newspaper was augmented by the increasingly large and ornate buildings in which newspaper proprietors housed their organizations. Canada's economic expansion at the end of the century caused the leading newspapers to move to larger and more lavish quarters. In April 1895 the Toronto *Globe*, which had been gaining ground in circulation since the merger of the Toronto *Mail* and Toronto *Empire* at the beginning of the year, acquired a new building for $21,000.[57] That same year, Hugh Graham of the Montreal *Star* paid $50,000 for a property on St James Street, "the principal street of the city." Graham noted that the *Star* was the "only English daily possessing this advantage."[58] In 1898 John Ross Robertson built a new building valued at $35,000 for the Toronto *Telegram*.[59] Even smaller newspapers such as the Brantford *Expositor* and the Hamilton *Spectator* built four- and six-storey buildings to house their bustling concerns.[60] For publisher E.J.B Pense, writing in 1899, the proliferation of increasingly grand newspaper edifices showed that the press had finally arrived in the world of business and finance and was truly a "pillar of society."[61]

Located mainly in the most desirable business districts of their cities, the buildings were valuable properties in their own right. The worth of the buildings soared as the business districts in which they were located expanded and Canada's cities prospered during the Laurier "boom" years. As newspaper operations grew, larger premises were required to accommodate additional machinery and more employees. Sometimes the financial choices involved were difficult to make. The Manitoba *Free Press*, for instance, badly needed a new press. But its acquisition entailed raising additional funds because housing the new press required larger quarters.[62]

A new building, however, could proclaim to the world a newspaper's success and potential for growth. The Ottawa *Free Press*, long the city's weakest daily, bought three houses in 1907, altered their interiors, put on new fronts, and built a four-storey reinforced concrete building at the back. "It was," recalled the newspaper's publisher, "I think the second reinforced concrete building erected in Ottawa. We had to bring in a Montreal contractor to put it up. The excitement of a new building helped us and we convinced merchants and readers that we were on the go."[63]

Land and business values skyrocketed during the first decade of the twentieth century. In 1902 the Southams paid $120,000 for their new premises in Ottawa, and in 1905 the Toronto *Star*, which was finally turning a good profit and paying dividends to its shareholders, invested more than $150,000 in a new building.[64] In 1913, the Vancouver *News-Telegram* spent $225,000 on a new building, a figure four times as great as the largest amounts spent at the beginning of the century.[65]

The size of newspaper buildings continued to grow, and the premises were often built to house other businesses. In 1912 the Vancouver *News-Telegram* converted part of its building into quarters for other businesses "to take advantage of high rents."[66] Newspaper investments in land and buildings became increasingly speculative as publishers sought to profit from the real estate boom of the early years of the twentieth century. For example, the Montreal *Herald* built a $350,000 eight-storey building and the Vancouver *World* built an eighteen-storey highrise, billed as "Canada's first newspaper skyscraper."[67]

The Southams had taken the lead in treating newspaper real estate as a speculative investment. They, too, had built their buildings beyond the needs of their newspaper operations and rented out the excess space. For example, they rented out four of the Ottawa *Citizen* building's six storeys for a profit of $5,000 in 1905.[68] They found real estate so profitable that in 1911 they invested $327,000 in real estate in Calgary and later built an eight-storey building to house the *Herald*, a development announced with the headline: "BIG REAL ESTATE DEAL MEANS THAT THE HERALD WILL HAVE SPLENDID

NEW HOME IN BUSINESS HEART OF CALGARY."[69] The business manager of the *Herald* complained that "most of my time is being taken up in showing people desirable offices" in the newspaper's new building.[70] The real-estate venture, however, paid off: in 1909, their real estate accounted for less than half of their newspaper empire's assets of $1,678,000, but by 1913 it was worth more than $2 million out of total assets of $3 million.[71]

The national economic upswing of the Laurier years, which began in 1896, boosted the profitability of many newspaper operations. The Toronto press, for example, did not earn significant profits until the late 1890s. In 1898 four Toronto newspapers turned a profit, and in each case profits exceeded one-third of gross revenues. In both 1902 and 1906 (when figures are available), at least three Toronto newspapers out of six showed a profit.[72]

The dominant newspapers in local markets consistently earned profits from 1900 to World War I.[73] The exceptions were during times of economic downturn, such as 1909–10 and 1913, when either losses or a drop in profits reflected national business conditions, and during the first years of World War I, when a serious economic downturn occurred.[74]

A look at several Canadian cities during the twentieth century's first decade reveals the beginning of a pattern in which certain newspapers became and remained dominant in their markets by winning the competition for circulation and advertising and consistently showing a profit. Most of these newspapers still dominate their local markets in the 1990s.

In Ottawa the *Citizen* and the *Journal* usually showed a profit, while the *Free Press* lost money.[75] The Manitoba *Free Press* consistently made money, while the *Telegram* and the *Tribune* more often than not were in the red.[76] Several Toronto newspapers – the *Telegram*, the *Globe*, the *Mail and Empire*, and the *Star* – made money but the *World* and the *News* were perpetually in financial trouble.[77] The Montreal *Star* was, by all accounts, the most financially successful newspaper in Canada, having made Hugh Graham one of the nation's wealthiest men.[78] The *Gazette* of the same city probably made money, given its monopoly of the business market after the *Herald* moved to afternoon publication in 1896.[79] *La Presse* and, to a lesser degree, *La Patrie* enjoyed financial health, but the same could not be said for the *Herald* and the *Witness*.[80] In London the *Free Press* prospered, the *News* failed, and the *Advertiser* seems to have had good years and bad.[81] The Hamilton *Spectator* made a profit from 1877 to 1924.[82] The *Herald* and *Mail* of Halifax consistently "made good" in the early years of the twentieth century.[83] In 1908 the Vancouver *Province* claimed to be making $30,000 a year on a circulation of 10,000 to 12,000.[84] In Calgary the *Herald* flourished at the expense of the *News* and *Herald* once ownership was assumed by the Southams. The Edmonton *Journal* also flourished at the expense of its competitors.[85] Lethbridge publisher W.A. Buchanan reportedly made $7,000 on an initial capital investment of $30,000 in the *Herald,* while the Southam's *News* bled red ink.[86]

Even for the profitable papers, however, it took money to make money. During the late nineteenth century, as mentioned earlier, the rapidly rising costs of acquiring new technology placed enormous financial pressures on the publishers. In 1903 J.S. Brierley cautioned Montreal Liberals about to launch a new French-language daily that they should watch out for "heavy fixed charges."[87] As publishers' financial needs were satisfied less and less by financing from political sources, they became increasingly dependent on help from financial institutions. Indeed, for many newspapers, survival depended on access to outside capital sources. P.D. Ross was on the brink of insolvency in 1891–92 but was rescued by loans from the Bank of Ottawa and another investor.[88] In 1916, E.N. Smith's Ottawa *Free Press* almost collapsed when its bank had failed, thus cutting off the newspaper's access to a line of credit: "The difficulty of getting accounts transferred to another bank until ... the Bank of Commerce took us in, had given some of us the treacherous spots that awaited concerns without adequate resources."[89] The Halifax *Herald* would not have survived a disastrous fire in 1912 if a friendly banker had not made a substantial loan.[90] More and more, what counted was not the newspaper's editorial stance or position in the political party's pecking order but its margin of profit and the publisher's access to credit.

Financial considerations thus forced the publishers to act like businessmen. Their behaviour became "entrepreneurial," as defined by Lewis Fischer.[91] This meant that the publisher had to become more of a risktaker, gambling that the money he raised to finance new machinery and plant expansion would be recouped through the growth of additional business made possible by the expansion. This could be hazardous because the hoped-for increase in revenues was often uncertain even if the new machinery and plant expansion did help to raise circulation. There was also a time lag between spending on plant improvement and reaping the rewards of the investment. As in other businesses, success rested on the publishers ability to anticipate economic trends.

The Lethbridge *Herald*'s W.A. Buchanan was a good example of a publisher who was forced to spend large sums of money to stay competitive because of business conditions and market rivals. In 1907 Buchanan bought expensive printing presses that exceeded his immediate requirements because he predicted "many years of growth." Soon after, he acquired new stereotyping equipment to keep ahead of his competitors.[92] J.H. Woods of the Calgary *Herald* confronted a typical dilemma. In 1908 his printing press was too small for the *Herald*'s needs, but he was reluctant to "incur the expense and liability involved in the installation of a stereotyping press." The trouble, he noted, was "that our circulation may force us to it before our earning capacity warrants it." He did not want to buy the press because he could not "afford the extra expense until business conditions improve. At the same time the *Albertan* has a stereotyping press, and the *News* is advertising that it is going to get one in the next fall. Of course, our present duplex is better than anything they have had in the past, but we will not be able to maintain the circulation of 7,000 on our present facility."[93]

It was also vital for publishers to have access to capital. P.D. Ross's seventeen-year struggle to put his Ottawa *Journal* on a sound financial basis showed the vital importance of access to capital for a publisher. Ross needed capital to tide him over some rocky financial patches, such as the previously mentioned mistake of buying a poor set of typographical machines and being forced to replace them with linotype machines in 1892. From his initial purchase, in partnership, of the newspaper in 1887, the *Journal* was kept afloat financially by loans from such key Ottawa financial figures as the Bank of Ottawa's president Charles Magee and businessman N.S. Sparks, by investment from sawmill owner George Perley, and by timely personal loans from Ross's mother and brother. It was only in 1904 that Ross paid off his debts and assumed complete control of the *Journal*.[94]

The transformation of newspapers into big businesses meant, as J.S. Willison observed in 1913, that newspaper ownership was now beyond the reach of working journalists.[95] Interestingly, those working journalists who acquired control of their newspapers in the first decade of the twentieth century – P.D. Ross, Walter Nichol, Joseph Atkinson, and William Dennis (none of whom started out wealthy) – had one thing in common, namely, access to capital on extremely favourable terms. Ross, for example, was able to assume full control of the Ottawa *Journal* in part because his financial backers eventually forgave part of his debt on the stock allotted to him.[96] Nichol, editor of the Vancouver *Province*, purchased the newspaper from owner Hewitt Bostock under a special reduced-price arrangement financed by the Canadian Pacific Railway.[97] Atkinson received an annual salary of five thousand dollars, two thousand of which was paid in stock. He was also given first-purchase rights on any shares that other shareholders wished to sell. Since the shareholders comprised only the small group of investors who had bought the *Star*, this agreement allowed Atkinson to to take control of the newspaper in 1906 by purchasing the shares of a deceased shareholder, which gave him a majority of the shares.[98] As a reporter for the company that owned two Halifax dailies, the *Herald* and the *Mail*, Dennis was allowed to purchase shares on an instalment plan and in 1897 was given an advantageous deal to purchase a controlling interest in the company from its principal owner.[99]

Most newspapers were dependent on loans, as the Manitoba *Free Press*'s E.H. Macklin revealed in a plea to the newspapers's publisher in 1900: "It would relieve me greatly if I had the assurance from you the Banking arrangements would be completed in time to meet the Hoe draft which falls due December 26."[100] The *Free Press*'s rival, the Winnipeg *Telegram*, had to raise an additional $27,000 for equipment to remain competitive.[101]

Bankers and wealthy financiers thus replaced the politician as the most important benefactors of newspaper enterprises. For example, the Southams, who had now established branches in Montreal, Toronto, and Ottawa, were vulnerable to financial considerations. The Ottawa branch, who were proclaiming their independence from politicians and "partyism," were not quite so independent of bankers. In the worsening business climate of 1913, they considered selling their Alberta properties because, as Harry Southam wrote to his brother Wilson, the Bank of Nova Scotia "may ... insist upon considerable reduction in our loan. If this contingency should arise, conditions would be so adverse that we would be up against it with a vengeance."[102]

The Canadian daily's shift from political mouthpiece to industrial entity accelerated as more and more businessmen invested in the press. Rising capitalization costs meant that only the wealthy were able to purchase newspapers. The paper-making Riordon family's ownership of the Toronto *Mail* and the Toronto *News* and the takeover of the Toronto *Globe* in 1882 by retailer Robert Jaffray and financier George Cox represented the thin edge of the business world's wedge into newspapers.[103] Canadian General Electric founder Frederic Nicholls's purchase of the Toronto *Star* in 1896, investment tycoon Clifford Sifton's takeover of the Manitoba *Free Press* in 1898, pork baron Joseph Flavelle's purchase of the Toronto *News* in 1902, stock promoter B.F. Pearson's acquisition of five Maritime newspapers in 1906, and financier T.H. Purdom's assumption of control of the London *Advertiser* in 1908 underlined the business world's increasing intersection with newspapers.

Beginning in the 1890s it became more and more common for syndicates of businessmen and wealthy politicians to buy newspapers. Often they financed their purchases through joint-stock ventures. One venture that pointed the way towards the future involved a syndicate of Conservative party businessmen-politicians, who banded together in 1894 to take control of the Toronto *Empire* by purchasing all its 200,000 common shares.[104] As the cost of buying newspaper businesses – even small ones – rose, syndication grew in popularity. It was also popular because it allowed risk to be spread among a number of investors. It was also used to reduce financial risk. [105]

By 1920, in response to intensified competition for readership, crowded markets, and increased machinery and labour costs, successful publishers had greatly reduced the political component of their newspapers and made them first and foremost businesses. The next chapter will explore the introduction by publishers of business methods of organization and the editorial consequences of these changes.

3 Publisher Power and the Rise of the Business Manager

As newspaper operations everywhere grew in size and value between 1890 to 1920, publishers adopted the new administrative practices that were sweeping the North American business world. Many newspapers were turning into such large and complex organizations that publishers were no longer able to oversee all the details of newspaper operations. Increasingly, they hired professionals to handle special tasks within the organization, and as a result, the status of editorial employees was reduced while those in the business office increased.

By the end of the century widespread literacy, a consequence of school reforms earlier in the century, and rapid urbanization had led to the formation of a new mass audience for newspapers. By 1891 Canada's literacy rate was eighty-five percent. Its urban population rose in the same decade but skyrocketed from 1901 to 1911 with an increase in urban population from 2,014,222 to 3,272,847. The percentage of urban population to the total Canadian population had risen from 37.5 percent to 45.4 percent.[1] This new audience was increased by the expansion of white-collar professions, the rising numbers of clerks and assistants in stores and offices, and the increase in leisure time for skilled workers. The audience for newspapers was no longer limited to élite, prosperous males but now included women and children. The staples of mid-nineteenth-century newspapers, political comment and commercial news, no longer sufficed for these new readers, who increasingly demanded entertaining and sensational editorial content.

By the late nineteenth century an administrative revolution had occurred in business methods and organization throughout North America in response to intensely competitive and crowded market conditions and rising capital and labour costs. According to Harry

Braverman, the purpose of such business philosophies as "scientific management" was to promote efficiency and reduce fixed costs, especially the rising costs of labour.[2] Michael Bliss notes that "Taylorism" (as the movement became known after its best known practitioner, Frederick Taylor) entered Canada in the early twentieth century through branch-plant managers and lectures from "brainstorming" advocates.[3] The latest and most effective methods of personnel accounting and organization and the "departmentalization" of business enterprises also made their appearance in Canada at this time.[4]

To implement these practices, business proprietors relied on a key employee, the professional middle manager – Alfred Chandler's "visible hand."[5] In Canada the transition from nineteenth-century small-scale entrepreneurial capitalism to twentieth-century corporate capitalism created the conditions for the rise of corporate bureaucracies headed by salaried managers. The growing size and complexity of business enterprises compelled owners to delegate responsibility for daily operations to managers. After 1900 corporate administration became a specialized activity as managers rationalized corporate structures by developing rigid employee hierarchies with clear lines of authority and implemented new accounting procedures to control production and labour.[6]

Canadian publishers eagerly adapted the new business philosophy. The Canadian Publishers' Association, for instance, became noticeably more business-conscious. Formed in 1859 to lobby for lower or subsidized postal rates and less restrictive libel laws, it existed at first mainly as a social club for members. "Members came from coast to coast," one observer noted, "to discuss mutual interests and problems, but mainly for the purpose of social intercourse."[7] Particularly popular were the yearly excursions to remote Canadian destinations, often underwritten by the railways as public relations gestures to the journalists.

But hard times in the late 1880s, exacerbated by greater competition (including price cutting in newspaper subscriptions and job-printing bids) and increased operational costs, changed the CPA's focus. Business matters became more pressing, causing the publishers' organization to "introduce practical discussions as an impetus to success in business."[8] Lofty talk about journalistic ethics and the profession's higher calling gave way to practical lectures and workshops encouraging more scientific business management. A participant at the 1894 CPA convention no doubt voiced a widespread sentiment when he declared that "business must be prime."[9] By the late 1890s the publishers were attending convention sessions devoted to such business concerns as the precise cost of advertising space, the economic aspects and effects of linotypes, the latest bookkeeping methods, the right equipment for the business office, the most efficient office organization, and so on.[10]

The industry's journal, *Canadian Printer and Publisher*, was especially tireless in advocating modern business methods. In a typical article published in 1895 it advised newspapermen to "study business details" because "business management is too often the weakest part of a newspaper office ... little if any attention is devoted to the details of the cost of every department at work. The publisher is apt to be blissfully in the dark as to what his space is worth, how the cost of each issue of the paper compares to its selling price, and exactly what margin there is between cost and profit on the various revenue producing departments." The journal applauded several newspapers that had their office management organized by a "competent accountant, who can lay out the whole programme."[11]

The *Canadian Printer and Publisher* relentlessly promoted greater efficiency in newspaper publishing, and John Imrie, its editor, preached the benefits of "cost accounting" and proper bookkeeping methods and shocked the membership by charging that most publishers did not really know whether they were making or losing money. Imrie organized a "cost education campaign," through which he spread the cost-accounting gospel to scores of Canadian newspaper establishments.[12]

The new ideas about cost accounting soon travelled even to the remote hinterland. At the 1911 CPA convention, for example, D. Smith of the Fort William *Times-Journal* presented a paper entitled "Business Management-Subscription Prices, Collections, Credits, Other Systems." Summarizing the lessons of departmental cost accounting, he said that business management started at the front office, where "all the machinery of keeping track of the inflow and outflow of the concern should be closely checked ... [so] that the concern should make profit on the transaction. In order to do this there should be an efficient bookkeeping staff and the books should be so kept that at the end of each month the manager should know the gross earnings of the newspaper, job department and circulations separately; the wages paid out and the paper and material consumed, the footing of the different columns showing at a glance how much was earned or lost in each department."[13]

Not adopting the new business methods could prove fatal. Veteran Toronto *Star* newsman J.H. Cranston recalled the haphazard business practices of Jim Livingstone, the business manager of the short-lived Hamilton *Post*, who belonged to the "old school of journalism."

Livingstone was a "keen sportsman" and an "assiduous follower of the ponies" who believed that the best way to run a newspaper was to hire some good men and let them do the work while he scurried around collecting enough money for their wages. He worked only when "absolutely necessary" – that is, on Thursdays and Fridays, when he collected accounts and sold advertising space. The men in the plant always got their money first, but if Livingstone was short, not a wheel was turned in the press room until he arrived with the pay packets. The editorial staff often had to accept post-dated cheques. Needless to say, after the first few months the *Post* exhausted its bank credit, and the paper folded in 1901 after only six months in existence.[14]

In the increasingly fierce competitive environment of the early-twentieth-century newspaper, slipshod business practices such as Livingstone's could not be countenanced if a newspaper was to be commercially successful. The Southams certainly demonstrated this when they bought the Edmonton *Journal* in 1911. They immediately brought in a management consultation expert, Albert Haynes (whose hiring was in itself a sign of changing times), who discovered that the newspaper was "losing money ... and lacked system and organization throughout." Haynes proposed sweeping changes, beginning with reorganization of the Southam's western Canadian properties (the *Journal*, the Calgary *Herald*, and the Lethbridge *News*) into a joint-stock company so that the newspapers could be operated on a "more scientific basis."[15]

As for the *Journal* itself, Haynes found that "departments are not clearly enough defined and inter-related; the records are inaccurate and badly kept; and valuable assets lost sight of altogether. Too little care is given to credits, and collections are woefully in arrears."[16] He recommended replacing the amateur business office with professionally trained clerks because "the work would be more efficiently done by a much smaller staff." Haynes further advised that "in accordance with the established policy of all well-conducted newspapers," the administration of the newspaper should be divided into two distinct departments, with a managing editor in charge of an editorial and mechanical department and a business manager to direct a circulation and advertising department. He also proposed having a separate cashier-accountant who would audit collection figures independently of the collection agents.[17] Haynes's reorganization was a success, and the *Journal* was soon turning a healthy profit for the Southams.[18]

The new administrative methods alleviated "heavy and uncontrollable overhead," as the Calgary *Herald*'s J.H. Woods found in

1915. The *Herald*'s year-old cost-accounting system, Woods remarked, allowed the owners "to keep track of our business every day, so that on any one day we can tell practically up to the night before whether or not we are making money in that month." He added that "it is by economies and careful watching of details (and not only by extraordinary advertising situations) that money in the newspaper business is to be made."[19]

Many publishers, especially the most successful such as Joseph Atkinson, William Dennis, Hugh Graham, Walter Nichol, John Ross Robertson, and P.D. Ross, readily embraced innovations in accounting and administration and began to concentrate more and more on the business side of newspaper operations. The Montreal *Star*'s Graham was involved primarily in the business side throughout his career, first as a bookkeeper at the Montreal *Gazette* and later at the *Star*, where a succession of journalists, beginning with Graham's partner George Lanigan in 1869, ran the editorial side.[20] William Dennis, proprietor of the Halifax *Herald*, reorganized the paper on the principles of "economy and efficiency" and "survival of the fittest." Among other things, he moved his office from the editorial room to the floor where the business office was located. For Dennis, "sentiment was a thing of the past" and the *Herald* was a "pure business."[21]

Joseph Atkinson was an even more ardent advocate of new business methods. He began on the editorial side as a reporter for the Port Hope *Times*, moved to the Toronto *Globe*, and then worked as an assistant editor at the Montreal *Herald*.[22] When he became publisher of the Toronto *Evening Star* in 1899, he insisted that the newspaper be run essentially as a business, not as a party organ, despite the expectations of the newspaper's Liberal party backers.[23] Initially he oversaw both the business and editorial sides of the paper, but by 1907 this was proving too arduous. Accordingly, University of Toronto graduate John R. Bone was hired as managing editor, and from that point on Atkinson devoted himself to the business side.[24]

Much of the Toronto *Star*'s success was credited to Atkinson's use of new administrative methods.[25] Department store magnate Timothy Eaton and financier George Cox, both *Star* stockholders, convinced Atkinson to keep separate budgets for each department of the newspaper so that the profits of one would not hide the losses of another. This approach allowed the owners to have a clear sense of each department's performance and also enabled them to improve manager and employee productivity, as responsibilities could be traced and measured. To keep employees working hard, Cox further advised putting "each department on such a close budget that it will be next to impossible to keep within it." Atkinson also adopted Eaton's practice of reviewing departmental expenditures on a daily basis. If a department's expenditures exceeded income by too great an amount, the department head was instructed to reduce his costs promptly or face the consequences.[26]

But not all newspaper publishers were so forward-looking. In 1911 John Nelson, manager of the Vancouver *News-Advertiser*, urged the more traditional newspaper publishers to follow the example of their colleagues who had adopted "scientific management." He commented that too few publishers had as yet "emerged from the purely literary excursion in which [newspaper publishing] used to be regarded into the commercial enterprise which it is today. The modern newspaper is a manufacturing plant whose saleable commodity ... is an inch of white space, a line of agate type. The half tone illustration, the feature story, the expensive editorial, are mere cogs in a machine the purpose of which is to render more valuable the paper's sale unit – an inch of white space."[27]

Publishers who ignored the newspaper's business side certainly paid a price for their failure to adapt. The collapse of the Toronto *World* is a case in point. In the 1880s and 1890s, under publisher W.F. "Billy" Maclean, this was the most innovative and one of the most popular newspapers in Canada. It introduced a breezy, investigative style of journalism more in tune with Toronto's growing reading public.[28] After 1900, it entered a period of persistent financial crisis, which was attributed to Maclean's "divided ambitions"; he simply spread himself too thin, trying to be a full-time politician and part-time land speculator while operating the newspaper. Hector Charlesworth believed that the *World*'s failure in 1921 would have been averted had Maclean concentrated on publishing. As it was, "it didn't help the paper's future that Maclean robbed the *World*'s till to pay off the debts of other investments rather than reinvesting the money to improve the paper."[29]

After taking control of every aspect of the business operation, successful publishers then turned to removing the politicians from positions of influence over their newspapers. Whereas publishers had once sought the consent of Liberal or Tory leaders before placing people in senior positions on their newspapers – as the Toronto *Globe* did with J.S. Willison in 1890 and the Montreal *Herald* with J.S. Brierley in 1894 – this was done less and less by the first decade of the twentieth century.[30] Many influential publishers, including "Billy" Maclean, P.D. Ross, John Ross Robertson, and Clifford Sifton, were essentially self-made men who believed in rugged individualism and hard work as the keys to success in the newspaper world.

Fiercely independent, they jealously guarded the prerogatives of their position and permitted no interference in the operation of their newspapers. Montreal *Witness* publisher J.R. Dougall, for example, worried about accepting five free shares of Sun Life Insurance and said that, had he thought ownership of the shares would compromise his independence, he would have returned them.[31]

P.D. Ross's desire to be free of outside pressures led him to reject a Liberal scheme in 1903 to turn the Ottawa *Journal* into a government "organ" and amalgamate it with the Ottawa *Free Press*. Ross remarked: "Even though it would be a good thing financially for me ... I continue possessed with that inclination to be purely my own boss which has hitherto given me more satisfaction in life than making money. As a government organ, and with a partial responsibility for the money of Liberal shareholders, my editorial wings would be clipped to a considerable extent, morally if not by contract.[32]

Being "my own boss" was a sentiment shared by other publishers. But as the newspaper businesses grew larger and more complex, publishers could no longer personally oversee every aspect of their operations. Increasingly, their role was confined to laying down general policies, while day-to-day concerns were delegated to specialized professionals. The biographers of Joseph Atkinson, W.A. Buchanan, John Ross Robertson, and Clifford Sifton all make this point.

Nevertheless, publishers still exercised a great deal of power in the day-to-day running of their newspapers. At the Manitoba *Free Press*, for instance, publisher Clifford Sifton was vigorous in directing policy. When J.W. Dafoe was hired as the newspaper editor in 1901, he underwent several long interviews with Sifton in Ottawa. Until Sifton retired from active politics as Laurier's lieutenant in charge of the western Liberal party, Dafoe was bombarded with instructions on a near-daily basis. Even afterwards Sifton's correspondence contained occasional admonishments, instructions, and direct commands to Dafoe.[33] At the Toronto *Star*, Joseph Atkinson's approval was necessary for every editorial published in his newspaper.[34] Gregory Clark remembered overhearing one *Star* editor on the telephone murmuring "yes, yes, yes for 10 minutes while through the receiver I could hear old Joe's voice laying down the law."[35] The publishers of the Toronto *Star* and the Toronto *Telegram* were both known for their vigorous use of the publisher's prerogative, as John Ross Robertson's biographer Ron Poulton points out; "while Robertson lived," Poulton writes, "everyone at the *Telegram* walked softly."[36]

As publishers expanded their business activities beyond their newspapers, it became even more difficult for them to devote themselves to the myriad details of newspaper operations. Many dealt with their properties in the manner ascribed to long-term Vancouver mayor and *World* publisher L.D. Taylor, who, according to a contemporary, was "not connected to the literary end of the paper, but has control and dictates the policy and passes on all doubtful points."[37] Those who could not avoid "divided ambitions" – especially the growing number of businessmen who were buying newspapers – solved the problem by hiring business managers to handle their newspaper's commercial operations. In the 1890s, for example, financier and Liberal bagman Robert Jaffray delegated the *Globe*'s business affairs to F.A. Acland.

Clifford Sifton adopted a similar approach towards administration of the Manitoba *Free Press*. During Sifton's early days as the paper's owner, he was too busy in Ottawa as Laurier's Interior minister to bother about its daily operations. For that reason, in 1898 he hired Arnott J. Magurn, an eighteen-year newspaper veteran, as managing editor and assigned W.J. Somerset to be business manager. Magurn, like other nineteenth-century editors accustomed to having complete financial and editorial control, unleashed an expensive circulation campaign by publishing special editions and expanded issues more frequently. Alarmed at the rising costs that resulted, Sifton instructed Magurn to reduce the newspaper's expenditures and to consult with the business manager regarding all financial decisions. Moreover, for the moment Magurn was to curtail publication of all extra editions, large, expanded, and illustrated. Magurn protested that it was the managing editor's responsibility to decide how the news should be presented, and that such decisions should not be guided by business criteria. Accepting Sifton's orders, Magurn argued, would effectively remove the word "managing" from his title. Magurn held that advertising copy should not drive out news copy, which would be the result if he were limited to twelve pages on Saturday, as Sifton required. Before long, Sifton fired Magurn and hired a more cooperative editor, J.W. Dafoe, as well as an astute business manager, E.H. Macklin.[38]

A few years later, Sifton highlighted the importance of a good business manager in a letter to J.S. Willison, whom he advised not to assume financial control of the money-losing Toronto *News*: "Unless you had a peerless manager, such as Macklin, who could take the whole load off your shoulders and who has the business genius for making money, the load on you would be intolerable and would seriously interfere with your health and editorial efficiency."[39] This was good advice, but Willison rejected it and the *News* remained in poor financial health until its demise in 1920.

By the early years of the twentieth century the business manager had become the key newspaper employee, eclipsing the nineteenth-century star, the editor. The rise of the business manager was reflected in that most important yardstick of success, salaries. By 1903, when the Toronto *Globe*'s manager J.F. Mackay surveyed the state of Canadian journalism, it was apparent that business managers and top advertising agents were more highly prized and consequently earned more than their editorial colleagues. For newsmen this rankled; as Mackay himself commented: "I have known men connected with the business office of large dailies who had never got through an entrance examination and who could not write two sentences correctly, drawing two, three, and four times as much salary as university graduates working on the reportorial and editorial staffs of the same paper. Men who can turn in advertising contracts can command their own price; men who can write classical essays are a drug on the market."[40]

The advent of the business manager led to a more rapid rate of expansion of the newspaper business office in comparison to the editorial office. At the Toronto *Telegram*, for instance, nine employees were working in the business office in 1891, including a cashier, a debt collector, an advertising agent, and six clerks and accountants. The editorial office supported fifteen employees (a managing editor, a news editor, nine reporters, two proofreaders, and two stenographers), and there were fourteen employees in the circulation department. Ten years later, however, the number of workers in the business office increased by eight, the newspaper having added a business manager, a bookkeeper, an assistant bookkeeper, a second advertising agent, a secretary, and several clerks. On the other hand, the editorial office staff had increased by only three.[41] At the Toronto *Star* the number of employees in the editorial department rose from eleven in 1899 to twenty-three in 1905, while its business office staff quadrupled from three to twelve. There were no circulation workers at the *Star* in 1899, but twelve had been acquired by 1905.[42]

As newspaper circulation grew, staff sizes increased, and their organizational structures within newspaper offices became more complex. For small newspapers such as the Ottawa *Journal* in 1884, a simple organizational structure divided into business, editorial, and press/composing offices was sufficient.[43] But as it and other newspapers evolved into operations printing several thousand copies a day of eight-, twelve-, and sixteen-page editions, running them became more complex. The *Journal*'s administrative organization had expanded to six departments by 1899 – editorial, proof-room, composing, press, circulation, and business.[44] Similar changes occurred at other newspapers such as the Toronto *News*, the Toronto *Telegram*, and the Calgary *Herald*. By 1915 increases in circulation numbers and advertising volume at the medium-sized *Herald* necessitated an expansion of the number of departments at the newspaper from six to ten.[45]

A comparison of salaries at the Ottawa *Journal* in 1884 and 1899 illustrates the shift in importance from the editorial to the business side. In 1884 the newspaper's business manager was paid twelve dollars a week and the advertising solicitor received ten dollars, while the editor received twenty dollars. By 1899 the business manager's salary had doubled to twenty-four dollars and the advertising agent's had risen to twenty dollars plus commission, but the managing editor got just twenty dollars.[46] At the Calgary *Herald* in 1913, the advertising manager received $294 a month, but the city editor, the editorial staff's highest-paid member, earned $216.[47]

R.S. Somerville, the Vancouver *World*'s managing editor, wrote in 1918 that the men who set the standards of values in the newspaper world "almost always sat in their swivel chairs in the business department."[48] When Toronto newsman C.F. Hamilton received a tentative offer in 1911 to be editor of the Winnipeg *Tribune*, he stipulated that "I should want control, eg. as against the business manager."[49]

As the demands of business began to triumph over editorial considerations, conflicts of the Magurn-Sifton kind became more common. For example, the Toronto *Globe*'s editorial office struggled in vain against the rising influence of the business office. In 1908, the newspaper's more business-oriented directors wanted to get rid of the illustrated section of the Saturday *Globe* because it was not profitable. Business manager J.F. Mackay convinced them not to, arguing that they could not expect a profit from all parts of the paper. It did not make sense, for example, to look to editorial-page advertising to pay the salaries of the four editorial writers.[50] The directors, however, ordered other "curtailments," including a reduction in the size of the magazine section. According to M.O. Hammond, *Globe* editor Stewart Lyon hated "the domination and curtailment policy of the business office. He wants the editor to be editor and have more say, but apparently the money changers are to rule."[51]

Stewart Lyon was right to be pessimistic about the increasing weight of the business office. In 1910 the *Globe* reorganized its affairs so that overall policy would be set and final decisions made by its board of directors, which consisted of major shareholders. But the management of the *Globe* was carried out by an executive council, made up of editors and the business manager, that met once a week. Significantly, the executive council chairman was the business manager and not the editor in chief.[52]

In 1913 the *Globe*'s board of directors wanted to discontinue the three specific editorial sections – the special Christmas issue, the weekly edition, and the weekly illustrated feature – that chairman Robert Jaffray dismissed as "not paying their way." On behalf of the Christmas issue, which featured stories and poems by Canadian writers, Lyon argued that the *Globe* should be encouraging Canadian literature. Nonetheless, the Christmas issue was axed along with the weekly section, despite Lyon's protest that doing so "would seem a retreat from the legacy of George Brown." Hammond, who edited all three sections, complained privately that when he had started at the *Globe* in the 1890s, he thought of his work as a "career," whereas now it was reduced to a mere "job."[53]

Hammond's reaction reflected a growing perception among the editorial staff, especially reporters, that their interests were diverging from those of the publishers. In the nineteenth century reporters and publishers had pursued common political goals. As noted earlier, nineteenth-century reporters could dream of owning their own newspaper one day, but by the early years of the twentieth century changes in the industry meant that they had a much slimmer chance of attaining that objective. Reporters began to feel like mere employees, and not very well-treated ones at that – a sentiment expressed in numerous attempts to found journalists' unions. In 1900 Montreal reporters failed in their attempt to form a newswriters' union, to be made up of editors and reporters and allied with the International Typographers' Union (ITU).[54] A similar effort fell through in Toronto two years later.[55] Other early attempts also failed, probably because of a "certain distaste" that many news reporters felt for "organization along union lines as being a supposed negation of the professional status to which they aspire."[56] Nonetheless, daily newspaper reporters in Montreal and Toronto clearly overcame their qualms after World War I and organized newswriters' unions affiliated with the ITU.[57]

Business prerogatives also encroached in other ways on the editor's formerly sacrosanct domain, the news pages. Montreal *Gazette* general manager E.F. Slack noted how advertising demands for "preferred positions frequently made it difficult for the editorial management to turn out a typographically attractive paper. They prevented the real news of the day from being properly displayed."[58] The Manitoba *Free Press*'s Dafoe also complained that the sports page was disfigured by advertisements "strung across the top of the page," which prevented effective placement of news. He added that the *Free Press* was the "most cut-up paper in Canada," and that he needed "many open pages to properly display and classify news."[59] The Toronto *Globe*'s M.O. Hammond fought a similar battle in 1907 over the placement of advertising because he believed there was an important principle at stake.[60] He was right: this was a struggle over whether editorial or commercial imperatives would govern the conduct of the newspaper.

In addition to favouring business staff over editorial, publishers assumed tight control over their editorial staffs, despite the myth in newspaper circles that editors and reporters have always enjoyed a substantial degree of independence from their publishers. Hamilton *Spectator* city editor John Wodell recalled that he never received a direct order from publisher William Southam.[61] But Wodell was chosen precisely because he saw eye to eye with the publisher.[62] Other editors had a similar relationship with their publishers; Flavelle, for example, once exclaimed to his editor J.S. Willison that he could not "help being impressed by agreement" on almost every subject they discussed. On another occasion, Flavelle thanked Willison for having "killed," without being asked, two items prepared by *News* reporters over which he would have had a "bad time" if published.[63] With rare exceptions, J.W. Dafoe also agreed with the policies of his publisher, Clifford Sifton.[64]

When editors disagreed with their publishers, however, it was evident who was boss. As noted earlier, Dafoe's predecessor, Arnott J. Magurn, jealously guarded his hard-won editorial prerogatives and was fired for defending them. M.O. Hammond recalled an incident where the Toronto *Globe*'s fiercely independent editor Stewart Lyon was handed a poem read by J.W. Bengough at a luncheon sponsored by publisher Robert Jaffray, who liked the poem and wanted it published the next day. "It won't go in tomorrow," Lyon answered. "We're running the *Globe*. Mr Jaffray can run the luncheon." But despite the bravado, Lyon complied with Jaffray's wishes.[65] Even as prominent an editor as J.S. Willison was occasionally taken to task for acting too independently. In 1907 Willison privately opposed the Ontario government's hydroelectric policy in a letter to the Toronto *News*'s chief owner, provincial minister of Lands, Forests and Mines Frank Cochrane, who coldly answered, "[I] ... need scarcely assure you that I would not like to see the *News* against the Government in this matter."[66] To offer a final example of the power wielded by publishers, Hugh Graham of the Montreal *Star*, who was the Conservative party's chief fund raiser, compelled his editors to act as his political spies and henchmen, gathering information and running other political errands for him.[67]

Contemporaries were well aware of the declining influence of the newspaper editor in the early years of the twentieth century. In 1905 the *Canadian Printer and Publisher* lamented that there had been no great Canadian editors since George Brown and concluded that the "power of the purse" was to blame. The journal observed that "the smart businessman has driven out the conscientious exponent of great principles, the apostle of forlorn causes, the artist in prose." The journalism of daily newspapers, it warned, was "in danger of degenerating into a mere trade, worked in the same way, and by much the same methods, as a department store."[68]

Also writing in 1905, the *Gazette*'s R.S. White summed up the consequences of the developments outlined in this chapter. In the past, the newspaper's "primary purpose" had been to mould public opinion. The "editorial mind," he continued, "had been the controlling influence. The business office was of minor consideration, important doubtless on one day of the week – pay day – but a sordid, rather contemptible sort of place for the other five. We have changed all that. To-day the business office dominates seven days in the week, and the editorial mind must be subservient to its necessities. In other words, the newspaper has become a mere commercial enterprise like any other business having as its main purpose the accumulation of wealth."[69]

4 It Pays to Advertise

The ability to attract advertisers was crucial to the commercial success of the Canadian daily newspaper between 1890 to 1920. The growing importance of advertising revenue dictated changes in the internal power structure of the newspaper, which led to the publisher's dominance over the editor and the triumph of the business office over the editorial office in daily operations. Publishers became less concerned with politics and more with raising circulation to gain advertising. Circulation growth became the yardstick of a newspaper's success and advertising became the means of its financial survival.

The Toronto *Star*'s Joseph Atkinson had a clear understanding of how important circulation was in attracting advertisers, and according to B.K. Sandwell, "he went out to get it in every direction, conscious that once he had the biggest circulation in Toronto no advertiser could afford to stay out of his paper no matter how much he disliked it."[1] A popular 1901 manual on how to build a successful newspaper advised that "as an aid to securing advertising, the paper should ... always endeavour to convey the impression that it is growing continuously and rapidly."[2]

One of the first to adopt this strategy was the Montreal *Star*'s Hugh Graham, who began publishing daily circulation figures on the editorial page in 1884. Four years later the *Star* offered five thousand dollars and a six-month subscription to anyone who could disprove the newspaper's circulation claims. In 1892 the newspaper claimed that its circulation figures were backed by a sworn disposition.[3]

Publication of figures, however, did not become common until the mid-1890s, when newspapers in Toronto and elsewhere copied the *Star*'s practice. Within a few years the leading dailies were featuring their circulation figures on the front page. Circulation rivalry often became the occasion for boasts and taunts. During the week of 11 January 1899, the front page of the Vancouver *Province* proclaimed that the newspaper had the largest circulation in Vancouver, larger than that of its two rivals combined. The *Province* offered to donate one thousand dollars to the Vancouver General Hospital if anyone could dispute its claim. Throughout 1902, the Toronto *Telegram* declared that its "circulation books [were] always open for inspection."

As time went on, circulation claims became increasingly comical. The Brantford *Expositor* proclaimed in 1905 that it had "the largest circulation of any Canadian daily published in a city of 35,000 or less." The St Thomas *Evening Journal* proclaimed that it had the "largest circulation published in the smaller cities of Ontario," while the Chatham *Evening Banner* trumpeted the "largest circulation of any daily published west of London."[4]

Competition over circulation reached absurdity when the Vancouver *World* sued the Vancouver *Province* for libel in 1906 because of the latter's claim that it had twice the circulation of the former. Although the judge dismissed the action, he still found the *Province's* assertion to be erroneous.[5] If nothing else, the *World's* lawsuit underscored the vital importance of circulation. In 1911 the Montreal *Herald* contested the Montreal *Star's* claim that it had a circulation five times greater than that of any local competitor. In this instance, the matter did not go to court, and after some initial skirmishing both sides dropped the issue.[6]

That the *Province* inflated its circulation figures would not have surprised anyone in the newspaper industry. Only very successful newspapers like the Montreal *Star* enjoyed a reputation for honesty in this regard. Most published circulation figures were fictitious, as new owners often found to their dismay. E.N. Smith was shocked to discover in 1903 that the circulation numbers of the newly purchased Ottawa *Free Press* were "padded to an absurd degree."[7] When Joseph Atkinson took over the Toronto *Star* in 1899 he discovered that he had been misled into believing that the newspaper's circulation was twice the true figure of seven thousand. The owners of the Toronto *News's* circulation in 1902 also claimed a circulation twice as large as what the books showed. Unlike Atkinson, however, Flavelle and Willison decided to charge advertisers space rates according to the inflated figures.

The rise of advertising agencies in the 1890s and the growth of national-brand advertisers eventually persuaded the Canadian newspaper industry to adopt a more honest approach towards the publication of circulation figures. In this they were influenced by the

American movement in support of publication of audited circulation statements. The movement, which began in 1899, culminated in 1913 in the establishment of the Audit Bureau of Circulation (ABC). Advertisers in both Canada and the United States were increasingly demanding high-quality information on newspaper circulation and on readership demographics, and the birth of ABC was an important step in achieving this aim. In Canada the *Canadian Printer and Publisher* fulminated against circulation figure "abuse" and called for the appointment of an official circulation auditor, a call that the CPA endorsed in 1906.[8] Although some Canadian newspapers began to publish audited statements, many publishers balked at revealing true figures. In 1908 the Southams estimated the Vancouver *Province*'s actual circulation at only 10,000 to 12,000, not 15,000 as claimed. As late as 1915 J.S. Willison privately declared that "no paper in Toronto issues anything like an honest statement of circulation."[9] The excessively competitive Toronto newspapers were among the last in Canada to join the ABC.

In 1914 the formation of the Association of Canadian Advertisers, whose avowed goals were to investigate newspaper circulation figures and to establish standards for assessing circulation, persuaded many reluctant publishers that they had to abandon their old practices. At the CPA convention held in 1914 the newspapermen adopted a formula that called for verification of circulation statements, publication of an official directory, and adoption of a standard circulation blank. This last was especially important since it would prevent "juggling of figures and the presentation of them in such a way as to give a wrong impression."[10]

Newspaper publishers soon learned that failure to provide accurate circulation figures could threaten their business. In 1916 the Canadian Manufacturer's Association (CMA), which apparently placed great emphasis on circulation audits, requested that the Southams provide circulation figures for the Hamilton *Spectator*. When the Southams refused, the CMA became "suspicious ... that Toronto newspaper circulation in Hamilton was greater than suspected" and began to think that the Hamilton market might just as easily be reached through Toronto newspapers as by advertising in the *Spectator*.[11] CMA pressure explains in part why twenty-seven of the larger Canadian dailies had joined the ABC by 1917, and why, two years later, the largest fifty-three Canadian dailies (out of 125) were members, representing a circulation of 1,525,000 out of a total of 1,950,000.[12]

The audit movement was one expression of the newspaper industry's new enthusiasm for "scientific" business methods at a time when established ideas about the newspaper's role were giving way to the desire for profit and to the demands of advertisers. The years after 1890 saw the rise of the newspaper business manager and the appearance of specialized circulation professionals. By 1904 circulation managers had a column devoted to their concerns in the *Canadian Printer and Publisher*. Canadian circulation managers joined the American National Association of Managers of Newspaper Circulation, and the *Mail and Empire*'s W.J. Darby was even elected its second vice-president in 1904. Canadians attended the association's annual conventions, one of which was held in Montreal in 1910. There, Canadian managers read papers with such titles as "Circulation Value of Serial Stories" and "Are Sporting and Other Extra Editions Conducive to Permanent Circulation Gains?" As these titles suggest, circulation managers increasingly sought more precise information about the usefulness of special features in attracting circulation.[13]

In 1917 the Canadian circulation managers formed their own national association. At its first convention, the leading speaker claimed that the circulation manager had grown from a "necessary evil" into a true "producer," and that the circulation manager's efforts promoted a "free and untrammelled press," independent of corporate and political entanglements.[14]

Beginning in the 1890s, circulation managers pursued aggressive marketing strategies to attract new readers. In 1894 the Montreal newspapers gave away illustrated books. In Toronto even the stately *Globe* had to acknowledge the demands of commerce by following the *Empire, Star, News,* and *Mail* in offering pictures and flower seeds as promotions. At the Manitoba *Free Press*, business manager E.H. Macklin promised new subscribers reduced rates and a patriotic painting depicting General Botha's surrender to the Canadian forces in South Africa. To those who resisted his pleas to renew their subscriptions, he sent a letter pointing out that the *Free Press* carried the latest and most extensive local news, attractive special features, and Sam Hunter's cartoons ("alone ... worth the price of subscription").[15] Macklin advertised his subscription offers in eighty-five western-Canadian newspapers, paid commissions to local agents for new subscriptions, and cajoled postmasters into promoting the newspaper in their communities. Macklin's tactics contrasted sharply with those of his predecessor, W.J. Somerset, who did little more than send threats of cancellation to readers whose subscriptions were about to expire.

Joseph Atkinson was another firm believer in circulation promotion. Within a month of acquiring the Toronto *Star* in 1899, he offered readers a fifteen-colour picture of South African war hero

Lord Roberts, which they could have by sending in six cents and a coupon from the newspaper. Other promotions featured portraits of Queen Victoria and the Prince of Wales and a book about the controversy over the authorship of Shakespeare's plays. This was just the beginning of a flood of "premiums," as such inducements were called. Other newspapers commented sarcastically on the *Star*'s promotional schemes, but Atkinson remained unmoved. When the newspaper offered its readers a thousand-dollar accident insurance policy in 1901, it stated that "the *Star* has no apology to offer ... the object is to place the paper in the homes of 30,000 people within the next year."[16]

Part of the strategy for increasing circulation involved using rudimentary marketing concepts, such as finding out what the subscribers thought of the paper and what sections they disliked or liked. The Ottawa *Journal*, for example, distributed a questionnaire to subscribers; the competing *Citizen* and its owners, the Southams, thought this "a very good way to find out what your subscribers like and dislike in your paper. It also ought to flatter them, and make them more friendly towards the paper by consulting them."[17] Other papers, such as the Toronto *Globe* in 1910 and the Manitoba *Free Press* and Calgary *Herald* in 1914, used professional canvassers to locate new subscribers.[18]

Contests became popular as knowledge of their circulation-boosting powers spread. In 1911, the *Canadian Printer and Publisher* began to run an occasional "Circulation Contest" column, which usually described about a dozen such stunts. The number of contests increased sharply during World War I, and the schemes grew more elaborate as newspapers tied local merchants into contests. Merchants were persuaded to offer reductions on goods upon presentation of coupons from the newspaper in exchange for free advertising space, which partially offset the costs of the reductions. The Calgary *Herald* in 1913 even induced the Canadian Pacific Railway (CPR) to offer reduced fares to those with coupons, which were also good for price reductions and prizes from other participating merchants.[19]

The variety of contests began to stretch the imagination. Readers were asked to count the circles in an illustration; they could win prizes for having the most freckles, being the ugliest man, prettiest girl, or most successful businessman, or possessing the biggest fish. Some schemes involved a "Mysterious Millionaire" who travelled around Montreal or Toronto giving prizes to anyone carrying the *Star*. The gifts became more lavish and expensive – ponies, boats, automobiles, one hundred acres of farmland, a new home. One Montreal *Herald* promotion in 1912 offered anyone who got twenty-five paid-in-advance subscriptions a trip to the seaside. Other prizes in the same contest were a trip to Europe, a player piano, and an automobile. In the early 1900s such contests became more expensive, costing the papers $2,000 or more to run. Their costs rose steadily, however, and in 1919 the Winnipeg *Telegram* spent $78,000 in "highly intensive circulation promotion."[20]

When the campaigns worked they did wonders for circulation, and the costs of running them were offset by additional revenue from subscriptions and increased advertising. The Ottawa *Citizen*'s "trashy inducements" helped it to outdistance its competitors in 1900 with a circulation of about nine thousand,[21] while campaigns by the Manitoba *Free Press*, coupled with an aggressive and extensive advertising campaign, helped the newspaper to break even in 1901 and consistently run a profit after that.

Contests worked because they increased circulation, which meant that advertising rates could be raised. The campaigns could backfire, however, as the Toronto *News* discovered in 1903 with its "Newsman" who made the rounds of neighbourhoods giving away gifts in return for subscriptions. This was discontinued "owing to failure of advertising staff to procure necessary advertising to cover the expense of the gifts."[22] Its contest for the most popular commercial traveller failed because the travellers tried to fix the outcome. The lavish 1912 Montreal *Herald* contest seriously weakened the company financially as it failed to bring in sufficient advertising and subscribers.

The battle for circulation pointed to the key importance of advertising; from the days of the earliest eighteenth-century Canadian newspapers, advertising has consistently helped pay the bills. In 1905 the Toronto *Star* published an article that surveyed changes in advertising at the newspaper since 1896. Not only had advertising volume trebled, the article reported, but the quality of advertising had also improved. In 1896 most advertisements were of the "fire ... retiring ... or moving sales" variety. Advertisers on the whole could rely solely on the strength of their name or reputation to attract customers. But that was not enough in 1905, the *Star* observed, because increased competition now required business to advertise more often and to present more information in their advertisements. Advertisers also had to cater to a new kind of consumer – "a generation that have learned to look for advertising as they have their daily food."[23]

Advertising revenues have been a constant factor in the growth of the industry. Not only did advertising monies rise steadily in actual figures but their percentage of overall newspaper revenue also rose consistently, most dramatically in the 1890s. In the period from 1870 to 1890, the average percentage of revenue from advertising varied from 40 percent to more than 50 percent. In the 1874 Toronto *Globe*, then the largest paper in Canada, advertising accounted for 47 percent of total revenue. In 1885 it accounted for 45 percent of total revenue for five Toronto dailies. But by 1898 advertising's share of revenue had risen significantly for the five dailies to 73 percent.[24]

Clearly the 1890s were the breakthrough years in which advertising became the most important aspect in newspaper publishing. A number of socioeconomic and technological factors converged to bring this about, leading to the structural transformation of the newspaper industry as it became an integral part of the economic system. The rise of advertising revenue was a result of the increased business activity during the "Laurier boom," in which Canada experienced rapid industrialization and urbanization, as well as the need for an increased market for consumers. Goods were integral to this change. Basic consumer goods such as clothes and household items had either been produced in the home or sold in bulk at the general store. In the 1890s, manufacturers began to produce these goods on a large scale while at the same time distinguishing their products from other similar ones through brand names, which were promoted through advertising. Improvements in transportation and the postal service permitted manufacturers to reach a growing national market, while advances in newspaper technology and content allowed the dailies to become the main vehicle through which the manufacturers marketed their goods to the new consuming public. The linotype's versatility and speed also enabled more publishers to reduce the daily price to one cent, so that practically anyone could afford one, thus expanding the mass audience. The possibility of changes in advertising copy and formats on a daily basis, again facilitated by the linotype, further encouraged retailers and manufacturers to advertise in newspapers.

In 1895, it was estimated that the cost of distributing flyers was six dollars per one thousand as compared to one cent per one thousand for a four-inch newspaper ad.[25] Salada Tea owner Peter Larkin, for example, had tried advertising through signs in stores, on billboards and streetcars, in theatre programs, and through demonstrations at grocery stores and exhibitions in 1902. But, he asserted, none of these were as "effective as the trade journals and the daily newspapers." Larkin placed a different advertisement daily in more than five hundred papers, providing information on sales, price changes, and new products – in effect, making the advertisements part of the news.[26]

Before 1890 advertising had consisted largely of single-column insertions selling generic goods and services, usually the reproduction of business cards. Display advertisements that used two columns or more were rare, as was content that went beyond the functionally descriptive to the conceptual (i.e., "lifestyle" advertising of the kind that associates romance, for example, with the purchase of chocolates). The few illustrations that appeared usually consisted of a few line drawings or unclear images produced from woodcuts, and little more than the name of a firm or product.

That had changed by the 1890s, when lower advertising rates made it possible for advertisers to buy more space to promote their goods. As the decade progressed quarter-, half-, and then full-page ads became more common. In Toronto the average size of display advertisements more than doubled from 3.1 column inches in 1883 to 7.1 inches in 1906.[27] Drygoods and retail merchants, such as Eaton's in Toronto and Morgan's in Montreal, led the way in display advertising. Their ads were broken up into sections (like the stores themselves) in which different sorts of sale items were described. As engraving processes improved, the descriptions began to be accompanied by drawings of the goods. Other retail stores followed, some introducing attention-getting devices such as weather reports on the top of their ads, others adopting easily recognizable logos such as Simpson's use of the British ensign with R. Simpson superimposed over it. In 1891 twelve stores were advertising regularly in Montreal newspapers. By 1894 Morgan's was using as much as four columns of space. By the twentieth century full-page ads (usually the back page) for the giant department stores, Eaton's and Simpson's, had become commonplace in the large city dailies. Conventional wisdom dictated that the most effective way to advertise was to have large ads. The vice-president of the Montreal *Herald* advised that "big space should always be used. One big, bold advertisement is worth many small ones." Moreover, "the advantage of the big advertisement is that once the eye is arrested, the mind is at once placed in a receptive mood."[28]

The growth of display advertising led to a change in billing procedures and a shift of influence in newspaper advertising. In the 1870s the newspapers had begun to practice volume discounting, that is, charging less by reducing the advertising rate as contracted frequency of placement rose. At first, this applied to the same advertisement, usually a business card, which could be run unaltered over time (and using the same typesetting). But as display ads began to change on a daily basis and innovations like the linotype facilitated daily changes, the newspapers bent to pressure from frequent and large advertisers to give them the volume discount as well.[29]

Department stores and other high-turnover businesses, such as the national brand-name manufacturers, profited from the decreased costs made possible by volume discounting. Bigger concerns had an obvious advantage as their advertising rates were proportionately lower than those of smaller competitors, who advertised less. A large-space and frequent advertiser such as the T. Eaton department store, which by the first few years of the twentieth century was buying a full-page daily in the leading newspapers in several cities, commanded the lowest advertising rates. Other frequent advertisers also received the best rates. P.D. Ross charged E.B. Eddy $180 a year for one hundred lines in 1893 in the Ottawa *Journal,* while another company, P. O'Reilly, paid $200 for the same space.[30] The ad rate structure of the Calgary *Herald* in 1913 showed just how wide the price differentials could be, ranging from a high of seventy-five cents per inch for an infrequent advertiser to a low of forty-five cents per inch for its highest-volume advertiser, the Hudson's Bay Company: a sixty-six percent difference in price.[31]

Department stores were clearly very influential, especially after the turn of the century. Timothy Eaton forced Joseph Atkinson, owner of the Toronto *Star,* to initiate costly innovations to the newspaper's presses so that Eaton's ads could be run with a red banner. The *Globe*'s business manager altered the news to suit John Eaton in his campaign to induce him to advertise. The opening of Eaton's store in Winnipeg in 1905 caused the *Free Press* to expand its features, especially those catering to women, to attract advertising from Eaton's. Newspaper administrators learned that department store advertisements attracted readers just as much as the news, as a dispute between Eaton's and the *Free Press* showed. During a six-week battle over advertising costs, the paper lost eight thousand subscribers. Many of those who switched told the paper, according to E.H. Macklin, that although they had taken the paper for years "the 'Missus' wants to see the Eaton advertisement and as the Eaton advertisement is only carried in the *Tribune,* we have to take that paper and cannot afford to subscribe for two."[32]

With the department stores spending some three to five percent of their yearly income on ads, their advertising dollars loomed large in any newspaper's annual revenue. The new Hudson's Bay store's annual contract for the Calgary *Herald*'s back page paid $25,000 in 1913 – almost fourteen percent of the paper's local advertising revenue. Advertising by the Hudson's Bay also compelled other retailers to increase their advertising to compete, leading to additional revenue for the *Herald*.[33]

By the twentieth century, newspapers had become much more

aggressive in securing advertising and in creating a market for it. They now began to advertise themselves as an effective retail medium. For example, the CPA and the Association of Canadian Advertising Agencies combined in 1912 to promote the merits of newspaper advertising. Aggressive promotion extended to aggressive involvement in promoting their advertisers. After 1910 newspapers had become so involved in promoting advertised goods that the next logical step would have been actually selling them. The Regina *Leader* furnished special reports on any product or article on sale in the city to any national brand manufacturer who had advertised in the newspaper, but it went further by reporting on goods not yet available in Regina in order to encourage the manufacturer to provide and then advertise them. Other tactics involved special "dollar day" shopping festivals for the town's merchants. The St Catharines *Standard* sponsored the event by publishing a special supplement on pink stock. Interested merchants paid extra for inclusion and received an arrow for display in their store windows. The significance of the arrow was pointed out in the newspaper's columns, and in this way the public was encouraged to support those stores that contributed to the extra cost of the festival. The Calgary *Herald* organized a week-long shopping scheme involving a "refund-your-fare" offer in conjunction with reduced fares from the CPR, which allowed out-of-town shoppers within a radius of three hundred miles to get their train fare refunded at the *Herald*'s office if they could provide receipts showing that they had purchased a certain amount of goods from merchants who advertised in the *Herald*. The merchants benefitted from $150,000 in increased sales and the *Herald* from the $5,000 it induced them to invest in special advertising.[34]

As part of the push to increase advertising, newspapers created promotion departments. The Ottawa *Journal*'s promotion department was quite explicit in describing the lengths to which it would go to attract advertisers. Among other things, it would advise local merchants of new advertising campaigns; assist a manufacturer's sales department with placement of goods; encourage local dealers to give window and counter display space to items advertised; induce the sales staffs of Ottawa stores to promote advertised articles; check up on sales and assist the salesmen of the advertiser to secure proper distribution of their lines in Ottawa stores; and publish promotional material in the *Journal* to increase the interest of readers in responding to advertisers.[35]

The last item reflected a major change in the definition of news. Modern press mythologizers have made much of the idea that the rise of newspaper "independence" led to the eventual separation of opinion from news copy and the introduction of separate editorial pages. What has not been acknowledged is that with the increasing emphasis on the newspaper as a pure business, the line between news copy and business promotion was becoming increasingly blurred.

In a 1909 editorial, the *Canadian Printer and Publisher* was ambivalent on the question whether "editorial influence should be thrown into the balance to sway the purchasing power of [a] paper's readers in the direction of its advertisers." Significantly, it did not condemn the use of news columns to push goods but admitted instead that there was "no doubt that the paper which will undertake to educate its readers to read and answer advertisements will prosper surprisingly." It left it to the individual paper to decide whether the work of educating should be "conducted from the editorial or advertising departments."[36]

On average, advertising consistently made up more than 70 percent of total revenue for Toronto newspapers in the early years of the twentieth century, the percentage often rising to 80 percent or more during and after World War I.[37] In 1918 the overall average percentage of advertising to total revenue was calculated for all Canadian dailies to be 75 percent.[38] The Ottawa *Journal* illustrates the general trend. In 1891 advertising accounted for 62 percent of a total revenue of approximately $35,000, and 61 percent in 1892. Twenty-five years later, in 1920, advertising accounted for approximately 83 percent of a total revenue of $574,910.[39] The *Journal*'s total advertising revenue of $491,000 shows how advertising became the financial motor in turning the newspaper into big business.[40]

Despite protestations about the need to maintain the independence, freedom, and public responsibility of the press, advertising considerations were becoming paramount in newspaper operations. Newspaper space was for sale, and this concept overrode all others. The way newspapers dealt with the question of fraudulent advertising is a case in point. The issue of "fake" or "objectionable" advertising had plagued the industry since the nineteenth century, when the largest single type of advertisement carried by the dailies was for patent medicines. Some of these medicines, like "Dr William's Pink Pills for Pale People," were harmless concoctions, but others, such as those that claimed to cure tuberculosis, gave rise to cruel illusions and in some cases could be harmful to desperate sufferers. There had also been a rapid increase in advertisements for "fake" mining company shares, or prepaid clothing and furniture where no goods were ever sent. The issue of newspaper responsibility should take in determining which ads should be run had been debated within the industry for some time: in 1896 the CPA had called for the banning of certain kinds of advertising such as that for alcohol and quack medicines. Yet little action, if any, had been taken. In 1913 a *Canadian Printer and Publisher* editorial admitted that "it is a lamentable reflection upon the good name of the modern newspapers ... that [they are] also the agency through which much that is deceitful and sordid and even criminal is propagated and exploited." The journal charged that the newspapers had been "slow to realize the fact that they have virtually been acting as accomplices by publishing the ads."[41] Newspapers were reluctant to refuse such advertising because of the loss of income, particularly from patent medicine advertising, on which a large part of a newspaper's income rested. Defending such advertising in the Ottawa *Citizen* following a complaint from a medical doctor, Harry Southam said, "We were adverse [sic] to carrying any patent medicine advertising, but if we threw it all out, we would have to go out of business, as it amounts to about 20 percent of our business."[42] In 1911 the governing council of the Toronto *Globe* sought to get rid of "unpure fake advertisements" but, when informed that doing so would cost the newspaper $16,000 a year, decided to eliminate such ads more gradually.[43]

The experience of the Montreal *Witness* suggests just how important questionable ads could be. The *Witness* approached advertising from a moral standpoint, censoring dubious amusement ads and banning ads for liquor and patent medicines outright. Although founded in 1860 as a proselytizing Protestant newspaper, it became an innovative mass daily in the 1870s. It was one of the first penny papers and also the first to use newsboys for home delivery. Its policy of excluding patent medicine, liquor, theatre, and similar advertising, however, cost it dearly. It estimated that by 1900 it was rejecting $10,000 worth of advertising a year, a loss that was considered a major cause for its eventual sale to outside interests in 1913.[44]

Some papers of the period also failed to distinguish graphically between news and advertising copy. At first glance, the front page of the 25 September 1905 Toronto *World* has no display ads, but a closer examination reveals twenty small ads, including purchased marriage and death notices set in the same type as news copy and headlines for advertisements set to resemble those used to report on news. A genuine news story such as "New York Civic Election" is followed by "Dineen's Hat Opening," an ad set in the same typeface. Harry Southam noted that the *Spectator* often set regular news heads over an ad "so the reader cannot distinguish it from regular news."[45]

Some newspapers went further and actually wrote up advertisements as news. At the Canadian National Exhibitions of 1893 and 1898 there were complaints of "nefarious" practices by certain "harpies and blackmailers" in the Toronto press who were inducing manufacturers to pay them so much per line for write-ups of the products they were exhibiting.[46]

There was some question within the industry whether such practices were bad. In 1900 the *Canadian Printer and Publisher* wrote approvingly of the *Petrolia Advertiser* for devoting several columns to a commercial directory that contained several short news stories about various firms. The article noted that the biggest papers "do an extraordinary amount of the missionary work for their best advertisers. Often they successfully conceal the reading notice [list of advertisers] under the guise of trade news, which, after all, is often more interesting than a lot of trash which newspapers publish nowadays."[47] This attitude shows how advertising needs often blurred the distinction between "puffing" advertisers and straightforward business reporting.

Toronto *World* publisher W.F. "Billy" Maclean was shameless about the practice of trying to get increased reader attention for his advertisements by writing up their products as news. Often deals involved a *quid pro quo*. In 1909, for example, Maclean wrote puffs for a real estate venture in return for $1,500 worth of advertisements. Maclean was not alone in initiating these arrangements. W.J. Watson, the Calgary *Herald*'s business manager, described how on a holiday trip to Exshaw, Alberta, he managed to sell "a full page write-up of the cement plant [to the plant's owner] and got $300 for the write-up and [the purchase of] 500 copies of the paper containing same. If we could do that once a week it would help the profits along."[48]

Sometimes favourable coverage was given in the hope of getting paid advertising in return. For example, in 1905, when Bell Telephone started its "Telephone Talks" advertising, Maclean wrote to the company demanding advertisements because the *World* had given the company positive coverage during the 1905 Royal Commission investigation of the company's activities. When the company did not comply, the paper severely criticized Bell, accusing it of monopolistic practices and poor employee relations.[49]

Equally serious in terms of editorial ethics was the practice of ignoring or censoring unfavourable news concerning major advertisers, something to which no paper seemed to be immune. J.F. Mackay, the Toronto *Globe*'s business manager, maintained the large Eaton's department-store advertising account in part by "suppressing news that J.G. [Eaton] fancied would hurt him."[50] News suppression was also the norm in the Southam chain, especially when it touched on their printing business. At various times Fred Southam, who was in charge of printing, admonished those who ran the Ottawa *Citizen*, the

Hamilton *Spectator*, and the Calgary *Herald* for printing negative articles about his customers. J.H. Woods's apology to William Southam in 1909 made clear that publishers paid attention to such requests, especially after the *Herald* "got into Fred's bad books, owing to the publication of an item about the Grand Trunk Pacific. This paper has endeavoured as far as possible to avoid such subjects as might be matter for discussion between him and his customers in Montreal."[51]

The commercialization of news columns increased when publishers became involved with boosting civic growth in their respective communities. Since growth and progress, usually synonymous in their minds, figured so largely in their financial success, the publishers were understandably open to becoming self-appointed spokesmen for and boosters of the economic growth, progress, and well-being of their communities. Most publishers used their newspapers unashamedly to "boom" their communities. Not illogically, they reasoned that growth of their community would result in increased prosperity and growth for their newspaper.

Civic boosterism was not news, and the possibility of mutual benefit had been recognized for some time. At an 1899 CPA convention, the publisher of *Canadian Printer and Publisher*, J.B.S. Maclean, had justified such mutual back scratching. Instead of calling his address "How Newspapers Can Increase Their Revenue," he said, it should really have been titled "Newspapers and the Development of Canadian Resources," because "if our resources are developed newspapers will increase their revenue... Newspapers are prosperous when the communities in which they are published are prosperous. Communities prosper when money is being made and spent freely. Money is being made steadily by the fullest development of the industries and resources of the locality. The fullest development is brought about by public sentiment and interest. Sentiment and interest can best be created by the newspapers."[52]

The Lethbridge *Herald*'s W.A. Buchanan took this lesson to heart. From its first number, the front page carried the slogan "Watch Lethbridge Grow." Issue after issue boosted Lethbridge and Alberta industries and gloried in the industrial, farming, and population growth of the area. When the *Herald* became a daily in 1907, Buchanan announced that its policy was "to advocate the best interests of this city, this district and the province." But Lethbridge's businessmen had to help, he cautioned, and that meant they had to "support our advertising columns as much as you can ... It costs money to operate a daily in a city the size of Lethbridge, and we are depending on the loyalty of the citizens to local institutions to assist us in keeping the *Herald* up [to] the very highest standard. We will do our utmost to help the city advance, and that ought to mean something directly and indirectly to every individual in the city."[53] Buchanan was also the chairman of the city's Board of Trade publicity committee, as were many other publishers in their communities.

In 1910 publishers in western Ontario organized a campaign to boost the region, under the slogan "Stay in Ontario," designed in part to meet the aggressive promotion of western Canada by newspapers in the west. In the same year the New Brunswick publishers met to inaugurate a similar campaign for their province – "How to Make New Brunswick Prosperous."[54]

Under J.W. Dafoe, the Manitoba *Free Press* took the entire West for its constituency. The paper published regular reports on smaller centres from the Lakehead to the Rockies, while feature articles on various towns and industries appeared frequently. The *Free Press* noted any sign of progress or growth in articles on forestry and tree planting, mining, ranching, hydroelectric power, railways, and industrial development.

In a telling example of how business considerations and boosterism influenced the news, the Calgary newspapers were in a dilemma, "not wholly unfamiliar to others," over whether or not to publish the news in 1911 that several hundred unemployed men were seeking municipal relief. The newspaper that published the information was criticized by the others, which argued that the publication of such information is "calculated to do harm to the community by driving off capital and furnishing other parts of the country with arguments for use against the West."[55]

Commercial promotion had clearly entered the news columns of Canadian papers and was expected to provide benefits to the newspaper as well as the industries being promoted. A *Canadian Printer and Publisher* editorial admonished non-advertising merchants to examine the benefits that accrued to them through the local paper's efforts towards stimulating growth and development: "The optimism of the editorial columns, the faithful reporting of signs of industrial progress in the community, and the clear, forcible exposition of the community's commercial and social advantages make the local paper one of the best forms of municipal publicity."[56]

Newspaper boosterism assumed gigantic proportions in the early twentieth century. At first only the largest dailies in the biggest cities issued special editions devoted to promoting their communities, such as the Montreal *Herald*'s special 1892 issue on the "commercial growth of Montreal."[57] But by the turn of the century, newspapers such as the Winnipeg *Tribune*, with its thirty-two-page hymn of praise to the city's industrial growth, began to follow suit.

The specials grew larger: to celebrate its move to a new building in 1905, the Toronto *Star* of 21 August 1905 produced a massive and lavish sixty-four-page issue celebrating the industrial development of Ontario. In ensuing years, a plethora of special editions celebrating economic progress were issued, some as large as eighty-four to 148 pages. Typical was the 130-page "Prosperity" edition in the 1913 Calgary *News-Telegram*, of which it was said, "Every page indicates Prosperity in good, solid advertising and faith and enthusiasm in well-written forceful write-ups."[58] Smaller papers such as the Medicine Hat *News* or the Vernon *News* also took up the practice. The *Canadian Printer and Publisher* introduced a "Special Editions" column that, by 1910, regularly listed a dozen or more entries a month, the majority of which were local promotional editions.

Publishers found such special editions increasingly profitable. They gave advertising departments an excuse to solicit ads not only from regular advertisers but also from concerns that did not normally advertise and also led to increased circulation. The Toronto *Star*'s lavish 1905 special industrial edition was responsible for one-half of the newspaper's profits for the year. In 1908 the Toronto *Globe*'s special editions on the pulp and paper industry made a profit of $4,500. Special editions apparently provided its chief source of profit.[59]

Newspapers used any excuse to publish a special edition. Although the specials focused on a variety of subjects ranging from fashion, finance, tourism, and automobiles to crop surveys, the perennial favourites featured publication anniversaries featuring the date the newspaper was founded or relocated. For instance, a Calgary *Herald* business manager justified his latest special edition – from which he expected "to derive considerable revenue" – on the basis that the big event of moving from the old quarter to the new is sufficient excuse ... and we are sparing no effort."[60]

What passed for news in these specials amounted to little more than advertisements or promotion of special interests presented in a news format. The Toronto *Globe* celebrated its sixtieth anniversary on 2 July 1904 with a forty-four-page special devoted to the growth of Canadian industry. One large article extolled the Crow's Nest Pass Coal Company but did not mention that the *Globe*'s publisher, Robert Jaffray, was its major shareholder. By World War I links between newspapers and commercial supporters had developed even further. For example, the fifty-six-page "Prosperity Edition" of the Kingston *British Whig* published in 1916 toasted the Allies in colour and depicted local industries, the city and surrounding communities, and local social activities. The issue was the climax of the newspaper's year-long "Community Building" project. The paper benefitted through "the special advertising," which was on a "scale commensurate with the edition's size and importance. Page advertisements were many, and unusual advertisers were generous buyers of space." More significantly, however, the entire issue – "the compilation of facts and figures, the writing of editorials, the selection of articles, the make-up etc." – was prepared by the business office. The editorial office had nothing to do with it.[61]

The newspaper's transition from political to commercial vehicle is clear. J.W. Dafoe described this evolution in 1912: "The function and power of the newspaper had changed greatly. Formerly the editor of a newspaper was primarily a local fighter for a political party. Now the newspaper is recognized as an essential adjunct to the business activities of a community ... the better the newspaper the better the city."[62]

The commercialization of the news columns was abetted by the rise of national advertisers, which in turn led to the formation of advertising agencies. The first such agency, Anson McKim & Co., came into being after the Toronto *Mail* sent McKim, its agent, to Montreal in 1878 to drum up out-of-town or "foreign" advertising. Some of the advertisers McKim contacted wanted to advertise in Ontario newspapers other than the *Mail*. The *Mail*, through McKim, began providing newspaper rates and circulation for other Ontario newspapers. Many of these newspapers did not want to be represented by a potential rival, so in 1889 McKim severed his connection with the *Mail* to form Canada's first general advertising agency. Fittingly, McKim is credited with the conception that advertising could be sold like dry goods or any other commodity. By 1900, six Canadian agencies as well as some American ones were launching national campaigns.[63]

The formation of the ad agencies in the 1890s led to the professionalization of the advertising field. Increasingly, these agencies took over copywriting and layout from the newspapers or advertisers themselves, and the ads became more persuasive and effective. The ad agencies deserve much of the credit for transforming advertising content from the functional – a bare description of the product or notice of a sale with price – to the conceptual, where sexual, psychological, and lifestyle connotations are connected with products. A good example of the latter are the turn-of-the-century soap ads, which mixed the concepts of guilt and duty by suggesting that the housewife who did not use their product was exposing her family to disease, while those who did not only eliminated this risk but also saved money, time, and effort. By 1889 J.R. McConnell was already demonstrating a grasp of "concept" advertising: "It must not be forgotten that many new things have been introduced and a demand created for them by advertising – things which the public never knew they wanted until they heard of them through advertising."[64]

By 1920 advertising had become the financial motor of the newspaper industry. Competition between newspapers was no longer fuelled by politics as it was in the nineteenth century but by the need to build up readership in order to command higher advertising rates. As the financial stakes rose, competition between newspapers intensified and expanded to other areas. The next chapter will explore the strategies employed by newspapers to dominate their local markets.

5 Competition and Collusion

The emergence of the advertising agencies as well as the growth of national advertising and volume discounting intensified competition in the newspaper industry. At the same time newspaper publishers also negotiated among themselves to reduce this often "ruinous" competition in order to ensure a "living profit."[1] Alternating conditions of competition and collusion led to increased concentration in the newspaper business, a trend that was fuelled by the already high costs of market entry into the daily newspaper field.

Similar to other industrialists, publishers used four broadly based, often overlapping strategies to reduce and overcome competition: invade other markets, outspend the competition, buy out rivals, or alternately fight and collude with competitors. The "dollar daily" – so called because big-city publishers charged a minimal, almost giveaway, fee of one to one and a half dollars a year to out-of-town subscribers rather than the normal three to five dollars a year, beginning in the 1890s – signalled the emergence of "classically individualistic entrepreneurs who recognized no limits on their right to engage in any lawful business practice."[2] Several key publishers used such predatory pricing tactics in an attempt to dominate the industry. They also used their superior local positions (higher subscription prices and lower per unit costs) to invade small-city and rural markets in order to increase their circulations and gain more advertising revenues, as well as positioning themselves more favourably to take advantage of national brand advertising, especially from big department stores and mail-order houses.

Low federally subsidized postal rates on the railways helped to increase circulation beyond local limits, at the same time that the intense competition for circulation and shrinking opportunities for local growth necessitated the expansion of newspapers into other markets.

The dollar daily was sold at below-cost. During the 1890s, for example, one estimate suggests that the cost to customers barely covered the cost of the paper needed for three hundred issues, let alone editorial and production costs. By 1903, as production costs rose and papers grew larger, the Toronto *Globe*'s J.F. Mackay estimated that the $1.50 a year charged to subscribers didn't even meet the cost of the paper and that the newspaper lost from twenty-five to fifty cents per subscriber.[3] As the century wore on, subscribers paid directly for less and less of the newspaper. By 1912 the cost of the Manitoba *Free Press* to subscribers was four dollars a year less than the cost of producing the paper.

Substantially lower paper prices, widespread use of the linotype, greater advertising volume, and higher advertising rates made this phenomenon possible. The appearance of the first dollar daily, the Toronto *News*, in 1894 may have been closely related to the desire to increase paper sales, since papermaking was the principal interest of its owners, the Riordon family. Contemporary critics suggested that "Mr Riordon is anxious to sell the product of his paper mill and that is all he cares about."[4] Although newsmen called the Toronto *News* an "abortion" because, apart from a few alterations, it was a morning version of the evening edition, the concept was an immediate success. Initially the reduced out-of-town price caused the *News*'s circulation to soar past 42,000 in 1898, though the total shrank to 30,000 and lower in the next two years because of the introduction of competing dollar dailies.[5]

As the decade wore on, the steady growth of railway links helped big-city publishers to compete against the rural and small-town publishers. Even in the last century, railway access had greatly helped the large metropolitan dailies to penetrate the hinterland. The Toronto *Globe* attributed its large circulation in the 1880s largely to a special train that it leased to carry its morning edition to towns such as London. The Hamilton *Spectator* abandoned the morning newspaper market in 1895 because it found it difficult to compete with the Toronto dailies, which were sent to Hamilton on the morning train.

The dollar daily threat intensified after 1908, when the inauguration of the new postal service allowed country residents to receive the daily news "fresh and crisp" in the morning. In 1911 the Toronto morning dailies, the *World, News,* and *Globe*, made use of this new service by successfully arranging for the Grand Trunk railroad to begin a fast early postal run to London, Ontario. The "Flying Post" left Toronto at 2:55 A.M. and arrived three hours later in London, where it connected with the morning trains that left the city for the surrounding area. This enabled the morning dailies to reach subscribers in western Ontario from three to nine hours earlier than previously, or, as the Toronto *Globe* (5 March 1919) put it, "to be on the breakfast table 125 miles from Toronto." Rail expansion also helped the Montreal *Star* and *Witness* increase their circulation outside the city. In 1898, for example, the CPR's new line between Montreal and Ottawa made the Upper Ottawa Valley more accessible, while the 1902 merger of the Ottawa, Arnprior, and Parry Sound Railway with the Canada Atlantic short line and its subsequent absorption by the CPR in 1905 gave Montreal improved access to Ottawa's northern Ontario hinterland.

Newspaper canvassers for the big dailies of both Montreal and Toronto quickly took advantage of the improved post and rail services to aggressively solicit rural subscribers. The publishers of the smaller cities and towns now complained more than before about the "unfair competition" of the dollar dailies, which were undermining the twin pillars of their livelihood, circulation and advertising.[6] The early trains made local papers particularly vulnerable because the big-city dailies were now available to rural subscribers before the local papers (which could not be printed before the 11:00 A.M. mail deadline, meaning they were a day late). The dollar dailies were also significantly cheaper and offered a wider variety and choice of advertising, including mail-order advertising, a further lure to country dwellers. The ease of shopping by mail led to lost sales for small-town and village merchants, who in turn reduced their advertising in the local papers. It is no wonder that small publishers viewed the dollar dailies "with alarm,"[7] complaining that they were "an unscrupulous wrecking of legitimate newspaper interests."[8] Admittedly, some smaller publishers had introduced the bigger papers to their subscribers through the practice known as "clubbing," whereby a country weekly sold its own paper and either the Toronto *News* or the Montreal *Star* for $1.50 a year, with the weekly keeping half the amount of the daily subscription. Although this practice proved momentarily profitable for some, others rightly feared that a monster had been spawned in their midst and would soon devour them. One small publisher observed that clubbing reduced advertising in small towns because national manufacturers or patent medicines didn't have to advertise in the local papers – locals read the ads in the big-city dailies through the clubbing arrangement. Moreover, this created a "centralization" of business whereby advertisers and shoppers abandoned local areas in favour of the bigger urban centres.[9]

At the 1904 CPA convention publishers roundly condemned such big-city dailies as the Toronto *News* and *Star* and the Montreal *Star* for "dumping." Toronto *Star* publisher Joseph Atkinson admitted to the practice but said it couldn't be helped. "Other papers have been forced by competition and other reasons to go into this losing game, a losing game that I am in, and not for a longer time than I can help it."[10] Atkinson was being disingenuous; the dollar daily practice lost money initially but made money in the long term by allowing the publisher to charge higher advertising rates for the greater circulation.

The smaller publishers were clearly worried that business methods such as ruthless price cutting to drive out competitors, already common in other industries and leading to increased monopolization, would do similar damage to the newspaper industry. Out of desperation the Stratford *Herald*'s W.S. Dingman appealed to the editor of the Toronto *News* (then regarded as one of the "most aggressive" of the dollar dailies) to "reform the abuse":

According to present prices of paper I estimate that the cost of the white paper alone that is used in one copy during one year is in the vicinity of $1.50. That paper you sell outside of Toronto at $1, less commission, so that you net from each such subscription but some 75 cents to 85 cents a year. The loss is of course expected to be recouped out of advertising gained by increased circulation so obtained. Thus, besides encouraging the public in the disposition to grasp after something for nothing, the *News* is degraded to the rank of an advertising sheet, a class which is not recognized as entitled to the use of the newspaper postage rate. The methods of departmental stores have sometimes come in for severe criticism, and we are aware how unfavourably the reputation of John D. Rockefeller is regarded all over this continent at this hour, because of his Standard Oil methods, which are analogous to those of publishers who sell at $1 a daily the white paper alone in which costs 50% more than the gross price, and who do this in order to overcome competition and gain exaggerated circulation. I submit to you that this policy is out of harmony with the admitted high ideals after which the *News* strives in its treatment of public matters, and selfish and unkind toward contemporaries whose fields are restricted and who cannot [lose] on subscription revenue in the hope of recouping themselves by greater advertising charges.[11]

The complaints and pleas had no effect: newspapers were now clearly an industry, and their rules were those of the business world. Politics took a back seat to profits, as both Liberal and Conservative publishers took part in the "dumping" practice.

Agitation against the dollar daily continued at the 1906 CPA convention. Several publishers protested that the dollar daily violated the postal regulations governing second-class rates because of their heavy advertising and below-cost subscription rates. After the convention they pressured the federal government to recognize these violations. The question of postal subsidies harked back to the beginning of the CPA, which had been formed in part to lobby for them. In 1862 a delegation had been sent to convince the government that newspapers should be allowed through the mails without cost. Eventually the government accepted their argument that newspapers were educational matter and "public educators" and therefore entitled to reduced rates.[12]

In the early 1890s a dramatic increase in all-advertising circulars, proselytizing tracts, and increasingly bulky newspapers began to clog the mails and led to an alarming rise in the post office deficit. In 1889 the weight of newspapers carried free was 9,428,498 pounds; in 1891 it rose to 11,108,835 pounds, an increase of seventeen percent in two years. In 1897 it reached 16,557,490 pounds, a whopping increase of seventy-seven percent in eight years. These increases were considered the primary cause of the post office deficits of $800,000 in 1896 and $580,000 in 1897.[13] In 1898, Postmaster General William Mulock moved to institute postal rates for the newspapers in order to reduce costs and end abuses of the privilege. Terrified that their costs would skyrocket, the publishers raised a public outcry and attempted to rally their supporters in Parliament. Sir Charles Tupper defended subsidized rates for newspapers because of their educational value to the public. Another MP objected to higher rates as a "tax on knowledge." Mulock himself acknowledged that public opinion supported the cheap circulation of newspapers – it was the all-advertising circulars (many of which touted liquor and hotels) and the proselytizing tracts (he found one promoting "agnosticism" particularly offensive) that he objected to. These posed as *bona fide* newspapers, thus abusing the second-class-rate privilege.[14]

In 1889 John Ross Robertson, the Toronto *Telegram* publisher and MP, scoffed in Parliament at the notion of the newspaper as educator and wondered "why some newspapers, having a large circulation, should agitate and plead for the free circulation of newspapers." He noted that "three newspapers in Montreal and three in Toronto get considerably over one-third of the advantage consequent on this free carriage of newspapers." The end result, he said, was that newspaper proprietors had over sixteen million pounds of newspaper carried annually for free. "Why," he queried, "should the Dominion be called on to contribute to the revenue of these newspaper proprietors?"[15]

In the end, MPs and publishers agreed to an arrangement that eliminated the worst abuses but still preserved the second-class rate

– a mere quarter of a penny per pound of newspaper as opposed to thirty-two cents a pound for letter mail. To qualify for these rates a publication had to be a genuine newspaper that met the post office definition of a vehicle for the dissemination of news, a commodity that was sold to its subscribers for its news value, not distributed free or at a "nominal price."[16] Unfortunately for the smaller publishers, the post office never gave an exact definition of "nominal price." That omission was the loophole through which the dollar dailies flourished. The congestion problem that the amended post office regulations were supposed to address was never really solved, largely because Canada's booming industries increasingly realized that newspapers were the best medium through which to sell their goods.

The development of national brand names and department stores were particularly important in encouraging the widest possible circulation for metropolitan newspapers. The industry's trade journal, *Canadian Printer and Publisher*, which systematically took up the cudgels on behalf of the smaller dailies against the five or six largest ones, charged in 1902 that "the big city department stores in a bid to get the country trade have urged big city papers to expand their country circulation – often by reduced subscription rates in Toronto of 80 cents to $1.00 a year!"[17] In 1907 the CPP had opposed the proposed postal flat rate for newspapers on the grounds that the only "beneficiary would be a few big city dailies." It charged that some of these papers were "practically owned by the mail order concerns" (which in turn were controlled by the department store companies), and that "some which are not so owned receive a great deal of advertising support from them. The ambition of these dailies is to please their mail order owners and advertisers who are urging them to work up a national circulation."[18] In 1904, for example, Eaton's had advertised regularly in the eighteen or so small southern Ontario dailies, but in 1914 it confined publicity mainly to the biggest Toronto dailies. By then, the Toronto papers, which in 1904 had little outside circulation, calculated that at least half of their circulation was outside of Toronto.

Department store advertising also figured in the departure of daily publishers from the Canadian Publishers' Association, which had many weekly and trade journal members, to form their own organization in 1916. CPP worried that having their own organization would enable the bigger publishers to move even further into the "territories which are the natural fields of the small city daily and the country weekly" on behalf of the great department stores that wanted to see "the widest and largest possible circulation built up for the metropolitan dailies which carry their advertising."[19]

Circulation expansion of the Montreal and Toronto dollar dailies was nowhere more evident than in Kingston. Its location made it the battlefield on which the dollar dailies of the two larger centres met head on, as can be seen by Kingston's approximate out-of-town circulation in 1914:[20]

Montreal	*Star*	580	Toronto	*Mail & Empire*	250
	Gazette	15		*Globe*	220
	Herald	200		*News*	200
	Telegraph	75		*Star*	60
	Mail	50		*Telegram*	20
				World	19
Total		920			767

Considering that in 1913 the Kingston *British Whig* and *Standard* had only 4,232 and 4,017 subscribers, these figures show how threatening to small local papers the big metropolitan dollar dailies could be.[21] The figures also show how successful the Montreal *Star* was as a dollar daily, a success it enjoyed in markets as far away as the Maritimes. The *Star*'s pre-eminence was no surprise; by the 1890s it was already the largest and richest daily in Canada. Its circulation in Kingston was matched by its penetration of other markets, such as Ottawa's.[22] By 1913 approximately 40,000 of the *Star*'s 100,000 circulation was delivered by mail. The *Star*'s predatory tactics – it was the only daily charging the rock-bottom price of $1.00 against the $1.50 to $2.00 of other papers – alarmed many publishers at the 1904 CPA convention, and the paper's publisher, Hugh Graham, came under special censure. One critic charged that "it was never intended that newspapers should be distributed through the whole of Canada at a low rate to facilitate one man's accumulating the whole business. (Hear! Hear!). And I think the post-office arrangements could be attacked on the ground that no daily newspaper has a right to charge $3 to $4 in Toronto and $1 in Kingston. It is inequitably a fraud on the citizens of Toronto." But another publisher, the Sherbrooke *Record*'s L.S. Channell, defended Graham, making it clear that the practice of price cutting was likely to continue. "I don't blame Mr Graham. I think it is a straight question of dollars and cents to him. The extra circulation is all the better for his advertising end."[23]

By 1911 the *Star*'s invasion of the Maritimes was so marked that the region's publishers organized a petition asking the postmaster general to raise the postal rates for the dollar dailies. They also requested zoning charges that would allow them to continue to charge subscribers immediately outside the city the old rate but would effectively deny the largest metropolitan interlopers access to their markets because of much higher long-distance rates. The petition movement snowballed as the small publishers in central Canada joined the campaign. They were eventually joined by medium-sized publishers such as the London *Free Press* and the Ottawa *Citizen*. By 1913 over one hundred out of 135 daily publishers had signed the petition.[24]

In their complaints, smaller Canadian publishers were acting like other small businessmen at the same time as the biggest entrepreneurs were threatening to dominate industry after industry. Small businessmen pressured the government to regulate competition on their behalf and thus ensure fair play. In this case, they called on the federal government to amend the postal regulations in order to deny second-class rate privileges to the dollar dailies. The largest dollar dailies, they contended, were no longer newspapers as defined by the 1898 regulations since they now consisted primarily of advertising and non-news features (comics, women's pages, etc.); they had become advertising circulars more than vehicles of "news dissemination." Moreover, the $1.00 or $1.50 charge to out-of-town customers was arguably a "nominal price" – all of which disqualified them from the second-class postal rate.[25]

The publishers' cause was also aided by the railways, which clamoured for more subsidies to cover the losses that were incurred, they claimed, by the substantially larger editions they were forced to transport at the old rate. They were ignored by the Laurier government and by the Borden government, which followed in 1911. Government inaction was attributed to the power of the big dailies, especially the Montreal *Star*. One postmaster general, L.P. Pelletier, admitted that he "could not afford to fight the leading dailies."[26]

The dollar daily situation was not corrected until World War I, when the Montreal *Star* and other papers voluntarily raised the out-of-town subscription rates to two dollars or more. Factors such as wartime newsprint shortages, the general decline in advertising, and mounting rationalization (mergers and bankruptcies survived by the more efficient and profitable newspaper enterprises) may have contributed to the decision to raise rates.

The contrasting fortunes of the Montreal *Star, Herald, Witness*, and the later *Mail* and *News* at the turn of the century foreshadow the eventual rationalization of the newspaper industry in Canada as a whole. They also provide one of the best examples of the new breed of newspaper entrepreneur ruthlessly determined to control the market – the *Star*'s Hugh Graham.

From the beginning Graham ran the *Star* primarily to make

money. He was a pioneer in the use of such tactics as massive coverage of local events, numerous features, special correspondents, and the latest and fastest print technology so that he could outdo his opponents. As journalist A.H.U. Colquhoun attested in 1896, "Mr Graham spends freely on the paper and is willing at all times to pay well for the best that is going."[27] The *Star* consistently had the best and most complete news services and correspondents. It was the only paper besides the Toronto *Globe* to send two correspondents to cover the South African war, and in 1902 it shared the cost of establishing the Canadian Associated Press and its direct cable to Great Britain with John Ross Robertson of the *Telegram*.

Graham was the first to make circulation the criterion of success in the public and, more importantly, the advertiser's eye. Colquhoun noted that Hugh Graham's Montreal *Star* advertised its circulation figures even before it had outstripped its rivals in circulation. By the time it had the biggest circulation in Montreal, its previous forthrightness caused advertisers to "accept them as genuine without challenge."[28]

In the 1890s publishers in Montreal began to find that they had already expanded local readership to the limit. This exacerbated the competitive situation and was the main reason for the strenuous dollar daily efforts of the *Star* as well as its competitors, the *Herald* and, in 1909, the *Witness*. Montreal newspapers had felt the pinch of the "limited English market constituency" as early as 1894 and had added more features and extra editorial staff in an effort to compete. One observer noted that "eight or nine years ago their circulation was nearly as large as now, and their rate for advertising as good, yet their expenditure was almost 50% less."[29] Their problem was to increase advertising to make up for higher costs without having to raise the newspaper's price. The *Herald*, for example, lost one and a half cents on each one-cent paper. This loss was accounted for by its price reduction from two cents to one in 1894 coupled with increased staff and machinery costs. It had to be made up out of increased advertising at better rates. This in turn required a larger circulation, which was gained by a reduction in daily price leading to a wider market. As described earlier, the *Herald* was forced to move to afternoon publication in 1896 to use the railroad to reach the hinterland markets. This created a veritable dogfight in the afternoon market between the *Herald* and the *Star*, especially since the *Herald* also acquired the energetic services of James Brierley and the largest subsidies in the Dominion from the newly elected Laurier government.

To compete with the *Star*, the *Herald* aped its sensationalist style and pursued an aggressive circulation strategy of offering prizes, gifts, and other inducements to new subscribers. Between 1897 and 1908 Brierley also tried repeatedly to arrange a "fusion" of the *Herald* and *Witness*, arguing that, since the two papers were "moving in many respects along parallel courses," their union "would result in a journal far more successful in a pecuniary sense at least, than either can be under existing circumstances."[30] The *Witness*'s J.R. Dougall agreed with Brierley's logic, "particularly the duplication of expense and the competition at present involved. Increased circulation and the conservation of energies now wasted on competition should immediately result in a more favourable comparison with the 'Star.'"[31] But Dougall refused the merger, fearing that the distinctiveness of his paper would be lost and that its mission of promoting classic liberalism and proselytizing Protestantism – or, as he put it, its "anti-rum, anti-Rome, anti-corsets, anti-tobacco, anti-gambling, anti-combines and anti-tariff" position – would be lost in the pursuit of money making pure and simple. In this he represented the old "personal journalism" of the nineteenth century, when newspapers were used primarily as a pulpit or platform. According to Dougall, a newspaper's role was to "lead and [provide a] voice [for] the good people in their more important campaigns," and unlike the *Star* and the other business-oriented "people's" dailies, its editorial side always ruled the business office.[32]

This approach had worked for the *Witness* during the nineteenth century. In the early 1870s it was Montreal's leading English-language daily. But the advent of the *Star* as a "purely money-making" newspaper in 1869 eventually caused its downward slide. The *Witness* did not grow as fast as the brash, exciting, sensational *Star* because it refused to compromise its moral stance by accepting questionable advertising or sensationalistic news coverage. This meant no liquor or theatre advertisements and no news coverage that emphasized murder, mayhem, or sin. It also meant no extensive coverage of sporting news, especially horse racing, prizefighting, and other sporting events that encouraged gambling. While these strictures had begun to hinder the growth and prosperity of the *Witness* at the end of the century, they crushed the paper's fortunes in the early twentieth century.

The *Herald*'s entry into the afternoon market spelled the beginning of the end for the *Witness*. After 1896 the "killing competition" from the *Herald* caused the *Witness* to lose money every year, forcing its publisher to dig deeper and deeper into his pocket to make up the losses. By 1909 consistently dropping circulation and annual losses had taken their toll and forced the paper to change its sixty-five-year tradition of non-commercialism and adopt some of the tactics of the successful businesslike dailies. It promoted itself through a $10,000 circulation contest. It bought expensive new printing and typographical equipment, spruced up its layout, beefed up its city and business reporting staff, and opted for livelier and wider news coverage. And it became a dollar daily and dropped its out-of-town subscription price.

Ironically, the paper could not capitalize on the initial success of its dollar daily campaign, which doubled its circulation. It actually lost even more money because it could not offset its additional subscription losses by greater advertising; its nineteenth-century "journal de combat" nature and moral strictures prevented it from reaching new advertising markets in areas its publisher considered unacceptable. For instance, by advocating temperance it lost not only lucrative liquor ads but also ads such as those for cocoa, when the distributors (who also dealt in liquor) decided to punish it. Its principled advertising stand cost it an average of $10,000 a year in lost advertising.[33] The *Witness*'s "independent" nature also hurt it with the party faithful, since the *Herald*'s advertising agents had no hesitation in using Laurier's "name continually in appealing to advertisers of a Liberal complexion" – urging that it would please Laurier that "the organ should have the preference."[34] The end of the *Witness* in 1913 heralded the demise of the nineteenth-century advocacy press in early-twentieth-century Canada.

The *Herald*'s revival after 1896 also threatened the *Star*. After Brierley's takeover, the *Herald* rapidly moved from having the fourth largest circulation to having the second largest in 1901. In 1891 its circulation was roughly one-tenth of the *Star*'s (3,500 to 32,083) but by 1905, it had climbed to over forty percent of its rival's (23,473 to 56,453).[35]

For Hugh Graham, however, competition did not stop at price cutting and outspending his rivals: he persistently and secretly sought to buy out his competition in order to put a stranglehold on the Montreal market. As M.E. Nicholls wrote:

In the 80s under Graham's shrewd direction the Montreal *Star* became one of Canada's most successful papers. It acquired early domination of the afternoon English language field in Montreal and all efforts to break his grip proved unsuccessful. Graham was not only an able publisher, he was a finished strategist, and if he loved anything more than running the *Star*, it was in busying himself in the affairs of his competitors. When one of them appeared likely to become a dangerous rival, he raided its organization and took from it selected key men. He had something to do with the rise and the fall of nearly every evening paper that came into the field in his time. Sometimes the motive was political; more frequently it was to make the *Star*'s domination of the field secure.[36]

To cite one example, in the *Star* of 5 November 1884 Graham called on creditors to initiate bankruptcy proceedings against the shaky Montreal *Herald*, hoping that if it were declared bankrupt, he himself could pick up the pieces on the cheap.

During the economic slump of 1913, which slowed advertising and forced newspaper retrenchment throughout the country, Graham moved decisively against his two rivals. He secretly financed the takeover of the *Witness* by Charles Gordonsmith, a former *Witness* employee. Several months later, Graham bought out financier D. Lorne McGibbon's controlling share of the *Herald* for $110,000 and then forced the merger of the two papers into the *Herald-Telegram*. In order to prevent the establishment of a new strong Liberal competitor, Graham reversed McGibbon's earlier attempt to make the *Herald* Tory by allowing the paper to espouse a mild Liberal party line. Equally significantly, he took over the contract under which former *Herald* publisher James Brierley was paid $40,000 not to publish a newspaper in Montreal for seven years.[37]

Graham kept the *Herald* operating, but barely. It was part of a strategy to deny market share and thus make it difficult for new competitors such as the *Mail* and the *News* to become established between 1914 and 1917. Veteran newsman Leslie Roberts described the process in 1929:

Consequently, when the *Herald* ... threatened the circulation domination of the *Star*, and more particularly of the *Star*'s week-end offshoot, the *Standard*, Sir Hugh Graham, as he then was, forced sale of the *Herald* to himself, slaughtered its Sunday edition and relegated its week-day issues to the backwoods of journalistic pauperdom, where it has remained for more than ten years, scarcely alive.

No true newspaperman would have felled the *Herald*, once he acquired it. But to the present day business journalist who regards his newspapers only as founts of revenue, the emasculation of a virile paper is simply part of the day's work on the road to the next million dollars. By these methods has he contrived to keep his field clear of competition in his latter years ...

In the operation of his newspaper he has throttled opposition in order that his papers might thrive more vastly, and, when opposition has been stifled, he has permitted his *Star* ... to slump into the doldrums of journalistic hodge podge.[38]

Buyout was not the end of Graham's bag of tricks when it came to beating the competition. Indeed, the start-up of the morning *Mail* in 1913 and its sister paper, the evening *News*, the year after never really had a chance to get underway in the face of Graham's determined opposition. When the *News* applied for vital membership in Canadian Press (CP) in 1914, it was turned down because of Graham's veto. Graham also reportedly controlled Montreal's newsprint supply, and there were accusations that he starved his rivals of necessary supplies.[39]

In 1917 the *Mail* and the *News* finally succumbed, in part because of wartime inflation, a drop in business, and the high cost and scarcity of labour, but mainly because they could not compete against Graham's capital. And this, despite a reported million-dollar investment over their three-year attempt to survive.[40]

The rationalization of Montreal's market, during which effective competitors disappeared, also occurred in other Canadian cities. Market saturation, rising overhead costs, and the dollar daily phenomenon meant increasingly that after the 1890s only the fittest newspapers survived. Publishers in other cities employed competitive tactics similar to Graham's in that they spent money to destroy their rivals or, when all else failed, purchased or amalgamated with their competitors.

Some cities began to rationalize before Montreal. By 1895, for example, London had two established papers, the *Free Press* and the *Advertiser*, which seemingly had the market sewn up, each publishing morning and evening editions. Each possessed modern web presses and Mergenthaler linotypes, and each took train services – the CPR day service, and the midnight Great North-Western for the morning market. And they had successfully stymied four recent attempts to start rival papers by meeting the would-be competitors' price cuts. The respective strengths of the two papers also prevailed against their most serious challenger, the well-financed *News*, which managed to last until the turn of the century. From then on, London became a two-paper town with no new challengers.

In the smaller cities, the favoured tactic for controlling the market was to spend your rival into the ground. The Woodstock *Sentinel-Review*'s Andrew Pattullo had used this strategy in 1898 when faced with a new challenger, the *Express*, and a weekly turned daily, the *Times*. Determined to drive out his competitors, Pattullo hired a vastly expanded and expensive staff, including some Toronto journalistic heavyweights and a talented business manager. Pattullo also sank money into a state-of-the-art Cox Duplex printing press and a new stereotyping plant (which made a cast of the typeset page, thus avoiding the need to reset type), all of which set a pace that his competitors found hard to keep. Circulation rose sharply, and the *Times* was driven into collapse. The same thing happened later to the *Review*. Pattullo then cut his expenses and reduced his all-star staff to normal size.[41]

In Winnipeg and Calgary spending the opponent into bankruptcy was also used to help rationalize the market by the end of the war. In these markets, however, the dominant papers first sought to secure advertising and subscription rate agreements with their competitors. Initially the Calgary *Herald* and the Manitoba *Free Press* were unable to arrange such agreements because their competitors feared that they would be giving up their most effective means of competing – pricecutting. When in 1915 the Manitoba *Free Press* was unable to come to an agreement with the competitors for a citywide price hike in subscription costs to offset wartime inflation and extra costs, it unleashed an expensive competition for subscriptions that involved contests and the expansion of the paper's features and news coverage. By 1917 its campaign had forced its rivals, the *Telegram* and *Tribune*, to capitulate and agree to adopt the *Free Press*'s price hikes. The fierce competition also had the effect of seriously weakening the *Telegram* and the *Tribune*. Both were serious money losers at war's end, and the *Telegram* subsequently abandoned publication.

The Calgary *Herald*, in a market where there were three roughly equal competitors in 1908, used similar tactics to achieve domination by the end of World War I. When its rivals refused to collude, it had sufficient capital (provided by its owners, the Southams) to buy additional popular features and hire more staff to provide increased local coverage, which attracted more readers. Such resources were not available to its less well endowed competitors. The *Herald*'s publisher, J.H. Woods, explained that profits were lower in 1911 because of "considerable" expenses for extra features: "We feel that we do not want the *News-Telegram* to even commence to get a grip on this field, and I thought it was time we made a little splurge and improved our paper."[42]

The *Herald* was able to use its superior circulation figures as well as price-cutting practices to keep its main rival, the *News-Advertiser*, from increasing its advertising revenues. In 1909, after "hopeless endeavours to get the papers to raise their subscription rates" from three dollars to match its five-dollar rate, the *Herald* cut its own subscription rates to three dollars a year for an indefinite period. This had the effect of "cutting out a good many subscribers from the Calgary *News* and transferring them to us."[43] In 1915 it resorted to the same tactic when it offered discounts if advertisers bought space for three days a week and also offered an extra discount for cash with each order. Woods explained that "we offered this in order to cope with the cut rates that the other papers were giving for the purpose of securing business." The tactic worked, and Woods noted that "we get just now about 75% of the real money that is being spent by the half dozen largest retail advertisers in town."⁴⁴ This wasn't the end of Woods's ploys. In the same year he offered the paper's biggest advertiser, the Hudson's Bay Company, its lowest rate exclusively on condition that it not advertise in the *News-Advertiser*. By war's end, the *Herald* was able to dictate price rates for both subscriptions and advertising to the other papers. Not surprisingly, the money-losing *News-Advertiser* died in 1918 after a brief but futile change of name to the *Canadian*.

Although collusion was used primarily to reduce competition, raise advertising and subscription prices, and increase profits, the Calgary and Winnipeg examples show that it was also used as a weapon to gain market ascendancy. Clearly, in the *Herald*'s case, collusion tactics were actually competitive and ultimately predatory, aimed at maximizing profit and eventually at securing a monopoly position. As the dominant paper in Calgary – the only one that regularly made money – it could and did command advertising revenues and rates that were twice those of its competitors combined. The *status quo*, which the collusion agreements represented, only benefitted the *Herald*, especially in the long run, since it preserved a situation where one paper made money while ruling out the possibility of change.

In the twentieth century there was a growing belief among publishers that there were enough newspapers in Canada. They increasingly voiced their resentment of those who started new papers for political or polemical reasons, thus jeopardizing the investments of those publisher-businessmen already in the business. The CPP reflected this sentiment throughout the early twentieth century. In reporting the demise in 1901 of the Hamilton *Post*, for example, it noted that there were "too many newspapers in Canada."⁴⁵ It also printed statements by publishers who condemned the expansion of the number of dailies. J.F. Galbraith, publisher of the *Chronicle* in Morden, Manitoba, was a typical example. He denounced the "party politics" that fostered "papers that have been established for political reasons that never would have been contemplated as business enterprises." These papers, he contended, "not only demoralize business but they depreciate the real value of newspaper plants for, no matter what the real value of a newspaper plant may be, that value is destroyed when its earning power is not sufficient to pay interest and provide for wear and tear."⁴⁶

In some smaller cities publishers were finding that the "natural" number of dailies was two or even one, and that three definitely was too many. The owners of the Stratford *Herald*, the Dingman family, justified this trend ad follows: "This condition suits the public also, who do not feel complimented by being represented by half-starved, scrappy, local sheets."⁴⁷ As the twentieth century wore on, the problem of "too many papers" was increasingly solved through merger, amalgamation, or buyout.⁴⁸ The successful 1895 merger of the *Mail* and *Empire* provided a good example of how "fusion" could eliminate costly competition. Similarly, the merger of the St Catharines *Star* with the *Journal* in 1906 prompted the CPP to remark that the "St Catharines field should be greatly improved."⁴⁹ Other examples followed, such as the amalgamation of the four Fort William and Port Arthur dailies in 1910. Galt became a one-newspaper town in 1912 when the *Reformer* and *Reporter* merged on the grounds that Galt was "too small a place to support two daily papers"; the merger was "a move to turn two dead papers into one lively one."⁵⁰ After the 1913 economic slump J.K. McInnis sold his Regina *Standard* to the rival *Province* for "purely economic reasons and ... merely in accordance with the modern principle of conservation of both physical and monetary expenditure that is resulting in the amalgamation of all sorts of commercial and industrial enterprises."⁵¹

The economic hardships of World War I – declining business that led to less advertising; growing inflation, especially the rise in newsprint prices from $40.00 to $109.40 a ton; higher wages; and a labour shortage – accelerated newspaper mergers and amalgamations. Newspapers could not help but be affected by the decline in business that had begun in 1913 as a result of the faltering wheat economy, railway overexpansion, and the serious overextension of the manufacturing sector that drove many businesses to bankruptcy. During World War I production costs rose so much that many newspapers collapsed, leaving many communities with one newspaper instead of two or three. One observer described the near "panic" conditions at the outbreak of World War I when "contracts for many commodities, including advertising space, were cancelled in large numbers."⁵² To counteract this, the CPA asked its members to run a series of "Good Cheer" advertisements beginning 17 August 1914. J.H. Woods reported that at the beginning of the war, "business to date has been practically at a standstill owing to the war scare ... while the expenses of the war, extras etc., have been considerable."⁵² The Ottawa *Free Press*, which in 1913 seemed to be recovering financially, was severely weakened by the rising cost of newsprint, labour, and equipment and the decreased advertising caused by the war. It was eventually forced to merge with its rival, the *Journal*. Wartime inflation and the paper shortage were behind the collapse of the Winnipeg *Telegram* in 1920. The editor of the Montreal *Star* reported that the paper's operating expenditures, estimated to be one million dollars in 1913, increased by a thousand dollars a day during the war.⁵⁴ The Lethbridge *Herald* suffered because "credit tightening" contributed to a general business decline and stagnation. The *Miner* of Rossland, British Columbia, abandoned the daily field because of the "advance of paper costs, telegraph tolls, press reports because of the war."[55]

At first CPP clearly applauded the trend towards concentration, arguing in 1915 that "fewer papers" meant "better service" since there was a "great deal of over-lapping and duplication, and we believe that the time will come when it will be absolutely necessary for economic reasons for publishers to consolidate their interests with those of other publishers."[56] By war's end, publishers were clearly heeding this sort of advice. In city after city competing newspapers merged, all giving economic reasons for doing so. Typical was the 1918 amalgamation of the St Thomas papers into the hyphenated *Times-Journal*. CPP cited the reasons for "two such old and well-established newspapers" joining as "those which have been responsible for similar unions elsewhere – scarcity of labour and the excessive cost of materials which go into the making of an up-to-date daily paper." Significantly, the new entity, which replaced the two former Liberal and Tory organs, now was to be "conducted on strictly independent lines."[57]

Local monopoly was clearly regarded as the panacea for financial woes caused by too much competition for too little business. The Windsor *Record* waxed euphoric in 1917 about the benefits of being the only paper in town:

No more effective way of dealing with the white paper pinch and other problems pertaining to the increased cost of making a newspaper could be devised than by transforming two dailies published in smaller cities into one. There is abundant room in this province for such enterprise ...

Look at the saving to the merchant who feels compelled to advertise in both!

Consider the immense saving in white paper and the duplicating of everything that goes to make a paper.

Many of these papers owing to competition are now just making a fair living. What is going to happen to some of them, with the cost of newsprint already advanced 69%, to say nothing of other increases in expenses?

Woodstock and Windsor are fair examples of one-paper towns. These two papers are considered among the best small city dailies in Canada. They are abundantly filling the wants of their constituencies, and are saving the reading public and merchant considerable money, at the same time making a comfortable living for the publishers.

The other papers should think the proposition over.[58]

By 1918, Niagara Falls, Sarnia, and Stratford had become single-daily towns, and by the following year the trend had taken hold: of seventeen towns that had two dailies in 1911, only one had that many by 1921, and of nine that had had two in 1921, only one had two in 1931.

If merger was not possible, the favoured tactic was to buy out the competitor. The Niagara Falls *Review* explained that it purchased its competitor, the *Record*, in 1918 because both publishers realized that it was impossible for the two papers to have "decent returns on investment" given the higher production costs triggered by the war. It cost fifty percent more to produce the *Review* than it had two years earlier. "In the face of business-killing conditions the two papers have made every effort to keep above the current, but finally decided that the only business salvation was a getting together of some sort."[59]

In the biggest cities rivals were also purchased to clear the way for a monopoly in either the morning or evening market. After war costs forced P.D. Ross and the Southams to conclude that the Ottawa market could not sustain three dailies, they forced the merger and disappearance of the *Free Press* into the *Journal* in 1917. The same year saw the Vancouver *Sun* buy up the assets of the *News-Advertiser* because there was "no room for two morning dailies."[60]

Whether caused by merger, purchase, or bankruptcy, the result was the same – fewer and fewer dailies as the century progressed. The overall number of Canadian dailies had continued to rise until World War I, with increases mainly in the developing centres of the West, as growth was largely over in central and eastern Canada. In 1901, there were 114 dailies in Canada; by 1913 the number had risen to a high of 138. But wartime proved to be the big rationalizer. The first year saw nine dailies collapse, one in the East and eight in the West. By 1917 twenty had disappeared, and by the war's end, thirty-six dailies had fallen. By 1921 there were only 109 dailies in Canada. This trend continued after the war and in 1938 there were only ninety. The toll included some venerable and once-mighty concerns, including some thirty- and forty-year-old ventures such as the Toronto *World* and its colleague the *News*, the Winnipeg *Telegram*, Calgary *News-Advertiser*, Brantford *Courier*, Hamilton *Times*, and Ottawa *Free Press*.

The dailies that failed were not replaced by new ventures, in part because of the high costs of operating a large urban daily. In the few instances attempts were made to introduce new dailies, all were unsuccessful. The Saint John *Star*, which opened and closed in 1910, was typical of the length of time most new dailies survived during this period. In 1915 the Vancouver *Times* and *Evening Journal* survived only for forty-three and forty-four days respectively. The Montreal *Mail* and *News* were unusual in that they managed to last three years.

Not even access to large amounts of capital could stave off this decades-long trend, as the Southams discovered when their ill-fated Lethbridge *News* proved unable to compete with the well-established *Herald*. Joseph Atkinson lost in excess of $500,000 between 1922 and 1926 in a vain attempt to supplant the *Free Press* in London and start a newspaper chain at the same time.[61] And *Mail* backers lost a million dollars trying to break into the Montreal market.[62]

Newspaper attrition was furthered by the conscription debate and the election of a Unionist government, which disrupted traditional party allegiances and severely reduced patronage, making it even harder for the partisan press to function and increasing the emphasis on the economic aspect of newspaper publishing.

The trend towards fewer papers and increased monopoly and concentration was often abetted by advertisers. In 1912, for example, a proposal to start a paper in Berlin, Ontario, was quashed after advertisers signalled that they did not intend to use the new paper.[63] St Thomas advertisers were pleased by the merger of the city's two dailies.[64] And the long-term failure of the Toronto *News* was laid firmly at the feet of the major department stores, which systematically reduced or removed their advertising from it in favour of the stronger Toronto dailies.[65]

With decreases in competition and increased concentration in more newspaper markets across the country, the time was ripe for the development of Canada's first corporatively linked chain of newspapers – the Southam chain. The idea was not new; the American Scripps and Hearst chains had shown the way. In Canada, however, while papers in different cities might have had a single owner, such enterprises did not really constitute a chain as it is understood today – a permanent, centrally managed corporation that administers linked newspapers. Rather, before the Southams, they amounted to little more than one entrepreneur temporarily owning several newspapers.[66]

The Southam family's early newspaper holdings did not at first constitute a chain; indeed, their claims that the chain came about by accident ring true. The motivation behind their early expansion from Hamilton to other cities was that the new properties would contribute to what they considered to be their main business, printing. As one son said to family patriarch William Southam after their western expansion in 1908, "The moral effect of these two western papers would be a valuable adjunct to your general printing business." As late as 1915 another son could still observe that "the original idea in buying a chain of newspapers was that they should all work together for the common good of Southam Ltd – the common good now, as for years past, being the boosting of the printing business."[67]

Moreover, they occasionally were tempted to sell the newspaper properties, some as late as 1913, which suggests that they were not consciously creating a chain.[68]

What became Canada's first national chain of newspapers started in 1897 when William Southam, who controlled the Hamilton *Spectator*, sent his sons Wilson and Harry to purchase the Ottawa *Citizen*. Using Southam assets from the *Spectator* and Montreal and Toronto printing companies, the brothers eventually made the *Citizen* profitable after first absorbing $78,000 in losses between 1898 and 1901. Similar to the modern-day practices of newspaper magnates such as Rupert Murdoch, the Southams repeatedly used the value of their properties as collateral to raise money to take over and bankroll other newspaper properties. They were able to pay $15,000 in cash for the Calgary *Herald* in 1907, promising to pay a further $45,000 using their creditworthy properties as security. The Southams liked to spread the risk when absorbing other papers. When William Southam bought into the *Spectator* in 1878, he did so in partnership with William Carey. The Calgary *Herald* was purchased with J.H. Woods, who put in $3,000, as well as with other participants who provided smaller amounts. The same pattern occurred with the Edmonton *Journal* and the Lethbridge *Herald* in 1912.[69]

Following their western purchases, it appears that the Southams decided consciously to build a "national chain" across the country by purchasing additional properties in Montreal and Vancouver. And they decided to separate the printing business from the newspapers. J.H. Woods was enthusiastic about the chain proposal, observing that a "chain of papers such as you suggest would be the biggest power in the Dominion, besides being an immensely valuable property."[70]

The chain made sense. The need to cut costs for the western papers, because of intense competition in their locales, forced a corporate restructuring that enhanced the benefits of chain ownership. Accordingly, in 1912 a central organization was created, Canadian Newspapers Ltd, to put the three dailies under one corporate structure. The aim was to spread the risks – both the *Journal* and the Lethbridge *Herald* needed immediate ten-thousand-dollar infusions of cash – while simplifying them at the same time. The purpose of the new structure was to use the assets of the profitable Calgary *Herald* as the short-term guarantee for the liabilities of the other two, and the assets of Southam Ltd as the long-term guarantee for Canadian Newspapers Ltd overall.

Some advantages of chain newspaper ownership had already become apparent to the Southams. In 1907 the *Spectator* and the

Citizen reduced editorial costs by printing the same editorials often and "clipping" syndicated features and stories from each other. When the Southams bought a minority interest in the London *Free Press* in the same year, they realized further advantages of multiple ownership. These included "the exchange of information regarding offers of new business" and perhaps the three papers joining "in having a Toronto office, or a Toronto representative for looking after new business."[71] The Calgary *Herald* benefitted immediately from Southam ownership as the Southams were able to arrange for it the much lower newsprint prices they paid for their papers.

Canadian Newspapers Ltd, however, systematized benefits by formalizing the arrangement in a permanent corporate structure. All three papers were run from a central Calgary office, so that administrative expenses were shared and savings realized through volume purchases of supplies and equipment. Personnel and equipment were also shared as the need arose, thus avoiding duplication. The papers could now afford a full-time circulation manager who sold ads on a provincewide basis and organized joint promotions. The new structure also permitted editorial savings and an increase in quality through the hiring of an expensive "crackerjack" editorial writer, who would have been too expensive for one paper to support.[72]

The formation of Canadian Newspapers Ltd marked the beginning of the organization of Southam newspapers into one corporate structure devoted to their development. As noted above, the "principal objective" of putting the first three newspapers under one corporate roof was to use the stronger *Herald* to keep "the other two afloat until they were in a better financial position."[73] But the overall benefits of the restructuring persuaded the Southams to extend the same structure to the rest of their newspaper properties.

Another advantage of chain ownership became clear as the papers standardized their size and format. As J.R. Booth, the Southams' paper supplier, told them in 1911, by ensuring a longer run of paper, thus allowing more time to set it properly, standardizing resulted in a better-looking newspaper. There would also be less danger of shortage, since one paper could make up the shortfall of another. The "saving in the cost of paper as time goes on will far more than compensate them for the present expense [of standardization]."[74]

The Southams always consulted among themselves through circular and shared letters between Hamilton, Ottawa, Montreal, and Toronto on the effectiveness of syndicate material, paper and equipment prices, administrative practices, editorials, and so on. By 1911 more and more information was being compared as corporate standardization advanced. It took until 1915 to complete effective standardization and bring the western papers in as equal partners, at which point all the Southam newspaper statements and accounting systems were "standardized as near as possible." All information was exchanged so that the western papers "could compare their departmental costs with ours, as we do theirs with ours." Special meetings were instituted to "govern the newspaper ends of our business with the idea that all of us could perhaps gain something from a general talk on the newspaper situation."[75] The value of comparing standardized shared information quickly manifested itself. It allowed Wilson Southam, for example, to notice that the western papers had heavier expenses than the *Citizen*, the higher cost of doing business in western Canada notwithstanding. He urged the *Herald*'s business manager to come to the *Citizen* to take some "valuable pointers" from a cost management expert the *Citizen* had hired to improve its administrative methods.[76]

In addition to the pricecutting, predatory collusion tactics, modern business methods, and superior access to capital by which the Southams dominated their markets, they also consolidated their position by purchasing competitors. In Ottawa they shut down E.N. Smith's *Free Press*, which for years they had secretly controlled with P.D. Ross. Luckily for Smith, P.D. Ross allowed him to merge with the *Journal*.[77] In Hamilton, they bought the *Times* in the hope of merging it with the *Spectator*, and when that proved unworkable they closed the paper in 1920. In the same year, after buying the Winnipeg *Tribune*, they immediately bought its rival, the *Telegram*, for $100,000 and shut it down after absorbing its physical assets.

The dominance of the Sifton-owned *Free Press* of Winnipeg was threatened by the Southams' purchase of the *Tribune*. After being rebuffed in a bid to remove competition, the Southams loaded the *Tribune* with all the features and advantages that their chain could afford. Faced with this competitive onslaught, the Sifton family had the choice of selling the property or starting its own chain. It chose the latter course, beginning with the purchase of two Saskatchewan dailies in 1925. And the example of the successful Southam chain may have been the reason why Joseph Atkinson bought the London *Advertiser* in 1923.

The rise of the Southam chain fundamentally changed the dynamics of the Canadian newspaper scene. By 1919, the pre-war situation of lively and competitive markets had changed so dramatically that the CPP, which had so loudly campaigned against the inefficiency of competition, now changed its tune. It did not like the postwar landscape of monopolies and worried about the consequences to cities like St Thomas and Brantford, which could support two dailies but did not. It feared that the public's need to know would be sacrificed to business considerations and the quest for profit:

One thing that is necessary above all else is a free press, a paper that can say what it thinks without counting the cost. Surely, perhaps slowly, we are moving toward the point where the mediums that should be vehicles for public expression are being stifled and laid away simply because they have not earned more than it cost to run them.

The whole tendency increases the business pressure on the editorial columns. It makes men more fearful of failure. It makes them more ready to consider business interests in the conduct of their news columns or the drift of their editorial pages. And all the time that this is going on the public is the poorer and the more endangered.[78]

The foregoing indicates how deeply the newspaper industry had changed between 1890 and 1920 and how completely business had eclipsed editorial considerations. The industrialization of the newspaper – as symbolized by the contrasting fates of the editorially focused Toronto *News* and Montreal *Witness* and their rivals, the money-making *Stars* – was now complete. The intensely competitive markets of the 1890s had given way to the rationalized ones of the 1920s, as stronger publishers eliminated their weaker competitors through merger, amalgamation, or purchase in pursuit of higher earnings. The resulting fall in the number of competing dailies signalled a structural transformation in the industry whereby significant concentration characterized the market in many Canadian cities. Moreover, the steady expansion of the Southam chain showed that national combinations, not local dominance, would be the key to future newspaper survival.

6 Concentration

The growing concentration in newspaper markets paralleled developments in other industries. Describing oligopoly in Canadian industry, V.W. Bladen identified two kinds of market-regulating behaviour among competing companies in the same industry: where there are relatively few firms, informal agreement is common and occurs frequently under the leadership of the strongest company; but where the number of firms is large, more formal trade associations may develop. Newspapers displayed both types of behaviour. Locally, the small number of players in each city amounted to an oligopoly (or monopoly) whose members made informal agreements among themselves; nationally, the larger number of firms made informal agreements impossible, so formal trade associations were organized instead. The aims of these newspaper associations were similar to those of other industry associations, which according to Bladen were preoccupied with "fair trade practices" – "fair trade" being synonymous with the restriction of competition, including the "abandonment" of price competition.[1]

Like other Canadian businessmen, newspaper publishers at the end of the nineteenth century sought to reduce what they perceived to be ruinous and unrestrained competition in their field. By persuasion and coercion, they set up combinations to restrain trade with their rivals to ensure what Bliss politely called a "living profit."[2]

Controlling price competition, or pricefixing, had occurred earlier in the nineteenth century. Montreal newspapers set up a cartel in 1854 to fix advertising rates, and one of the prime concerns of the CPA in 1862 was to sustain a yearly two dollar subscription floor among its members. But it was only in the 1890s that there was any systematic attempt to control and fix prices to reduce expenses, end pricecutting, and raise profits.[3]

Combination became an attractive alternative to competition as newspaper publishers defended themselves against the newly formed advertising agencies' invasion of what was formerly their exclusive domain. The ad agencies were succeeding in inserting themselves as middlemen between the advertisers and the newspapers, thus appropriating a significant percentage of advertising income. Canada's first newspaper "combine" originated in Ottawa in 1895 in response to the machinations of the A. McKim advertising agency. Mckim had gone to one competitor, the *Free Press*, claiming that the opposition *Journal* charged thirty dollars for an advertisement (when it had actually cost forty-five dollars) and persuaded the *Free Press* to take his ad at the lower rate. McKim then returned to the *Journal* with his thirty-dollar ad, compelling the *Journal* to lower its rate to meet the competition. He repeated this tactic with the third rival, the *Citizen*.

Once they learned of these tactics, Ottawa publishers, who were normally not on speaking terms, held weekly meetings to set common rates and neutralize McKim's activities. The Ottawa accord set the precedent for subsequent agreements, usually more formal and comprehensive, to reduce competition.[4]

However, the 1895 agreement broke down when the well-funded Southam family purchased the Ottawa *Citizen* in 1898 and unleashed a new round of intensive and expensive competition. By 1900, tiring of a money-losing rivalry exacerbated by mounting postage, paper, and wage costs, Ottawa publishers revived their commitment to cooperation and agreed to raise subscription and daily prices and advertising rates. At a special publishers' symposium on how to increase profits under heavier expenses, the Ottawa *Journal*'s P.D. Ross extolled the benefits of cooperation, claiming that his paper had gained from $5,000 to $10,000 because of the 1895 agreement.[5] Fellow publisher E.J.B. Pense of the Kingston *Whig* pointed out that "it will not be easy for most of the papers to increase their rates without an understanding with their fellow publishers."[6]

In 1906 the Ottawa publishers strengthened their pact. For the next ten years the concord managed to hold despite occasional violations, but the principals still believed that it did not go far enough to ensure satisfactory incomes. They then forged a comprehensive agreement that rigidly controlled all aspects of competition. Under this agreement, the *Free Press* was absorbed by the *Journal* in 1917, leaving only one competitor, the *Citizen*. A formula was introduced by which one paper would receive financial compensation if the other exceeded it in advertising, circulation, or profit. The *Citizen*'s Harry Southam considered that the agreement eliminated "waste in the production and distribution of our newspapers" brought about "by the years of futile and senseless competition."[7] A new agreement in 1920 went so far as to stipulate that if either partner's circulation fell more than five percent below the other's, "the two companies shall co-operate ... to promote the smaller circulation."[8]

While the situation among Ottawa publishers was brought about through mutual agreement between roughly equal partners, a similar agreement was forced in Calgary and Winnipeg by the oligopoly's strongest member, the Calgary *Herald* and Manitoba *Free Press*. In Calgary it was not easy to make or adhere to advertising rate agreements, as developments between 1908 and 1918 reveal. At the end of 1907 the faltering Calgary *Herald* was taken over by the Southam group led by J.H. Woods. By September 1908, although the *Herald* had forged ahead of its competitors, the *News-Telegram* and the *Albertan*, Woods felt that receipts were not high enough. Nor would the dividends be adequate unless advertising rates were raised. It rankled that "keen" and "unscrupulous" competition forced the *Herald* to drop its display advertising twenty percent below that of its sister publication, the Southam chain's Edmonton *Journal*, though the *Herald*'s circulation was sixty percent higher. Woods was determined to redress this situation through price-fixing agreements. In 1908 he had made "several attempts to get the papers to come together for the purpose of raising the rates, and drew up a schedule which we thought would be satisfactory to all."[9]

Although occasionally rebuffed by other publishers, Woods persisted in the effort to reduce competition and raise prices and rates. Harry Southam advised Woods in 1910 to continue his efforts to convince his Calgary rivals to "arrange for united action" in order "to keep up a stiff rate."[10] Woods's persistence was understandable – it cost money to compete because rival campaigns forced the *Herald* to hire additional staff to solicit new circulation. He bemoaned the "aggressive" competition in Calgary and the "normal" situation in Ottawa and Hamilton, where price and rate agreements prevailed.[11]

The *Herald* saw price-fixing agreements as insurance against economic vicissitudes. In a 1912 letter to Woods, Fred Southam explained the importance of a joint increase in the subscription rate:

It is absolutely essential that some such arrangement should be made between the city papers in order to make them a financial success. At present things are on the boom and you are no doubt getting considerable revenue from special advertising. Should things slacken up at all you will have great difficulty in getting down expenses, while your advertising revenue would probably drop off considerably. It is altogether too much to expect the advertising to carry the very heavy subscription loss which you at present show.[12]

The *Herald*'s management tried again in 1912 to convince the *News-Telegram* and the *Albertan* to cooperate. This time it urged its rivals to raise subscription rates from three to five dollars, a move that would net the *Herald* $20,000 extra a year in circulation revenue. The *News-Telegram* tentatively agreed, subject to the *Albertan* joining, but the latter demurred because it feared a loss of circulation. For the *Herald* and the *News-Telegram* to go it alone would have given the *Albertan* "a chance to grab our circulation."[13]

The business downturn and reduced commercial opportunities engendered by the outbreak of World War I eventually led to permanent collusion among the Calgary papers. In 1915, for example, the *Herald* unleashed a costly circulation-boosting campaign, adding more features and greater news coverage, that finally convinced its rivals of the wisdom of a uniform increase in yearly subscription rates to five dollars. By 1918 the *Herald* clearly dominated the market. Its power enabled it to force renewal of the agreement and boost subscription prices again. These raises, which alone netted the paper an extra $21,000 for the year, indicate the profitability of collusion for the strongest paper.[14]

The *Herald* used its strength to push through advertising rate increases as well. It raised the rate of its largest advertiser, the Hudson's Bay department store, from 33.5 cents to 42.5 cents and assessed other advertisers at an even higher rate. The *Herald* had come far since its desperate negotiations with the Hudson's Bay in 1915, when the paper took a loss on advertising in order to ensure that the store's business would not go to its competitor; by 1918 the *Herald* no longer worried that the department store might threaten to switch papers for rate advantage: "If we absolutely have to do without the Hudson's Bay we can manage for a while quite well."[15] Furthermore, the newspaper unilaterally slashed the percentage paid to the advertising agencies from fifteen to ten percent. All these moves, helped by the strengthening of its position through collusion, allowed Woods to expect more than a seven percent profit in 1918.[16] By 1920 the *Herald*'s dominance was such that the *News-Telegram* was forced to close, leaving only one competitor, the *Albertan*.

In Winnipeg, too, the dominant paper was able to force its rival to collude and raise subscription prices. Like other Canadian newspapers during the war, the *Free Press* found its profitability curtailed owing to the wartime decline in advertising revenues and a hike in the cost of newsprint. Because the subscription price did not cover newsprint and distribution expenses, as editor J.W. Dafoe believed it should, the *Free Press* raised its subscription rate to ten cents a week in 1915. Its competitors, the *Tribune* and the *Telegram*, refused to go along, resulting in a serious loss of circulation for the *Free Press*. Secondary dailies like the *Tribune* feared that substantial rate increases would encourage two-paper subscribers to cut back to one, and that the leading papers would reap the benefit. Indeed, the *Free Press*'s own readership canvassing bore this out. Beginning in October 1915, the *Free Press* cut its subscription rate and embarked on an aggressive and successful "newspaper war ... for the purpose of knocking a little sense into our friends."[17] In 1917 the *Tribune* and the *Telegram* gave in and came to a "definite agreement ... as a result of which the subscription rates of all the evening Winnipeg newspapers have practically been doubled."[18] The *Free Press* did well by these actions. The immediate effect on the smaller papers was unclear, but the long-range effect was that the *Telegram* disappeared in 1920 and the *Tribune* was taken over by the Southam chain. As in Calgary, these events showed how a dominant paper could force a colluding agreement that eventually strengthened its position.

Elsewhere in Canada, other publishers recognized the value of collusion. In 1915 the refusal of the Edmonton *Bulletin* and *Journal* to lower their rates caused the Hudson's Bay to withdraw its newspaper ads and rely instead on circulars and window displays. The gesture was shortlived, however, and it soon resumed advertising at the papers' stipulated rates. Publishers learned that if they stuck together, they could dictate rates to the advertisers, rather than the reverse.

Even in Toronto, the most competitive market in Canada, publishers sought to control competition. In 1905 pricefixing was considered by the *Star* and the *News*, both evening papers. From 1900 to World War I, the four largest dailies refused to pay commissions to the agencies for local advertising. This was galling to the agencies because all national advertising originating in Toronto was considered local. In 1916 the *Star*'s business manager asked the *World* to join the standard advertising rate schedule agreed upon by the other publishers, and managing editor H.J. Maclean replied: "We are for all practical purposes already in accord with your suggestion."[19]

The growth of the advertising agencies in the 1890s – there were six national agencies by 1900 – encouraged collusion among publishers, who came together in informal local and formal regional associations to "restrain" advertising rate competition and control the agencies. The Ottawa Valley Press Association was formed in 1896, partly in response to the divide-and-conquer tactics of the McKim agency. At their first convention, members complained about McKim's practices and low prices and agreed to standardize the prices of ad rates. The Eastern Townships Press Association, formed the next year, set ad rates at a new, higher level.

Publishers were particularly incensed by the twenty-five percent commission successfully instituted by the agencies. Noting that agents received only five to ten percent in Britain and fifteen percent in the US, they called for either a reduced commission or none at all; why shouldn't the advertiser pay the commission? they asked.

The main business of these associations was to prevent the undercutting of advertising rates (going below the newspaper's rate card) and to encourage joint rate increases. By 1900 increased machinery costs and higher postal rates created additional pressure for joint action on rate increases to pay for the extra expenses. Publishers repeatedly called for rate agreements at press association gatherings and gradually hammered out agreements. But universal adherence to the agreements proved difficult to achieve. One publisher complained in 1907 that while he had tried for a couple of years to stick to association rates, "I am still waiting for business. The agents say I am asking too much for my circulation ... Until we can get concerted action I don't see how we are going to make the agents come up to our rates."[20] The Western Canadian Press Association found, to its embarrassment, that its members were quoting rates one-quarter to one-half lower than those in the agreement to a secretly sponsored advertising agent.

Increased competition led the president of the Western Canadian Press Association to call for a strengthening of the association: "The condition of all can be greatly enhanced by a union of interests, so far as rates and prices are concerned."[21] The publishers, who were looking for fixed rates, considered that the higher rate was the "fair" price.

The momentum for joint action grew. The daily publishers formed their own section within the Canadian Publishers' Association in 1905 in order to "assert more group control" over advertising rates. In that year, the "organized" papers met for the first time with the "organized agencies" to negotiate rate agreements.[22]

Despite complaints that member papers were breaking the agreements, the efforts of the associations showed publishers the benefits of "competition abandonment." One publisher observed that "this whole question of rates is one of education. As a result of these discussions the rates and position of the newspapermen have been steadily improving."[23]

From 1907 to 1914, publishers negotiated among themselves and with the advertising agencies to come to terms on advertising rates.

By 1914 the publishers had finally overcome their own divisions and fashioned an agreement among themselves that in essence abandoned competition. No commission, discount, rebate, or drawback of any kind was allowed from the published rate card, nor could there by any preferential rates or terms. There followed agreement with accredited agencies on a standard contract for recognized agents. The contract eliminated "disguised" price competition, so called because differently worded contracts made advertising rate comparison difficult.[24]

Publishers learned to cooperate in other areas. As early as 1862, the CPA was to trying to sustain a yearly two-dollar subscription floor among its members. Competition in the 1890s drove the price of most dailies down to one cent. But the attrition, mergers, and absorptions of the war years made it easier to coordinate regional and even national agreements to raise prices. In 1917, several key publishers convinced the English-language papers of Quebec and Ontario to raise their subscription prices. That this did not occur by accident was made clear by P.D. Ross:

After leaving you [J.S. Willison of the Toronto *News*] I saw W.J. Douglas at the *Mail* office and found him apparently favourably disposed towards bringing the mail subscription rate of the *Mail* and *Empire* up to $4.

I think I stated yesterday that we had all the evening English papers of Ontario and Quebec in line except the Montreal *Herald*. I find I was wrong about Hamilton where the papers have not absolutely committed themselves. We have, however, verbal assurances that two will come in and have little doubt of the third.[25]

The same process occurred months later on the Prairies as the management of Southam papers in Calgary and Edmonton agitated for a regional circulation price increase. Indeed, Robb Sutherland of the Western Publishers' Association and Southam editor Bob Jennings of the Edmonton *Journal* undertook "missionary work" to convince their competitors to put the rate increases into effect: "We will not be able to increase our outside rate until they do, as we would be running up against both Edmonton and Saskatchewan on a differential rate."[26] Sutherland, who was also business agent for the western dailies, was given credit for the 1918 advertising and subscription rate agreements in Calgary. His activities revealed the extent to which collusion had been institutionalized in the newspaper industry.

The mounting cartelization of the newspaper industry became apparent as early as 1907 with the creation of the Western Associated Press (WAP) and its 1910 successor, the Canadian Press, which absorbed it. When the Canadian Pacific Railway Telegraph Company (CPR Tel) raised the price of its news service to its western customers, the three Winnipeg dailies formed the WAP to offset what they considered exorbitant price hikes by offering an alternate service. Tellingly, the three dailies agreed not to use business information revealed during talks to set up the WAP against each other. Eventually WAP drew in the majority of dailies from Manitoba to British Columbia. A clause in its agreement denied membership to a new daily if its existence threatened the livelihood of another WAP member. This practice was imitated by CP, formed as a publishers' cooperative to take over the wire-service and news-gathering operations abandoned by CPR Tel when it absorbed WAP in 1910. As historian J.A. Cooper observed, "the Canadian newspapers established their own combination – decently disguised as a cooperative."[27]

The publishers' ability to control competition in their specific marketplaces was enhanced by CP's power to restrict membership: without access to these services, a new daily could not hope to survive because CP also controlled the vital Associated Press news service. The CP board of directors, dominated by the big dailies, chose to interpret strictly the clause that stipulated that the board could deny membership if "the population or local conditions in any city or town did not justify an increase in the number of papers receiving the service."[28]

Montreal in 1914 was apparently just such a city: the newly established *Evening News*'s application was refused (because of the *Star*'s veto) on the grounds that a new evening paper was not desirable. (The *News* was finally admitted after a long, bitter, and highly publicized fight.) In 1911 the Vancouver *Sun* was forced to wait for two months before its application was approved, thus giving the morning *News-Advertiser*, which had had the morning field to itself for years, an additional competitive advantage.[29]

The public became aware that CP acted as a cartel after it rejected the application of a group wanting to start an Ottawa newspaper in 1923. Unfortunately for the publishers' cooperative, the group included Prime Minister Mackenzie King, and the rejection aroused criticism in the House of Commons, especially when the matter of CP's annual subsidy of $50,000 came up for review. John Ross Robertson described it as a "kind of tyrannical organization,"[30] while *Orange Sentinel* publisher Horatio Hocken wondered if CP's action violated the Anti-Combines Act. He questioned the fact that "a dozen men forming the executive committee of the daily newspaper organization can determine just where a newspaper shall be printed and where one cannot be printed." The Toronto *Telegram* supported Hocken and wondered "why the associated newspapers should be privileged to suppress competition with themselves." Thereafter, Parliament failed to renew the subsidy.[31]

Despite the parliamentary bluster, the Canadian government did little about the growing cartelization of the newspaper industry. The view underlying American anti-trust legislation – that industrial monopoly was inherently bad – was not shared in Canada, where government prosecutors had to prove that trade was being restricted or that monopoly was harmful to the public, a difficult thing to do. Historically, the size of Canada's economy in relation to that of the United States has led Canadian governments to ignore, if not overtly to encourage, the growth of big oligopolistic companies the better to compete on a continental scale. Canada's anti-trust policy was weak and generally not applied, and its regulatory body, the Board of Commerce, had a negligible impact on price-fixing associations.[32] In fact, government subsidies to wire services indirectly aided the attempts of the biggest publishers to dominate the industry. In 1902 the *Telegram*'s John Ross Robertson and the *Star*'s Hugh Graham set up the Canadian Associated Press (CAP), a press agency in London, to send British news to Canada because of widespread dissatisfaction with the anti-British bias of AP wire service reports during the Boer War. The federal government gave CAP an initial start-up subsidy of $15,000 and an annual smaller grant thereafter. CAP kept its rates high to discourage access by the smaller dailies and thus maintain exclusivity for the biggest publishers.[33]

In 1917, when wartime costs had become prohibitive and there were fewer papers to share the financial burden, smaller publishers, especially in the West, convinced the federal government to grant an annual $50,000 subsidy to pay for the increased expenses of transmitting news over the telegraphic gaps between Fort William/Port Arthur and Winnipeg and Calgary and the BC coast, and also to establish CP (which served at the time as little more than a publishers' holding company to handle the AP franchise) as a news gathering operation.[34] Although they themselves had earlier accepted federal subsidies, the Toronto and Montreal press magnates announced their "principled" opposition to the "subsidy hunters." In 1920 the same men opposed the smaller publishers' application for a federal subsidy for a direct cable link to Britain (which would negate CAP's usefulness), again ostensibly on principled grounds. However, the real reason for their opposition, according to J.W. Dafoe, was that the subsidies allowed the smaller papers to gain access to news that only the largest dailies, with their superior resources, could hitherto afford; hence their news "exclusivity" was threatened."[35]

It should be noted that the biggest dailies benefitted more from the rate structure for CP's services than from the subsidies. In each city newspapers were assessed a flat rate regardless of circulation. Big dailies thus had the advantage in that they could spread costs over larger circulation. This allowed the Toronto *Star*, for example, to invade Hamilton *Spectator* territory in 1915. Equal rates were a further example of the type of industry leadership practised by the biggest dailies.

Publishers were also moving towards collective action in their dealings with labour. Such action had occurred before, during the nine-hour dispute in 1872 between Toronto pressmen and compositors and a common front of newspapers led by George Brown's *Globe*, but this was an isolated incident; when disputes arose, proprietors negotiated individually with the organized pressmen and compositors.[36] But the expanding unionization of newspaper pressrooms in the 1890s resulted in most newspapers negotiating in city-wide units. In Toronto, for example, after several years of dispute with his compositors, the Toronto *Telegram*'s Robertson capitulated in 1892 and paid their union initiation fees. Robertson's unilateral act angered the other publishers because it set a precedent that their workers asked them to match. To prevent future occurrences, the Toronto publishers negotiated jointly. In 1902 the Toronto dailies "stood absolutely united" in discussions with the Toronto Typographical Union, and thereafter Toronto publishers, represented by the *Star*'s Joseph Atkinson, adopted a common front in negotiations with the union.[37] For one whose newspaper championed the cause of labour, Atkinson drove very shrewd bargains, showing once again that the bottom line for the Canadian newspaper was business, rather than political or social principle.

In 1901 the Ottawa publishers formed a union of their own, notifying the Ottawa Typographical Union that no individual publisher was empowered to negotiate any issue that affected the publishers' collective interest. In 1909 the Hamilton *Spectator* arranged strike-breaking services for its two rivals, the *Herald* and the *Times*, though it was not itself threatened by strike action.[38]

Publishers began to see the value of acting jointly on a regional and even national scale. For example, in 1905 they successfully dealt with the eight-hour day that printers were demanding by sending a delegation to meet with James M. Lynch, president of the International Union, who deferred the time reduction for another year and a half. In 1915, when a number of labour agreements expired at the same time, western publishers responded with unified action.[39]

Hikes in paper prices around the turn of the century also threatened the publishers' well-being and further encouraged them to band together. Prices escalated rapidly in 1899 from a low of $1.70 and a high of $2.10 per hundred rolls to $2.50 and $2.75. These price rises occurred immediately after the formation of a papermakers' union, which the CPA viewed as a papermakers' "combine." The publishers, led by colleagues who were MPs, successfully pressured the government to create the Taschereau Commission to investigate the price hikes. The commission determined that there was indeed a combine and that the price enhancements were "undue, unreasonable and oppressive." Later, the rapid rise in paper prices during the war again led publishers to pressure the government to freeze prices through 1918.[40]

The Canadian Publishers' Association itself was formed by publishers seeking to exchange information and protect their collective interests, as companies in other industries were doing all over Canada. Established in 1859, the Canadian Publishers' Association's membership originally comprised only the smaller Ontario dailies and weeklies. Then in the late nineteenth century the formerly aloof Toronto dailies joined, and other regional associations became affiliated with the CPA. External threats to newspaper prosperity such as the 1898 introduction of postage rates, the 1890s paper price hikes, high customs duties on printing and typesetting equipment, and mounting labour expenses accelerated the publishers' use of the CPA as a vehicle to promote newspaper profitability, although its aim was educational. With their distinctive needs, the daily publishers split off to form a separate wing of the CPA in 1905 and then formed an entirely separate organization, the Canadian Daily Newspaper Association (CDNA), in 1919. The CDNA ultimately succeeded the CPA.

Under the aegis of the CPA, publishers were in a better position to "influence legitimate legislation in our interest"[41] on postage, paper, and equipment duties and other issues that threatened their pocketbooks. As shown earlier, the "grievance" over postage duties was "old as the Association itself."[42] In 1898 when the publishers realized that Postmaster General William Mulock was not going to back down once postal charges had been reintroduced, they sought to have the government offset the rates with a reduction in the cost of printing materials. Every time the government threatened postal rate increases, the CPA organized resistance, sending a delegation to the postmaster general in 1912 and calling on its members to protest to the government by telegram.

In the formation of the CPA and its expansion into a dominion-wide publishers' association, the newspaper industry mirrored the organization and development of other Canadian trade associations, which were essentially cartels disguised as associations. The CPA's official history cites the association's efforts to reduce competition, especially its wartime bulletins encouraging members to raise daily and subscription prices in keeping with their colleagues who had already done so. Indeed, the CPA is credited with being the moving force behind the mass price hikes of 1917–18. It also waged a successful battle against the use of competitive and ultimately costly promotional devices such as premiums, special inducements, and contests to secure circulation.

The price-fixing nature of the association was embarrassing, however, in light of the general public antipathy to combines, a sentiment inflamed largely by editorial tirades against combination conspiracies and monopoly. It was doubly embarrassing given their strident campaign against the papermakers' alleged conspiracy to fix prices, as publisher E.J.B. Pense acknowledged: "Of course, people will say that newspapers who are running down combines should not themselves enter into or counsel advertising agreements."[43] The *Canadian Printer and Publisher* itself hinted at the hypocritical nature of the situation. After lauding the increased strength of the press associations, it cautioned: "These organizations are [not] formed merely for the sake of increasing prices."[44]

Newsman Edward Beck, juxtaposing CP's denial of a franchise to W.F. Herman with its complaints of a papermakers' combine, was more explicit:

[CP's] action in confining participation in its news service exclusively to those who are now participating therein seems to me to constitute a violation ... [and] an infringement of the guarantee of a free press, since it is manifestly impossible for anyone successfully to establish a daily newspaper in Canada if denied access to the Government-fostered news monopoly controlled by Canadian Press Limited. The question arises: has the Canadian Press Limited any moral or legal right to take public money ... and use it for the creation of a newspaper monopoly?[45]

Beck continued: "One of the chief grievances of the Canadian newspaper publishers made to the Government at Ottawa against the manufacturers of newsprint paper was that the manufacturers, so it was alleged, had used their power to prevent competition against the paper mills. If this is an offence when alleged against the paper mills, what does it become when practised by the newspapers?"[46]

To sum up, market competition had become so intense and costly by the 1890s that newspaper publishers sought to curb what were essentially money-losing practices by regulating the market through increasingly formal agreements. This meant collusion, most often in the form of price fixing. The inroads made by the agencies into the newspapers' advertising revenues caused the publishers to protect their incomes by banding together in regional press associations, whose aim was to raise rates, prevent undercutting, and reduce the agencies' contract percentage.

Ironically, the move to standardize rates hurt those smaller publishers who had initiated it in an effort to reduce competition and raise rates. Once standardized rates became commonplace and circulation figures more straightforward, it was easier for the advertising agencies to favour the big dailies rather than myriad smaller ones. This in turn further encouraged concentration and monopoly.

One characteristic of maturing industries, V.W. Bladen observed, was that once the competition-restricting trade organizations or cartels were in place, they were dominated by the larger members, who often used the organizations to extend their domination of the industry.[47] The newspaper industry fit this pattern: both the CPA and CP were characterized by competition restriction and other practices that encouraged domination of the cartel by its largest members.

7 Patronage and Independence

Concentration in the newspaper industry began with publishers asserting the independence of their papers from partisan control before World War I. Although political parties retained strong links with the newspapers, especially through patronage, the period from 1890 to 1920 was a transitional time during which publishers stripped the newspaper of its traditional political function and took complete control of their publications. The same competitive pressures that led to graphic innovations, sensationalism, and entertainment and reduced political comment also induced publishers to pull their papers from the orbit of political parties to concentrate on commercial obligations that often conflicted with political needs. The first step they took was to assert control by declaring the papers independent and blocking the politicians from interfering with newspaper operations.

Before World War I Canadians took their politics seriously, so much so that outside observers were struck by the belligerence of party rhetoric and the fury of electioneering. Gordon Stewart observes that the party system was important for national unity because it integrated regional groups into the transnational institution of the political party. The glue that held the parties together was patronage, and because the government was a major source of economic development and employment and the victorious party the dispenser of contracts and jobs, the stakes were high and the elections were bitterly fought.[1]

The key role of government in Canadian economic life ensured that political influence contributed to entrepreneurial success. As responsible government grew in the nineteenth century, patronage was used as a means to attract mass support for the parties. John A. Macdonald understood and exploited the nation-binding and election-winning powers of patronage, something the pre-incumbent Laurier deplored but later came to rely on himself.[2]

French social scientist André Siegfried noted in 1904 that the two great Canadian political parties were divided not by ideas or doctrines but only by "questions of material interest, collective or individual."[3] In short, to the victor went the spoils, and in the struggle for victory, "journalism and party politics were intertwined. The belief was general that the supreme function of a newspaper was to assert political authority." This was before the day when "financial, industrial or commercial undertakings on a grand scale" absorbed Canada's "ablest brains."[4]

Politics dominated the press throughout the nineteenth century, during which "it was almost impossible to be an editor without being a politician also."[5] The newspaper was the only mass medium at the time, so it is hardly surprising that the journalist exerted a considerable influence in nineteenth-century Canadian politics. Politicians and editors, when they were not the same person, had a symbiotic relationship that was at its closest during the late 1850s and early 1860s but still largely intact at the end of the nineteenth century. Because the editorial was the newspaper's most prominent feature, editors often found themselves "catapulted into political careers while politicians often found it necessary to become proprietors or patrons of newspapers."[6] Newspapers served politicians as the "fighting" organs that spread the message of their party and vehemently attacked their opponent's ideas. Often an aspiring politician would acquire his own newspaper to project himself into the limelight. Indeed, the extensive list of journalists who switched to parliamentary careers or went into the civil service suggests "journalism once vied with the practice of law as a stepping-stone to the assumption of power."[7]

The connection between newsmen and politics is well known. Before 1920 many politicians, from federal prime ministers to municipal aldermen, started their careers as newsmen. Although the political involvement of journalists lessened after 1900, politicians with press backgrounds were still commonplace. Prime Ministers Mackenzie Bowell and Wilfrid Laurier had published newspapers. Prominent publishers and newsmen such as Clifford Sifton, Frank Oliver, W.S. Fielding, R.S. White, Frank Cochrane, Robert Rogers, G.P. Graham, W.L.M. King, and William Templeman, among others, served as cabinet ministers between 1900 and 1920, and such influential publishers as John Ross Robertson, W.F. Maclean, R.L. Richardson and W.A. Buchanan sat in the House of Commons. Twelve MPs were connected to newspapers in 1896 (most as publishers) and fourteen in 1908. Premier George Ross of Ontario was a newsman and Premier W.D. Scott of Saskatchewan was a publisher. In 1902, nine of fourteen Ontario newsmen who ran for the ninety-eight-seat provincial legislature were victorious. Newsmen served as mayors in several cities in the early 1900s, including Toronto, Ottawa, Edmonton, Winnipeg, and Vancouver, while scores were elected to city councils.

Since newspapers were an essential adjunct to political influence in the pre-war period, many non-journalists such as Clifford Sifton, Joseph Flavelle, Robert Jaffray, Frank Cochrane, and B.F. Pearson bought papers. Even the "independent" papers that were founded or developed by journalists were strongly partisan. Indeed, Paul Rutherford suggests that prosperity and increasing government patronage helped bring the maverick "people's journals" – the commercially oriented papers like the Montreal *Star*, Toronto *Telegram* and Ottawa *Journal* – back into the partisan fold at the turn of the century.[8] Until World War I, although steadily weakening in importance in relation to a newspaper's survival and purpose, the press still benefitted through direct sponsorship of papers or journalists by party politicians (this could mean inducing party financiers to invest in faltering papers or create new ones), the granting of government advertising and printing contracts, the purchase of subscriptions and additional copies for propaganda purposes, information patronage (whereby favoured papers got prior access to public announcements and information), and the pensioning of journalists through civil service appointments.[9]

Such practices meant that the political parties retained some influence in the affairs of the press in the early twentieth century. Well-heeled party backers were largely responsible for the creation of new papers or takeovers of established ones from the 1890s on. The takeover of the *Globe* in 1882 by Robert Jaffray and George Cox showed the intertwining of politics and journalism. After George Brown's death, Lord Strathcona, a staunch Tory and backer of the CPR, sought to control the *Globe* to stop its criticism of the railroad. Jaffray and Cox took over the paper in part at the behest of the Liberal party. In 1896 both men were rewarded with Senate appointments.

Both political parties engaged in strategic takeovers just before elections to influence the vote. The Toronto *Star* was purchased in 1899 by such financial and political heavyweights as George Cox, tea king Peter Larkin, farm machinery baron Walter Massey, and Postmaster General William Mulock, so that Toronto would have a second Liberal daily in time for the 1900 election.[10] Similarly, the weekly Sydney *Reporter* was taken over by a Liberal group in 1899 and changed into a daily in order to defeat Sir Charles Tupper in the upcoming election.¹¹ In 1908 mining magnate John McKane and other Tories bought the Saint John *Telegram* and *Times*, both Liberal independents, to fight the Liberals in the election.¹² Other politically motivated groups started the St John *Standard* in time for the election of 1908 and refinanced the Edmonton *Journal*.¹³ Politics changed the ownership of the Dartmouth *Patriot* in 1910 and the Saskatoon *Phoenix* in 1914 and caused the appearance of the Fredericton *Daily Mail* in 1910 and the Vancouver *Sun* in 1911.¹⁴ In 1907 the Toronto *News* was taken over from J.W. Flavelle (whose massive losses showed that not even the wealthy could absorb the red ink of a major newspaper) by the kind of group that was coming to characterize newspaper ownership. A mix of politicians, businessmen, and lawyers, the group was headed by Frank Cochrane, a businessman turned politician (at the time, Ontario minister for Mines and Forests), and included industrialist A.E. Kemp, who was chief Ontario Conservative bagman, financier E.B. Osler, and prominent distiller George Gooderham. Their assumption of control turned the hitherto independent *News* into a party organ.¹⁵

The second type of patronage, the dispensation of public advertising and printing contracts, was a major factor in binding press to party. Obviously, patronage was far more important before 1890 when newspaper circulations were small. As James Moylan, the editor of the Regina *Leader*, said when asking a cabinet minister for a printing contract in 1872, "A few thousand dollars worth of printing is a small thing in your department, but it will go far to assist me."¹⁶ In an 1888 memorandum to Prime Minister John A. Macdonald, the publishers of the Halifax *Herald*, Saint John *Sun*, and Moncton *Times* requested more patronage since, as business ventures, party papers were "not now and have never been profitable, in no case, yielding the proprietors as large a return as the same capital, if otherwise invested, might have reasonably been expected to do."¹⁷ For some papers, government advertising or printing was the difference between bankruptcy and solvency.

Patronage of this kind was still important for key papers in the twentieth century. The Laurier government's expenditure on newspapers increased dramatically from 1899 on. In the 1900 election year alone, expenditures increased by fifty percent to $246,000. By 1904 they had risen to $386,000 and again to $644,000 four years later, a figure the Conservatives had almost doubled by 1912.¹⁸ Patronage helped the Manitoba *Free Press* become the West's ascendent paper. Not only did the paper benefit from owner Clifford Sifton's official advertising largesse but it had contracts (over $9,000 worth in 1903 alone) to print written matter from various federal ministries, including the Ministry of the Interior.[19] Patronage also helped the *Star* to gain dominance over the Toronto market, which may be why, as late as 1908, the *Star's* publisher was importuning Prime Minister Laurier himself to ensure that the now-prosperous paper remain on the official handout lists. Patronage ensured survival of the Ottawa *Free Press* and Montreal *Herald* during the early twentieth century. The former received more than $12,000 in job printing and advertising contracts in 1905, an amount that increased to $16,000 the next year, representing more than one-fifth the paper's income. *Herald* publisher J.S. Brierley admitted that he could not survive if the government changed hands since he received an annual subsidy of $25,000 from the Laurier government at the turn of the century, an amount that increased to over $51,000 in job printing and advertising patronage in 1902.[20]

Provincial governments contributed as well. The Manitoba government consistently kept the money-losing *Telegram* afloat, granting it $26,000 in contracts in 1910 alone. Between 1913 and 1914, BC's McBride government allocated $87,191 worth of advertising and printing contracts; approximately forty percent went to the government-supporting Victoria *Colonist* and Vancouver *News-Advertiser*.[21]

Federal and provincial governments also supported their press friends through large purchases of yearly subscriptions – in the nineteenth century this already amounted to hundreds of dollars – and by buying extra editions for propaganda purposes. For example, the federal government bought and distributed forty thousand extra copies of an edition of the Manitoba *Free Press* containing a speech by Prime Minister Laurier, and the Conservative government in Manitoba bought ten thousand copies of the Winnipeg *Telegram* in 1900 to hand out free to immigrants every two weeks.[22]

In the years around the turn of the century the Laurier government, through Clifford Sifton, spent hundreds of thousands of dollars to create a Liberal newspaper network to carry the party line across the Dominion. Sifton, a master propagandist, created a "Press Bureau" in his Interior Office to coordinate news items (which often contained carefully slanted pro-Liberal party views) for the dozens of dailies and weeklies on his official patronage list. The supply of articles was a hidden boon for many of the smaller publishers, who could not afford to send correspondents to Ottawa or elsewhere to dig up stories, and it represented a subsidy of sorts. The press bureau grew out of Sifton's appointment of A.J. Magurn, then Ottawa correspondent for the *Globe* and later *Free Press* editor, as "commissioner's secretary" to accompany an official expedition to the Yukon. The reports Magurn sent back to Toronto became news fodder for the country's Liberal press network. A little later Sifton established the press bureau in Ottawa. A contract to print ballot forms, government ballots, or other official information often proved an inducement for a paper to publish the Liberal "news" item. So successful was this network that the Conservative party set up its own in 1902.[23]

Government information was dispensed as a form of patronage until well into the twentieth century. In the 1880s it was "difficult" for an opposition correspondent to secure information from a public department because all announcements were reserved for party organs. Favoured correspondents had access to official information before it was submitted to Parliament. Thus, according to John Willison, "their despatches would be in telegraph offices before less favoured rivals could examine the reports."[24] In 1891 Halifax *Herald* editor and provincial Conservative party leader C.H. Cahan asked Prime Minister John Thompson for advance notice on a brewing Liberal scandal because "any news of this kind, when given to us exclusively, is of great assistance to the paper."[25] Journalist Arthur Ford recalled that news patronage was "one way a grateful ministry paid newspapers for support."[26]

Information patronage was no small matter, considering how "scoops" and exclusive information helped boost circulation in a competitive marketplace. *Globe* journalist M.O. Hammond, describing how the new Borden government affected his paper, noted: "This was the day of the big scoop. The *Mail* and the *World* had the list of the Borden Cabinet while the *Globe* did not. There was much surprise and indignation in the office ... The Laurier Government had time and again handed out the best news to the Globe."[27]

Government patronage also took the form of rewarding publishers and newsmen who had served their party with knighthoods or appointments to the Senate or civil service. Knighthoods, of course, were given to key party figures like Clifford Sifton and J.S. Willison. (Hugh Graham was the exception. Laurier got him a knighthood to neutralize the *Star* in the 1908 election.) Senate seats were only awarded to publishers or newsmen who were also politicians in their own right such as W.A. Buchanan, Mackenzie Bowell, or W.H. Preston, or to major party financiers or organizers like Robert Jaffray.

Those lower in the pecking order, generally editors and the occasional reporter (mostly Ottawa correspondents), were given civil service posts. Often the party-hack newsman, or "slave" as W.C. Nichol called him, would gather signatures of party members to support their request for a public position. It was by doing so that Fredericton *Herald* editor L.C. MacNutt became collector of customs in 1909. Other newspapermen would seek out influential party figures as sponsors. As A.J. Magurn, former editor of the Manitoba *Free Press*, put it in a letter to Sifton:

> The newspaperman is generally a politician and can expect nothing from the other side after he has compromised himself seriously year after year in hitting them whenever they raise their heads. I find it impossible to make any one believe that I can be either fair or impartial in the discussion of public affairs. I am labelled a Grit stalwart and cannot get away from it. I cannot regain the position I had here four years ago and it is nothing unusual or out of the way if I say to the party whose battles I fought in season or out of season for many years: "I helped you when you needed it most, now I want you to help me."[28]

Willison wrote to Prime Minister Borden requesting an appointment for his former Ottawa correspondent C.F. Hamilton. Borden professed to be "a little puzzled as to what we could offer," but he eventually appointed Hamilton assistant commissioner to the RCMP.[29]

Of the fifty-five or so appointments I surveyed (mostly from announcements in the *Canadian Printer and Publisher*), the most common were appointments as secretary to a federal or provincial cabinet minister (sixteen positions). The next most common were appointments to Customs, then to Marine and Fisheries. There were also deputy ministers of Labour and, provincially, of Education, a Dominion Statistician, postmasters, parliamentary librarians, commissioners of milk boards, a land title inspector, a registrar of patents, and a superintendent of the Toronto Institute for the Blind, sessional clerks, one Gentleman Usher of the Black Rod, several editors of official departmental publications, a Dominion trade commissioner, public works inspectors, and so on.

According to John Willison, it was customary in a party paper like the *Globe*

to ignore or give little attention to Conservative meetings. The Liberal meetings always had crowded houses. Their speeches excited tremendous enthusiasm. At Conservative meetings there were empty benches and perfunctory attention. I have known the *Globe* to give eight to ten columns to a Liberal meeting ... and less than a column to a Conservative meeting at least as well attended and addressed by speakers of equal attraction and distinction. Moreover, there was often deliberate misrepresentation of Conservative speeches and calculated suppression of passages which were regarded as damaging to the Liberal position.[30]

Such displays of partisan journalism were still very much in evidence in the twentieth century. Newsman Paul Bilkey observed that the press galleries of Queen's Park and Ottawa were still divided along party lines in 1903; even in 1911, as journalist Arthur Ford recalled, the set-up in the press gallery mirrored the partisan arrangement of the legislative itself.[31]

Political efforts to influence newspapers carried through into the twentieth century. Prime Minister Laurier issued instructions barely disguised as requests to J.W. Dafoe of the Manitoba *Free Press*.[32] The Conservatives established a committee to review Montreal *Star* editorials in 1907 and consult with owner Hugh Graham. The Southams were pressured into instructing Calgary *Herald* publisher J.H. Woods to cooperate more closely with the Conservative party in 1910.

Party influence still mattered. Reporters assigned to politicians often were little more than mouthpieces. W.H. Dickson, Ottawa correspondent for the *Globe*, had a typical experience in 1901 with Postmaster-General William Mulock and the Post Office report:

I got into [*sic*] the fact that he [Mulock] had a copy in his possession yesterday morning and went and saw him. I explained to him that I wanted a short summary in the Evening *Globe* and would go through the report myself for the morning edition. He asked me to return at one o'clock. On returning at that time I found he had dictated a synopsis of the report to his secretary ... Later in the day he asked me to let my report go in the shape in which he had prepared it. Not wishing to antagonize him I said "certainly" and did so.[33]

This sort of things occurred on both sides of the political fence. In 1908 C.F. Hamilton, Ottawa correspondent for the Toronto *News*, admitted that "my disposition is to keep pretty close to Mr Borden, so as to run no risk of upsetting his game."[34] Pretty close meant allowing the opposition leader to edit his copy. In 1911 the *Globe*'s M.O. Hammond asked Prime Minister Laurier which aspects of an impending election speech he wanted emphasized. Even John Willison, who had so bitterly complained of party control, was a willing accomplice of the Tory government. In 1911 he wrote to Prime Minister R.L. Borden that he sought a press gallery correspondent:

someone who will keep the Conservative member in touch with his constituents, who will take care to say things about him that can be quoted by his local press and keep him good tempered both towards the Government and ... towards the News. I also want to have far more attention paid to the work of the Ministers and what it means to the Government ... If, as I expect, we get within the next few weeks certain support which will enable us to get the additional plant we require and to produce the newspaper I am anxious to produce we should be able to do much better work than the *News* has ever done both in our interest and in the interest of the Government, *Indeed, I think the two interests are identical.*[35]

Many of the self-proclaimed "independent" papers entered the political orbit as well, prompting *Globe* editor John Cameron to remark: "I see now that 'the baser sort' of papers, notably those posing as independent go now for the *Globe* on every opportunity. I knew it would come, and only wonder that it held off for so long. Of all the papers in Canada, the Montreal *Star* is now most vicious against the Liberals. It is in very close touch with Tupper."[36]

Quite a few of the so-called independents were politically biased. When Joseph Flavelle and John Willison bought the Toronto *News* at the end of 1902, they claimed that they were founding Canada's first truly independent paper, one that would judge parties and individuals solely on their merit. In practice, however, the *News* behaved no differently from partisan papers. In every political contest from 1903 to 1917 Willison came down strongly on the side of the Conservatives. The supposedly independent Montreal *Star* did not hesitate to use its columns to roast Prime Minister Laurier on the reciprocity issue; the paper was consistently pro-Conservative, and by the late nineteenth century Hugh Graham was the chief Tory "bagman." The Toronto *Star*'s avowed independence did not prevent Atkinson from asking Laurier why the *Star* had mistakenly been taken off the patronage list for Liberal organs. The *Star* for the most part supported the Liberal party right up to 1917 (John Ross Robertson constantly referred to it as an "organ not a newspaper"), at which point Atkinson reluctantly broke with Laurier over conscription.[37] Willison himself in 1913 doubted whether there were six Canadian papers that quoted their opponents fairly. Clearly, "independent" was a sham label applied by papers hoping to capitalize on a widespread public dislike of "partyism," excessive partisanship and machine politics.

Veteran newsman Arthur Ford recalled how in 1913 he telegraphed his editor, J.H. Crockett of the Saint John *Globe*, seeking instructions on coverage of a major speech by Wilfrid Laurier on the contentious naval bill and another fairly minor speech by Tory minister Douglas Hazen. Crockett, an ardent Hazen supporter, wired back: "Ignore Laurier entirely. Send Hazen verbatim."[38] Crockett, however, was a throwback to the rough-and-tumble politics employed by the party organs in the nineteenth century. As early as

1900, Manitoba *Free Press*'s publisher Clifford Sifton was proposing a subtler form of political advocacy:

> The Government is not injured by the opposition papers' editorials, nor is the Government much helped by the friendly newspapers' editorials ... What actually injures the Government is some carefully concocted piece of alleged news which is prepared for the purpose of informing the readers of the papers that the Government has done something very offensive to the reader. It is not given as an attack upon the Government, it is simply given as an item of news ... I am quite convinced ... that the damage is done by the news columns and not by the editorial columns.[39]

Sifton's statement shows the change in emphasis from the editorial to the news column (whether or not for manipulative purposes), as well as the diminishing importance of the editorial to the publishers.

However, by the early years of the twentieth century the shift towards press independence was well underway. Even in 1899, Kingston *Whig* publisher E.J.B. Pense noted the "rapid growth" of independent papers.[40] By 1900 there were thirty-seven independent dailies with a combined circulation of 572,461, and seventy-seven organs with 660,699 readers.[41] This represented a significant change from the partisan world of the nineteenth-century newspaper. Between 1914 and 1930 the partisan press declined rapidly, while the number of independent papers continued to grow. Papers dropped their party affiliations, went out of business, or sold out to chains. The trend in Ontario was typical of Canada as a whole. There were forty-five partisan dailies in 1909, twenty-nine in 1919, and a mere eleven in 1930. The independent press, meanwhile, had risen from nine in 1909 to fourteen in 1919 and twenty-five in 1930.

From 1860 until well into the First World War, "independence" did not mean an absence of political affiliation. Broadly speaking, it signified the financial independence of proprietors who increasingly could afford to shrug off direct party control and who systematically sought to expand readership to ensure the financial success of their newspapers. The proprietors of the more substantial papers became powerful figures within the parties, where their nineteenth-century predecessors had been mere mouthpieces or political minions. One of the earliest independents, John Ross Robertson, declared in 1862 that "contrary to present practice, [the *Telegraph* will] ... give unswerving support to those who faithfully serve the interests of the city, irrespective of party and political leanings."[42] He spoke prematurely: Prime Minister John A. Macdonald chose to withhold patronage and thus doomed the venture. Upon taking over the Hamilton *Spectator* in 1877, William Southam reportedly told the Conservative party, "I will buy this thing and support you people, but I am running the paper, and I am not your servant."[43] In the prospectus for the establishment of the Winnipeg *Tribune* in January 1890, R.L. Richardson said the paper would be independent, but by "independence, we don't mean neutrality."[44] Rather, it would be Robertson and Richardson who would decide what to support or condemn, not the party. Richardson certainly made this clear in his unhesitating criticism of the Laurier government, and his insistence on his right to do so. "The hope of the country," he wrote in the *Tribune* in 1897, was "in honest outspoken papers that have the fearlessness to frankly admonish its friends when they are, or appear to be, doing wrong." The Laurier government was good, but it was not "immaculate" and deserved some "adverse criticism." The *Tribune*, he continued, "has not hesitated to acknowledge upon several occasions in the past, that the government did not fully live up to its opportunities."[45] The publisher was also in control of editorial policy at the Toronto *Telegram*, as John Ross Robertson made clear in his instructions to his reporters covering City Hall.[46] Despite their public stance of independence, however, both Richardson and Robertson were party stalwarts, the former representing the Liberals and the latter the Conservatives in the House of Commons.

Publishers of papers such as the Montreal *Star*, Toronto *World*, and Ottawa *Journal*, which were founded purely as commercial ventures and classified by *McKim's Newspaper Directory* as independent, were also actively involved in party affairs. J.W. Dafoe defined an independent as "any journal whose opinions are made on the premises by its owners and officers, and the making of which is affected only by considerations of public interest so far as they make an appeal and by the interests of the property itself."[47]

Independence also referred to political fair play or the opening up of the paper's news columns to the opinions of political opponents. John Willison is sometimes credited (certainly he credited himself) with introducing the unbiased news column in reporting the views of political opponents when he was at the helm of the Toronto *Globe*, the Liberal party's flagship, from 1896 to 1902. But earlier examples of impartial political news coverage could be found in the Montreal *Star*, Toronto *Telegram*, Toronto *Star*, and Ottawa *Journal*.[48]

The rise of the impartial news column showed that editors were distinguishing increasingly between the news column and the editorial, reserving "objective" news for the former and opinion for the latter. A Southam memorandum to its Ottawa *Citizen* correspondents in 1907 illustrates this practice as well as the political nature of independence at the time:

> A reputation for *reliability* and *fairness* in the news columns of the CITIZEN is the management's ideal which every correspondent should have in mind when writing his copy. We wish to have people think and say – "If you see it in the CITIZEN it's quite likely to be so." Of equal importance is it that the CITIZEN should have the reputation for printing, if not more, at least as much news as its contemporaries. Its reports should be complete and fair, and *free alike from bias on account of the reporter's predilections and the* CITIZEN's *editorial opinions.* Although politically the CITIZEN supports the policy of the Conservative party, correspondents should not allow this to interfere with their giving the CITIZEN impartial copy dealing with political matters. The CITIZEN is not the organ of any political party, or of any politician, but it is striving to be a high class, fair and reliable *newspaper* ... Both sides of every story should *invariably* be given.⁴⁹

By 1915, impartial news columns and the news column/editorial distinction were commonplace. According to E.F. Slack, the Montreal *Gazette*'s managing director, the business of a newspaper was to give the public fair and honest reports of the news of the day, uninfluenced by the editorial policy of the paper and unspoiled by any pressure from advertising. "Newspapers to-day are business propositions. The public expects them to give the news of the day as it happens, without colour or bias." Furthermore, "any paper which attempted to follow the lines that were in vogue even a few years ago would be an utter failure to-day."⁵⁰

Declaring independence also helped a paper to carve out a niche for itself in saturated markets. In the 1890s the Liberal-tinged Hamilton *Herald* managed to distinguish itself from the Conservative *Spectator* and the Liberal *Times* by declaring its independence. Even though Liberal party backers financed the purchase of the Toronto *Star* in 1899 with Laurier's encouragement, Atkinson still thought it best – in order to survive economically in Tory-dominated Toronto, with its established party organs – to advertise the paper as "independent" with the slogan "A newspaper not an organ."⁵¹

It was the Vancouver *Province*'s Walter Nichol, however, who tied the increasing influence of business considerations to the eventual demise of overt partisanship. In 1901 he noted how more publishers were producing newspapers in the strictest sense by "discarding entirely obligations of a political nature." This meant that "business, and not sentiment, was the watchword of the hour, and to this cry everything is made to conform." Advocating the separation of news and editorial opinion, he remarked, "If controversy is wanted, it could be found in the 'unattended' editorial columns or in the letters section, so that the newspaper could be devoted more exclusively to the recording of events." Moreover, "with the partizan [*sic*] feature eliminated from the newspapers, and with enterprise, accuracy and reliability made the *sine qua non* by the public, only the best and most intelligent would survive, and those which hang on to existence through drafts on the party pap bottle would have to succumb ... One thing is certain it would be business in the completest sense of the word."[52] Nichol clearly believed in the superiority of business and in the desirability of newspapermen acting like businessmen.

When E. Norman Smith, whose Ottawa *Free Press* was lavishly patronized by the Laurier government in the early twentieth century, muted its overt Liberal partisanship, the paper's circulation jumped significantly, a development Smith attributed to the paper's "independent" line.[53] As the generally Conservative Calgary *Herald* took an increasingly independent editorial stance, the "machine" Conservatives threatened to set up a straight party organ in competition if publisher J.H. Woods didn't toe the party line. Unfazed by the threat, Woods informed the paper's owners, the Southam family, that he'd like to turn the *Herald* into an "independent paper" with no party affiliation. It would fight western battles and criticize both political parties with equal enthusiasm. "That is the kind of paper I would like best to run and I believe it is the kind that will pay best in this country."[54] In its editorial stance the *Herald* often differed from other papers in the Southam chain, such as the Ottawa *Citizen* and the Hamilton *Spectator*. Indeed, divergent local market conditions made it impossible for the Southams to agree upon, much less to enforce, a common political stance in their newspapers.

Even smaller papers began to get the message. For example, R.G. McCuish of the Fort William *Evening Herald* said he turned "independent" because it was not wise "to give your paper to the politician at the expense of your business," and he advised other country publishers to "conduct their papers more as a business proposition" and to avoid being "tools of the politicians."[55]

The independence trend accelerated during World War I. Some observers claim that the establishment of the Union government blurred party differences such that it made little sense for the newspapers to wage fierce partisan battles. Many publishers believed that the move came about because of the need to close ranks in the face of total war. Such former partisan stalwarts as the Toronto *Mail and Empire*, Toronto *Star*, Guelph *Sentinel-Review*, Toronto *News*, and the *Globe* all markedly toned down their partisan rhetoric in favour of united non-partisan pro-war stands. The strongly Liberal Manitoba *Free Press* summed up the common sentiment in 1917: declaring itself to be "out of party politics" for the duration of the war, it now recognized only one duty – "that of serving the country with a whole souled devotion." That meant backing "unionist" candidates who would form a "win-the-war government."[56] But while patriotic fervour undoubtedly played a part, the economic realities of market rationalization during World War I – reduced business and advertising and newsprint shortages, which caused the number of newspapers to shrink through merger and bankruptcy – probably had more to do with the newspapers clearing their news columns of party bias and moderating their editorial thunder.

In the twentieth century the bigger publishers, thanks to the mounting financial might and mass influence of their publications, not only were able to resist political pressure (as J.H. Woods did despite the Southams' promise of more Conservative support, and as Graham did in maintaining the *Star*'s neutrality in the 1908 federal election): they also became politically influential and powerful in their own right. Indeed, Graham, the owner of the largest and richest English-language daily, "obviously aspired to play a dominating role in politics from behind the scenes as a puppet master manipulating the politicians."[57] His scheming was legendary. In 1904, for example, he served as treasurer in a $1.5 million plot hatched by the Mackenzie-Mann interests to buy Liberal newspapers in a bid to overthrow the Laurier government. His "whisper of death" campaign against Conservative party leader Arthur Meighen was a notorious example of his ability to cause havoc in party affairs.[58]

Other publishers meddled as well. Joseph Atkinson, nicknamed "Whispering Joe," became quite influential in Liberal party circles and was instrumental in writing the federal party platforms of 1911 and 1916. Significantly, the Toronto *Star*'s real independence began to manifest itself when Atkinson finally achieved majority control of the paper in 1913.

Publisher independence from party strictures became increasingly evident from the 1890s on and constituted a major difference between newspaper partisanship in the nineteenth and twentieth centuries. The Riordon family's independent handling of the Toronto *Mail* was the primary reason for the setting up of the *Empire* in 1887, while from the 1890s on, Robert Jaffray's growing resistance to party dictates on behalf of the Toronto *Globe* led to the Liberal party's takeover of the *Star*. Business rather than party considerations increasingly determined the course of a publisher's actions. William Dennis, the proprietor of the Halifax *Herald* and *Mail*, is a good example. Before he took them over in the late 1890s, the two publications were floundering despite heavy infusions of Conservative patronage. A staunch Conservative himself, Dennis lost that revenue when Laurier came to power. After 1896 he concentrated on making the *Herald* and the *Mail* into paying propositions by adopting modern business methods and the journalistic practices of such popular papers as the Montreal *Star* and the Toronto *Telegram*. In 1911 his once-moribund properties were described as "the best financial propositions in Eastern Canada."[59] A contemporary description of how Dennis "made good" is instructive:

Both papers are widely read. For a small province, their circulation is big. There is a reason for this. Dennis caters to the people. He chases up popular subjects. While his papers advocate the principles of the Conservative party, he refuses to be led or guided by the party managers. He opens his columns to the exponents of ideas not cherished by Conservative bosses. It gives both sides the political news and curious as it may seem, he manages to get and print important news from the Liberal camp long before the press of that party know anything about it. As a consequence, his publications are read by Grit and Tory alike and another proof of Dennis' deep solicitude for No. 1 comes to the front. He gets the circulation, and circulation commands the advertising and the advertising commands the cash.[60]

Expanding readership and, thus, advertising revenues, became more important than party needs, signifying the progressive weakening of the political content of newspapers in favour of entertainment. The same considerations governed the actions of another Conservative publisher, Charles Blackadar, who by 1917 had muted the "violently" partisan nature of the *Acadian Recorder* because the paper had made little or nothing out of patronage and his advertising patrons were to be "found in both political camps."[61]

Patronage no longer had the power to bind press to party. Even the Laurier and Borden governments' massive increases in direct newspaper patronage masked the weakening hold of the parties and the changing nature of newspaper partisanship after 1890. In short, the more financially independent the press became, the more the politicians spent to control it.

The actual figures are misleading, however, because they incorporate a large percentage of payments to independent printers and not newspapers. In 1914 Richard Southam complained that the increasingly Liberal *Citizen* was harming Southam Printing patronage contracts with the Borden government. Wilson Southam replied that the Southam interests still received $31,000 while the most richly rewarded party organ, the Montreal *Gazette*, received only $24,000. Moreover, the Mortimer Printing Company, which had no newspapers, received $88,000 worth of business, "which seems to show that the work goes largely to the man that is on the spot when the work is ready to be given out."[62] To be sure, political expenditures over and beyond printing payments represented substantial increases and helped bind some papers to the party. But the figures appear less impressive when spread over a number of papers or when measured against the enormous revenues that most big-city dailies earned from the 1890s on.

Thus, patronage does not fully explain continued partisanship since most party newspapers received very little – generally a few hundred dollars' worth – in the way of printing contracts or advertisements and announcements, while many received nothing at all, as one publisher complained bitterly in a letter to Laurier.[63] In 1899 only twelve papers received more than a thousand dollars in patronage. A favoured few got most of the money. In 1901 the Montreal *Herald* alone received eighteen percent of all the money disbursed. In 1902 the *Globe*, then the most important Liberal paper, received $2,600. But this was nothing compared to yearly revenues already in the hundreds of thousands of dollars. The $10,000 the *Globe* received in 1910 did not change this equation.[64] Party disbursements were of decreasing significance as big-city dailies boomed in the twentieth century. It was precisely the biggest and financially most successful dailies, the ones the parties most wanted to influence, that were the least susceptible to patronage.

Business conditions hampered the relationship between newspapers and parties from the 1890s on. Independents and "party organs" alike were controlled by people who increasingly resented political direction. They were far more concerned with their mass audiences and ensuring continued growth in circulation and advertising revenues. As for the journalists who worked for them, once-strong party discipline gave way to a growing sense of professionalism and autonomy as they themselves were increasingly alienated from the aims and needs of the businessman qua publisher.

The anomaly of the partisan paper in Canada was that newspaper proprietors, though connected to a party, still had to make a profit. This meant pleasing a wider audience than the party faithful. Yet because they contributed to the newspaper through direct party patronage (captive subscriptions, subsidized editions for election propaganda, and provincial or federal government patronage if the party achieved power), the faithful believed it was their right to direct the policies of the paper.

This situation made it difficult for journalists because they were serving two masters, the public and the politicians, whose needs and interests often differed. The Toronto *Empire*, widely regarded as the most partisan paper in Canada's history, is a case in point. As noted earlier, it had been created expressly as a Conservative organ in 1887 when John A. Macdonald grew disaffected with the independent ways of the the *Mail*. An *Empire* journalist, Hector Charlesworth, remarked that the paper had "a large and able staff, and had it been conducted independently of interference from party chiefs would have undoubtedly in the end outstripped its rivals." But neither its reporters nor its editor "felt safe from incurring the dislike of some politician with some personal axe to grind, who through his stock subscription or his prominence in the party gave him the right to interfere."[65] During Charlesworth's thirteen months on the paper, two city editors were fired simply because they had printed stories that had displeased one particular faction. Moreover, "non-political news of an important character was constantly suppressed at the request of some party magnate or other, a fatal policy in a field in which so many newspapers were competing."[66] Unable to please two masters, the *Empire* had lost $150,000 by 1895, at which point the party leaders decided there were too many large papers in Toronto and allowed the *Mail*, another money loser, to absorb the *Empire*.

The failure of the *Empire* showed the weakening of political influence on the press. When Joseph Atkinson agreed to publish the *Star*, he cited the fate of the *Empire* to underscore his bid for a paper run on business principles and based on profit rather than political considerations, as demanded by such veteran politicos as Postmaster General Mulock. He argued in a letter to Laurier that the *Star* "can only be useful politically if it has the confidence of its constituency and by having regard to its commercial success a Liberal paper enables itself to give greater service to the party." He objected to the notion of a reliable, subsidized paper that was to be used for purely political purposes. "A newspaper is a good ally but soon becomes useless as the subsequent organ of a party."[67]

There were other signs of declining press partyism. J.S. Willison, then editor of the Toronto *Globe*, complained in 1901 of political criticism and interference from the Liberal party. In a letter to Clifford Sifton, he defended the growing use of objective news coverage and took exception to "the assumption of every Liberal politician that I am his hired man, that he has the right to criticise and condemn me, and he has the right to dictate or shape my course as a journalist."[68]

Thus, by 1900 the seeds of independence had been sown and publishers had loosened the grip of the political parties. The process was hastened by the establishment of the dominion-wide Canadian Press news agency, which made full and impartial parliamentary reports available to all the press. The blurring of party lines during World War I, especially under the Union government, further weakened the partisan propensities of the newspaper. Moreover, as shown elsewhere, the wartime decrease in the number of papers translated into oligarchic or monopolistic newspaper markets. Newspapers were reluctant to antagonize segments of their politically heterogeneous audiences and thus jeopardize advertising revenues through strident partisanship. Even the most overt party organs increasingly became personal vehicles for their owners, whose whims they responded to even if it meant betraying the party to which the paper was attached. Financial independence allowed for political independence. Editor Arthur Wallis of the Conservative party's *Mail and Empire* complained in 1906 that he could not do any "really effectual work" on behalf of the party because of the "Riordan interests being in receipt of government favours of one sort or another."[69]

In the twentieth century, then, bribes seemed about the only way that political parties could bring the powerful publishers on side. Laurier was forced to bribe Robert Jaffray after he was "hurt" by the Toronto *Globe*'s defection on the separate schools issue in 1905.[70] As *Globe* editor M.O. Hammond recalled, "The *Globe* is more friendly to the Government these days and their making of Mr Jaffray a Senator ... seems to have secured for themselves a stronger ally."[71] Hugh Graham went very easy on the Liberals during the 1908 election, prompting Conservative leader Robert Borden to remark that Graham's recently acquired knighthood was "a circumstance which will convince the whole Conservative party that Sir Hugh was bought."[72] Bribery also weakened the Conservative hold on the *Citizen*. C.F. Hamilton of the *News* wrote to Willison: "You don't know how to conduct a party newspaper. The Ottawa *Citizen* does. It did not put a line to show that there was a Conservative party in existence until the Conservatives gave it $1,000 out of their campaign fund. They are sure it got a larger sum from the Liberals, as they vow it put its best reporters on the Liberal meetings. The day after the fight it plumed itself on its 'fairness.'"[73]

The *Citizen* became even less overtly political as Wilson and Harry Southam focused increasingly on entertainment. As time went on their editorial intervention decreased. During World War I they intervened only once, asking the *Citizen* to support Henry George's single-tax proposition, an issue dear to the hearts of rich men. Clifford Sifton had become progressively less involved the *Free Press* after his retirement from active politics in 1905, but he too was induced to intervene editorially over the issue of taxing the rich. When the paper began a series on taxing businesses, he told Dafoe that he categorically would "not permit the *Free Press* to lead such a campaign."[74] The normally pugnacious Dafoe quickly dropped the offending series.

Where before publishers had been cogs in the party wheels responding to directives from the party executive – especially from prime ministers – they increasingly took on the role of power brokers, often working outside the party. Canadian involvement in the Boer War is a case in point. In conjunction with the Montreal *Star* the Toronto newspapers, especially the *Globe*, were instrumental in forcing a reluctant Laurier to send troops to South Africa. Willison and Jaffray themselves put enormous pressure on the prime minister. Similarly, the *Globe* did not hesitate to abandon Laurier on the separate schools issue, thus placing itself on the side of the Conservative Hamilton *Spectator*.[74]

In sum, from the 1890s until well into the First World War, publishers were distancing their publications from political parties, although the publishers themselves remained partisan. By declaring independence they signalled their determination to take control of their publications away from the politicians. While newspapers still served as political advocates, publishers instituted more subtle methods of transmitting political messages in order to expand their audiences and turn a bigger profit. As competition and concentration lessened the number of dailies, and as the remaining ones grew bigger and more prosperous, the publishers became powerful in their own right and used their publications to influence political parties.

8 Joining the Élite

With patronage diminishing in importance after 1890, the question remains why most newspapers remained politically tied before World War I. Patronage accounted increasingly for small, often negligible, portions of the revenues of most city dailies, with the exception of a favoured and financially troubled few. Government and party subscriptions had begun to drop in significant proportion to total income as the major dailies, which had expanded their readership far beyond the politically faithful through the addition of popular entertainment features, added tens of thousands to their circulation in the early twentieth century. Senatorships and civil service appointments for loyal partisan journalists were few and far between. Yet the politicization of the formerly independent and maverick "people's press" proceeded apace,[1] as did the creation, around the turn of the century, of the Liberal and Conservative newspaper networks. It has been seen, however, that while many papers were purchased or created for political purposes, no direct patronage expenditures could cover the costs of even a medium-sized city daily like the Ottawa *Free Press*. Indeed, massive subsidies failed to save either the *Free Press* or the Montreal *Herald*, the main beneficiaries of Laurier government patronage.

The key to continued newspaper partisanship and politicization lies in the changing nature of newspaper ownership from the 1890s on. Those who controlled the successful big-city dailies were increasingly representative of the business/political coalitions that were spearheading Canada's industrial transformation. Newspapers became the spokesmen for these interests. As O.D. Skelton noted, newspaper independence increased as "business outweighed politics," but a paper "became independent of party only to become dependent on advertisers, or the organ of railway or corporation interests."[2]

"Interest" politics explains why three prominent Ottawa Conservatives lent money to P.D. Ross and the Ottawa *Journal* in 1891. They were not trying to create a party paper because there already was one, the *Citizen*. Ross, moreover, was too independent to be controlled;[3] the *Journal*'s eventual conversion to Conservative organ in 1904 occurred because Ross himself had also become a politician.[4] The fact was that Ross's benefactors controlled local concerns that were involved in mining and pulp development. They sought cheap power,[5] and Ross, who subscribed to this brand of conservatism, fought for their interests through the *Journal* and through his activities on behalf of public hydro. Ross was not "bought"; he did not have to be since he, like Atkinson, wished to join the rich. Both eventually succeeded. It is was this "club" that induced Ross to run for alderman and also for mayor.[6]

P.D. Ross exemplified the changing nature of newspaper ownership. Well-heeled party backers were responsible for most of the newly created newspapers or takeovers of established ones from the 1890s on. The setting up of the *Empire* as a joint stock venture in 1888 and its takeover by the *Mail* group headed by the Riordon family was an early example, likewise the *Globe* takeover by Robert Jaffray and George Cox; both illustrated the intertwining of politics and journalism. Strategic takeovers to assist a party during an election were almost always undertaken by coalitions of politicians and businessmen. Politicians, many of them lawyers, did start newspapers in the nineteenth century. So did many newsmen and printers who had worked their way up through the ranks and were eventually able to buy their own publications, start a new one, or buy a small paper. In 1908, after half a century of experience, William Buckingham, editor of the *Nor'Wester* in 1859 and later editor of the Stratford *Beacon*, remarked on the "number who made themselves careers" in the printing office "school," and who eventually became editors and proprietors of their own newspapers.[7]

In the twentieth century, however, newspapermen of this kind were "becoming fewer all the time for the newspaper field is no longer the recruiting ground of former days. Graduation, the chance to rise step by step has gone."[8] Individuals could no longer hope to own newspapers unless they had enormous wealth, like J.W. Flavelle and B.F. Pearson, or a position from which they could tap into the enormous patronage potential of the federal government, like Interior minister Clifford Sifton, or significant backing, like Joseph Atkinson and W.C. Nichol. The increasing purchase of newspapers by syndicates and the fact that few new papers were successfully established point to the corporatizing trend in newspaper publishing.

From the mid-nineteenth century onwards, newspaper work represented a chance for ambitious men to advance in the political world. By the 1890s, journalism also served as a path to success and wealth in the business world and provided an entrée to the political-business nexus that governed Canada. Men like Hugh Graham, John Ross Robertson, W.F. Maclean, and William Southam blazed the way for another generation of go-getters like Walter Nichol, P.D. Ross, Sanford Evans, and Joseph Atkinson – a lucky few who had started as reporters and gone on to work their way up to become editors. As such they had the chance to meet and represent political-financial interests and then, if they were able and clever, harness those interests to back them in their purchase of newspapers. Reporters dreamed of striking it rich. According to one observer, attempts to found a Toronto journalists' union in 1902 failed because reporters were "too imbued with capitalist notions and desires to be one [a capitalist]."[9]

In 1897 Walter Nichol remarked that the key to success in the newspaper business was to become a newspaper proprietor. Writing and reporting were too "hard and exacting" and the rewards "pitifully" small. There was no future for an older reporter, who was "either cast aside like a crushed orange or given some employment in a subordinate capacity." But patronage rewards for party "slaves" were rather few. "Owners alone," he concluded, "are rewarded by the labour of others."[10]

Nichol then went west to seek his fortune. At first joining the gold rush, he soon discovered that newspapers were a better vein to mine. In 1898 he became editor of the Vancouver *Province* under the tutelage of the wealthy federal Conservative MP Hewitt Bostock. The paper also had CPR backing, and eventually Nichol was able to buy out the paper in 1902. Under Nichol, the *Province* pioneered the popular breezy features style of journalism that eventually transformed even the strictly partisan press. For Nichol, the consistently profitable *Province*, which soon had the largest circulation in BC, was a springboard to success. By the time he sold the paper to Southam interests in 1923, he was president of an insurance company, director of several mining companies, and lieutenant governor of the province.[11]

Networking was essential to a newspaper's value in those times. The influence of a newspaper represented a valuable commodity that translated into contacts and connections with the monied world, which in turn led to money-making possibilities. P.D. Ross used his paper in this way, dabbling successfully in mines and streetcar advertising. That is why the 1906 instructions to the *Journal*'s city editor stipulated that "merchants must not be interviewed on business matters without first seeing Mr Ross [and if he approves] subsequently obtaining from Mr Robertson a list of those to be so interviewed."[12] J.H. Woods used insider connections and knowledge gleaned through the Calgary *Herald* to build a good real estate base by buying land in advance of sizeable railway purchases.

A significant number of publishers used the connections and prestige conferred by their newspapers to further their personal political ambitions, thus adding to their influence, especially with businessmen seeking favours from government. Indeed, many publishers were involved in politics to a degree that defined them also as politicians. As noted earlier, P.D. Ross ran successfully for alderman and unsuccessfully for mayor of Ottawa. John J. Young started out as a journalist in 1885 and went on to become editor of the Regina *Leader*, then of the Moosomin *Spectator*. Eventually he became chief editor and, finally, proprietor of the Calgary *Herald*. During his time at the *Herald*, he sat as an alderman and also represented Calgary East in the provincial legislature. Once he had milked the political-commercial connections inherent in newspaper ownership, he left journalism to concentrate on business. After selling the *Herald* to Southam interests in 1908, he became quite wealthy developing his gold and silver mining interests and gradually acquiring extensive cattle ranch holdings.[13]

W. Sanford Evans is a another case in point. A minister's son (and grandson of Senator Sanford), Evans graduated from Victoria College in Toronto and acquired a master's degree from Columbia University. He was taken on as a reporter by the *Mail and Empire* and had worked his way up to editor by 1900. During this time, he was active in the Conservative party, becoming chief organizer for fruit producer E.D. Smith in the 1897 provincial election campaign. Evans clearly sought success wherever he could find it. He married Irene Gurney, the daughter of stove manufacturer and former Toronto mayor Edward Gurney, who pulled strings with loan companies, introduced him to financiers, and occasionally lent him money to help him during his early career.[14]

Around the turn of the century, Evans left the *Mail and Empire* to become treasurer of the National Cycle and Automobile Co. He was soon squeezed out of the business and became unsatisfactorily involved with a Toronto-based publishers' syndicate that produced literary weeklies. However, as he confessed, he was "eager for any kind of business," and this led him to renew his involvement with newspaper work.[15] Through his political and social contacts he learned that Winnipeg's Tory organ, the *Telegram*, was up for sale.[16] In November 1900 he signalled his desire to become managing editor with an interest in the *Telegram* to a Winnipeg contact, R.T. Riley. Evans realized that "money would need to be invested before it paid," but the Tories were in power provincially, Manitoba was growing, and he believed that with "good managing and good editing," he would be able to "reap a reward."[17]

The reasoning behind Evans's interest in the Winnipeg *Telegram* reveals the interplay of business and political considerations that underlay so many newspaper takeovers at the time. Riley's reply is equally revealing and also shows how the network operated. He wrote that the *Telegram* had never been a success, partly because the Conservatives had been out of power for twelve years but mainly because the paper lacked "good business management." Riley enclosed an assessment of the paper by W.B. Somerset, a former business manager of the *Free Press*, who believed that there might be a "constituency for a moderate Conservative paper in the West now that the 'FP' is so ultra Liberal." But not, he cautioned, if the paper remained "principally political." Success depended on the new owner being able to "make it commercially valuable as an advertiser"; this required "time and money in working up a circulation." Adequate capital was necessary to tide over "its uncertain tenure of life for a long period." And, of course, there was a political "prejudice" to overcome.[18] Somerset's cautionary remarks about the political nature of the *Telegram* show the extent to which financial considerations prevailed.

Evans understood this. In summarizing his reasons for wanting to take over the paper, he attributed its past failure to management "by a committee of the party rather than by private individuals, and it has not been managed on business principles." He added that in addition to the newspaper work, he was attracted by "good opportunity" and the "inducement" he had had from the party to secure a nomination to run for either a provincial or federal seat.[19]

In January 1901 the paper was handed over to Evans "free of debt for the value of the plant taken at a very moderate valuation." Nonetheless, he was worried about the *Telegram*'s annual running debt of $20,000.[20] The Mackenzie-Mann interests, which had helped in the actual purchase, were unable to provide more money so Evans was forced to raise additional capital through the sale of $50,000 worth of debentures (corporate bonds backed by the general credit of the issuer rather than by a specific lien on particular assets).

With the new Conservative government in power under Premier R.P. Roblin, prospects looked good. Evans worked hard to make the right political and financial connections and put himself on a good footing with the movers and shakers of Manitoba. He networked and socialized, persuading the attorney general to arrange provincially financed special editions and meeting with the premier to secure job printing patronage. He spent an evening with the wealthiest man in Winnipeg and dined with various government ministers. At one such dinner, he received instructions on how to cover the new railway construction proposals.[21]

This incident was not isolated. In his letters to his wife, Evans reveals the extensive interconnection between politicians, railway interests, and the newspapers. In consultation with William Mackenzie he wrote in support of the Mackenzie-Mann interests in Manitoba, going so far as to publish a special supplement of 25,000 copies outlining their views. Throughout the period of competition for new railway lines, Evans was in constant contact with Mackenzie and his ministers, even attending cabinet meetings on the railway issue.

The politics of the railway battle was complex and Evans had to tread carefully. The Conservative caucus paid for four thousand extra editions between February and May 1901, and Evans realized that "if the Government is defeated on this measure or if the scheme does not work well the fight will be longer and harder still."[22] Moreover, he was angling to get an AP franchise, which was held, of course, by the CPR, and he was worried that opposing the CPR might jeopardize his application. Although committed to the Mackenzie-Mann camp, he pulled his punches with the Canadian Pacific; as he wrote to his wife, "I attacked them without making them too mad."[23]

Evans struggled on and in 1904, capitalizing on one of the "inducements" that brought him out west, he ran for Parliament during the federal election. When he lost, his father-in-law advised him to abandon newspaper work and "concentrate ... on making a fortune."[24] Evans took Gurney's advice and sold the *Telegram* to frontmen for Conservative Robert Rogers in 1905. He promptly plunged into business activities, employing all the contacts he had gained through his newspaper work. He started the Winnipeg College of Music and an investment house and then set up a real estate firm, asking the "headmen" at Canada Permanent (which had underwritten loans for him) as well as Mackenzie and Mann for inside information on whether and where their companies were planning to expand their Winnipeg operations.[25]

Undeniably, his *Telegram* stint helped Evans financially and politically. Robert Borden himself noted his work on behalf of the Conservative party and promised to reward him accordingly. Borden went so far as "to interest some eastern friends" in Evans's real estate proposals.[26] Evans parleyed his opportunities into a sizeable fortune and then returned to political life. He was elected mayor of Winnipeg in 1909 and 1911 and afterwards sat for fourteen years in the provincial legislature.

Evans's career shows how the business and political worlds intersected at the newspaper. The political connection, which had been there since the 1850s, largely overshadowed the business connection until the late nineteenth century, when the transformation of business in Canada, along with the transformation of newspapers into businesses, brought business squarely into the newspaper world. A newspaper career could now provide access to the financial political élite that dominated Canada.

That publishers were part of this élite was apparent in 1912, when a Winnipeg committee of three (including businessman Sir William Whyte and the *Free Press*'s J.W. Dafoe) asked that a Toronto committee be set up to make the question of naval defence non-partisan. The Toronto meeting was attended by about twenty-five business luminaries including Sir William Mackenzie, Sir Joseph Flavelle, Sir Edmund Walker, and the publishers of the six Toronto daily newspapers.[27]

A look at the careers of eighty-six newspaper publishers between 1890 and 1918 shows how actively they were involved in politics and business (see chart 1). Indicative of their political involvement is the fact that more than half (fifty-eight percent) could be considered professional politicians since they were elected to municipal office, provincial legislatures, or Parliament. This figure rises to sixty-five percent with the addition of publishers who ran unsuccessfully for their parties in provincial or federal elections. Almost one-quarter (twenty) had sat in the House of Commons, another one-fifth (seventeen) in provincial legislatures while eleven served as mayors.

The political involvement of publishers mirrored that of other businessmen at the time. T.W. Acheson found that half of the industrialists he studied had held some form of public office during their careers, about one in three occupying a major political office at the provincial or federal level. His finding that most industrialists in the smaller communities also participated actively in municipal government and on school commissions was also true of small-city publishers.[28]

Chart 1 also shows the publishers' extensive business connections. Half (forty-three) held directorships and investments. Publishers of the larger dailies held the vast majority (eighty-three percent) of outside investments, showing the intersection of big newspaper enterprises with other business enterprises. Conversely, among those who had no outside investments more than half were owners of

Chart 1
Backgrounds of Eighty-six Daily Newspaper Publishers, 1898 and 1912[a]

Cabinet Ministers[b]			Outside investments	43[c]
Federal	6		Big daily	13[d]
Provincial	5		Medium daily	21
Senator	8		Small daily	7
Member of Parliament		20	No outside investments	43
(Ran but lost)	4		Big daily	4[e]
MPP, MLA		18	Medium daily	12
(Ran but lost)	2		Small daily	27
Municipal Office		19	Origins[f]	
Mayor	11		Printer	15
City Council	13		Newsman	30
Board of Trade		9	Inherited	10
			No experience (bought in)	6
			Founder	16
			Unknown	11

[a] Sources: Morgan 1898 and 1912; *Canadian Printer and Publisher*, 1892–1920; assorted biographies.
[b] Some publishers are multiple entries politically, such as Frank Cochrane, who had served as mayor, MPP, MP, and as both provincial and federal cabinet minister.
[c] To be included, the publishers had to serve as presidents or directors of business enterprises outside the newspaper industry or have substantial shares or investments in them. The number here most likely is an undercount because of source inadequacy. For example, there is no mention in Morgan 1898 or 1912 of the substantial outside business interests of Frank Carrell, publisher of the Quebec City *Telegraph*.
[d] Big: a circulation of over 20,000 in 1912; Medium: 5,000 to 20,000; Small: under 5,000.
[e] Two of the richest and most powerful publishers of big dailies, John Ross Robertson and Joseph Atkinson, had no significant outside investments.
[f] Figures add up to more than eighty-six because a founder could also have been a printer or newsman.

small dailies. Of the five big-daily publishers with no outside investments, two (Robertson and Graham) were already in the tycoon class on the strength of their newspaper business alone; a third, Atkinson, was busy buying control of his company and would eventually become one of Canada's wealthiest men.

In sum, the survey reveals that publishers as a group participated widely in politics and business and that the owners of the bigger dailies were part of Canada's ruling élite. Most had worked their way into this position. Because of their enormously valuable newspaper properties, Graham, Robertson, and Atkinson became extremely wealthy men. Others augmented the considerable value of their newspapers with outside investments, as Southam did in steel, power, and printing, Ross in mines and a ticket company, Nichol in insurance and coal mining, and Stewart, Dennis, and the Southam sons in real estate.

The significant presence of businessmen in the publishing ranks is also clear from the survey, even though it counts only owners and not the many businessmen who, while not the principal owners, nonetheless still had important newspaper investments. Financier George Cox, who had stakes in the Toronto *Globe* and *Star*, is a good example. The following comprises a partial list of businessmen who either owned or had significant minority holdings in major newspapers.[29]

Francis Cochrane (Toronto *News*): mining, hardware
Senator George Cox (Toronto *Globe* and *Star*): finance
Robert Dunsmuir (Victoria *Colonist*): coal mining
Timothy Eaton (Toronto *Star*): department stores
Sir Joseph Flavelle (Toronto *News*): meat packing, finance, retail
George Gooderham (Toronto *News*): distilling
J.M. Gibson (Hamilton *Times*): utilities
A.E. Kemp (Toronto *News*): manufacturing
Peter Larkin (Toronto *Star*): food processing
D. Lorne McGibbon (Montreal *Herald*): rubber, manufacturer, real estate
John McKane (Saint John *Telegraph* and *Times*): mining
Sir William Mackenzie (Toronto *Star*, Winnipeg *Telegram*): railways, power, tramways
E.T. Malone (Toronto *Globe* and *Star*): lawyer, financier
Frederic Nicholls (Toronto *Star*): utilities, electricity
E.B. Osler (Toronto *News*): finance, stocks
B.F. Pearson (Halifax *Chronicle* and *Echo*, Saint John *Sun* and *Star*): insurance, finance, utilities, marine
T.H. Purdom (London *Advertiser*): lawyer, finance, insurance, tramways
Sir William Reid (Montreal *Telegraph*): railways
Riordon family (Toronto *Mail, News,* and *Empire*): paper
David Russell (Saint John *Times* and *Telegraph*): promoter
Sir Clifford Sifton (Manitoba *Free Press*): finance
Sir Frank Smith (Toronto *Empire*): retail grocery, railways
J.J. Stewart (Halifax *Herald*): banking
J.W. Stewart (Vancouver *Sun*): railways
William Van Horne (Manitoba *Free Press*): railways
Senator Josiah Wood (Montreal *Mail*): marine, shipbuilding

The list reads like a "who's who" of Canadian business and underlines the integration of the newspaper world into the highest echelons of the Canadian corporate structure. Many on this list, as the survey shows, also had significant political careers. For example, B.F. Pearson, the publisher of six Maritime papers and finance capitalist with involvement in shipping lines, utilities, and finance companies, was also a Nova Scotia cabinet minister. Another example was Hamilton *Times* publisher J.M. Gibson, a former Ontario attorney general and a principal owner in the Hamilton electric and street companies.

Yet if the most prominent publishers now had joined the economic élite, why did so many newspapers rail against monopoly, privilege, and "vested interests" during the period from 1890 to 1920? Why didn't the newspaper-owning élite suppress these attacks against their own class? The reason was that the newspapers never challenged the capitalist *status quo*. "Billy" Maclean, MP, owner of the Toronto *World*, and the most vociferous exponent of public ownership and nationalization,[30] allowed this broadside of 10 December 1909 in a special edition announcing a move to a bigger building: entitled "Allegiance to the Public Interest," the paper declared "unceasing war against capitalistic monopolies, against any endeavour to bring the many under subjection for the advantage of the few." It called for public ownership of all services and utilities that are "by nature monopolies." It denounced the transfer of public monopolies to private corporations as "detrimental to the community." And it argued that those private concerns that held public franchises should be under close public supervision and control. Stirring stuff, but in the final analysis mere rhetoric that neither called for socialism nor challenged capitalist ideology. Analyzing the Toronto *World*, *News*, and *Star* at the turn of the century, Thomas Walkom found that their populist diatribes focused on individuals – that is, on "boodlers" and rotten apples – and not the system. The underlying message was that once corrupt politicians and overly greedy capitalists were removed, anyone could strike it rich. The *World*'s attack on "vested interests" did not translate into a general attack on the wealthy; it supported "progressive" businessmen. Nor did populist appeals in the other papers amount to an attack on the socioeconomic system; indeed, Walkom concluded, the newspaper agenda for public debate excluded the topic of class conflict. Whatever conflict there was existed between good and bad people in a seemingly classless society, not between the impoverished many and the privileged few.[31]

In their support of the "progressive" businessman, newspaper publishers were in tune with the general desire to purge business and government of corruption and organize society more efficiently in order to avert the more severe social problems caused by rapid urbanization. The most influential publishers, after all, whether they started as newsmen, printers, or businessmen, were part of the Canadian economic political élite and subscribed to its fundamental belief in individual effort and creation of wealth as the driving force behind progress in Canadian society. Given that most were self-made men – including Robertson, Graham, Atkinson, Flavelle, Jaffray, Southam, Ross, Dennis, and Nichol – it would have been strange if they had thought otherwise. It was no coincidence that the newspapers were the prime exponents of the Horatio Alger myth and the economic optimism that pervaded the boom period under Laurier. Jaffray's Toronto *Globe* (17 December 1899) drew together this key moral message: commerce and hard work would be rewarded on earth, charity would be rewarded in heaven. Even Joseph Atkinson, whose detractors branded him as a socialist or worse, believed firmly in individual enterprise and material progress. The Toronto *Star* had high praise for the achievements of William Mackenzie upon his death, even though it had bitterly opposed many of his projects. The Toronto *Star* characterized the world as a progressive place, where business could be enlightened and where the rich could learn to use their wealth wisely. Atkinson supported progressivism, but within the existing business framework.[32]

Other influential publishers promulgated the same message in the pages of their publications. The social vision presented by the Manitoba *Free Press* under Sifton-Dafoe was ruggedly individualistic, oriented to hard work and progress. The duty of government was to facilitate progress by striking a balance between the requirements of capital and those of producers, labourers, and consumers. At the core of this vision was a kind of Social Darwinism in which the hardest working and most enterprising would be justly rewarded with the greatest wealth – the survival of the fittest through competitive free enterprise.

These sentiments were expressed not only by Liberal party stalwarts but also by Conservative party adherents, such as Joseph Flavelle and J.S. Willison of the Toronto *News*. Flavelle said that the paper should align itself on the side of progress and "courageous optimism," which meant supporting men or measures that brought to "syndicates, or groups, or cliques important possibilities of wealth."[33] As for Willison, "there is only one secret to success in life, that is hard work. And after all, human progress comes through in private initiative and genius for organization and production."[34]

In thought and deed, then, big-city newspaper publishers, including those with journalistic backgrounds, were now integrated into the Canadian economic and political élite. The dominant figure in the newspaper world was now the entrepreneurial publisher rather than Grant's nineteenth century editor-politician, and his activities were those of other businessmen.

9 Interest Politics

The growing presence of businessmen in newspaper boardrooms led to overall changes in the press's function. Publishers used the newspapers more and more to represent their personal interests, which often involved a complex web of related commercial and political ventures.

The press changed as the Canadian economy developed and expanded between 1864 and 1914 thanks to an informal but effective partnership between businessmen and politicians. The spheres of government, politics, and business were not separate: as the last chapter showed, there were wide areas of overlap, and it was "altogether natural that businessmen and politicians should have many connections."[1] Business was intertwined to an extraordinary degree with government at both the federal and provincial levels, and this was key to the development of newspapers at the time.

The federal, provincial, and municipal governments played leading roles in stimulating economic growth, and throughout the period under study businessmen turned towards governments for concessions, arrangements, jobs, and contracts – for patronage: The rhetoric of free enterprise notwithstanding, "business could not get along without the active cooperation of the state."[2] That is why so many businessmen entered politics, actively defending and lobbying for their interests in Parliament. Rodolphe Forget, a Conservative MP after 1904 and a president or director of twenty-nine companies, is a good example. Forget and other businessmen were all connected with economic concerns that were highly dependent on government regulation or support. "Political participation gained for these men protection and advantage in their private affairs."[3]

Because businessmen constituted the dominant class in Canadian society, they assumed that the state should be organized to meet their needs. But different levels of economic activity meant that different business groups (i.e., local manufacturers, resource extractors, or developers as opposed to national financial and transportation groups) had conflicting needs.[4] Most often these needs could only be satisfied by government action, and that meant businessmen had to persuade other politicians to their cause.

Businessmen were entering the newspaper business at the end of the nineteenth century not only to make money but also to use what was then the sole vehicle of mass communication to influence the public and garner support for their various financial interests, which desired support from any one of the three levels of government. It should not be forgotten that some businessmen were politicians in their own right, while many others were leading figures in their party, playing a financial and advisory role in party councils. Syndicates of investors undertaking financial promotion, especially of concerns involving public business, often comprised businessmen with substantial political interests. Two such syndicates were the Liberal business group led by Robert Jaffray and George Cox that took over the Toronto *Globe* in 1882 and the Conservative syndicate of Senator Sanford, Sir Frank Smith, and other Conservative businessmen who took over the Toronto *Empire* in 1894 to "put the paper on a paying basis."[5]

The first significant penetration by outside business into the newspaper world came from the railways. The symbiosis between railway and newspaper can to a large degree be explained by the interrelationship of public policy, public opinion, and the public purse. Because of their dependence on and competition for public subsidies, charters, and grants, the railways understandably sought to control and direct public opinion and deflect criticism, which in practice sometimes meant buying newspapers outright (usually in secret through intermediaries), or, if that was not possible, offering cash subsidies and other rewards for favourable coverage from their editors or publishers.

The central place of the railways in the economic expansion of Canada is well known. Railway construction spurred further economic activity.[6] The Southams' decision to buy the Edmonton *Journal* was influenced by railway expansion; as J.H. Woods advised: "I believe in the future of the city, and that now is the time to buy, as business values will rise as soon as the Grand Trunk Railway gets busy in that neighbourhood."[7]

From the beginning governments and the railway companies were inextricably linked, especially since retarded Canadian development and weak, uncertain private investment forced constant government bond guarantees and subsidies to back the new ventures. Indeed, long before the railway era public funds played a central role in the development of Canada's transportation system.[8] Politicians had always used newspapers for their political ends since partisan politics began, and as Canada industrialized her first modern industry did likewise, buying and using newspapers to further its political and financial aims.

During Canada's railway era, it was common knowledge that the railways either owned, controlled, or strongly influenced many newspapers. The Montreal *Gazette* consistently supported railway schemes in the 1860s and 1870s, but its support had a price. In 1870 Hugh Allan was one of the owners of the paper, along with the Whites. In return for their support for his railway promotions, Allan bankrolled the Whites' subsequent takeover of the paper. A prototype of the politically involved entrepreneur, Allan subsidized and bought newspapers to further those promotional schemes that required public assistance. According to Allan, "means must be used to influence the public and I employed several young French Canadian lawyers to write it up for their own newspapers."[9]

In 1853 Sir Allan MacNab stated: "Railways are my politics."[10] Half a century later in 1908, Calgary *Herald* publisher J.H. Woods said: "The policy of the *Herald* in Alberta politics [is] RAILWAYS irrespective of political parties or anything else."[11] Before World War I the centrality of railways to politics cannot be doubted, nor can the importance of railways to newspapers and vice versa. As Southam president P.S. Fisher pointed out in 1950, "In the days of railroad construction ... every different railway was interested in a paper."[12]

The CPR was notorious for its attempts to control the content of newspapers. It tried to silence its most persistent critic, the Liberal Montreal *Herald*, by taking control of it through frontmen in the early 1880s. For the same reason, it attempted to take over the Toronto *Globe* in 1882. By the late nineteenth century, the CPR was the corporate behemoth astride Canada; indeed, in its extensive economic and political range it almost rivalled the power of the federal government. Consequently, it vigorously protected its widespread interests. Although originally linked to John A. Macdonald and the Conservative party, the CPR hedged its bets with the accession to power of Wilfrid Laurier and the Liberal party in 1896. Already in 1895, CPR president William Van Horne sensed the coming national political change and actively sought to build bridges to Laurier. He cultivated J.D. Edgar and L.H. Davies, both leading Liberal politicians who were close to the future prime minister, and John Willison, a Laurier confidante and editor of the Toronto *Globe*, the leading national Liberal organ.

The purchase and subsequent sale of the Manitoba *Free Press* by Van Horne and Donald Smith, a major CPR backer, to Laurier's western lieutenant, Clifford Sifton, exemplifies the symbiotic relationship between railway promoters, politicians, and journalists. Despite repeated efforts to start or buy a party paper in Winnipeg after 1878, the Conservatives had failed to set up a successful rival to W.F. Luxton's independent Liberal *Free Press,* which had become the city's largest daily. In 1885 the paper's expansion required increased capital, which Luxton was forced to raise through incorporation as a joint stock venture with an authorized capital stock of $100,000. At the same time, John A. Macdonald talked the CPR's Van Horne into buying the floundering *Call* for $33,500. In turn, to reduce competition, Luxton purchased the *Call* in 1889 through the simple expedient of increasing his stock authorization to $133,500 and converting Van Horne's *Call* ownership into 335 shares of *Free Press* stock. In 1890 Luxton borrowed a further $40,000 – probably from Smith – to buy out his last Winnipeg rival, the *Sun.*

Initially, the CPR connection was beneficial to the *Free Press* because it gained exclusive access in Winnipeg to all the North American telegraphic news services through the CPR wire.[13] For their part, Van Horne and Smith were hoping that their link with the paper would help to deflect criticism of the CPR, please its political partners, and influence decisions on branch lines in Manitoba. In 1893, however, once Smith and Van Horne had gained effective control of the *Free Press,* they replaced the journalistically independent Luxton with their own man, Molyneaux St John, who worked for the railway's publicity department. A bitter Luxton explained why he was sacked in an article for the recently established independent Liberal *Tribune*.[14]

Nothing short of the Free Press being an instrument to aid directly and indirectly CPR schemes, meritorious or the reverse, and approve of CPR policy, good, bad and indifferent, would satisfy the directors, and simply because I would not accede to such a line of conduct for the *Free Press,* I am where I am today ... and my place will obviously be filled by passive persons necessarily responsive to every behest of the Canadian Pacific Railway. My successor, Mr M. St John, comes directly from CPR general offices in Montreal. He is simply being transferred from one CPR department to what is to be another.

The CPR, with its high-handed and exploitative ways, was already extremely unpopular with westerners and broadsides such as this did not help. Faced with a newly established rival, the *Tribune,* and hampered by its CPR connection and change of political allegiance from Liberal to Conservative, the *Free Press* began to lose public favour and money. Tired of the financial drain (the *Free Press* also needed to renew its aged press and plant) and desirous of pleasing a rising politician, Van Horne and Smith sold the *Free Press* in great secrecy to the then Manitoba attorney general Clifford Sifton in 1898. Sifton was already known to these men, since he had successfully moderated a dispute between the CPR and the Manitoba government when Manitoba premier Thomas Greenway had threatened to break with the railway unless the *Free Press* toned down its criticism. That Sifton was also a central figure in the ongoing Crow's Nest Pass Railway negotiations would not have hurt his bid either.[15]

Sifton bought the paper in part because the *Tribune* and its owner, the independent Liberal MP R.L. Richardson, were becoming increasingly unreliable (of Richardson it was said that he would denounce a railroad in a populist editorial then cheerfully accept a free railway pass or other gift and not see the contradiction).[16] Sifton also wanted his own paper through which to build a western political base. Railway politics hastened the break between the two men and prevented them from working together to build the *Tribune* into the Liberal party's principal western organ. Thus, in 1897 the *Tribune* supported Premier Greenway, who, seeking to break the CPR's monopoly, came out in favour of the Mackenzie-Mann proposal to link the CPR to the Duluth-Minnesota railway, a move that Sifton and the CPR opposed. Meanwhile, Mackenzie and Mann, no doubt eager to confound the CPR and to put their view across to the public, helped bankroll W. Sanford Evans, an ex-*Empire* editor, to take over the Winnipeg *Telegram* in 1900.

The CPR forged another link with the Liberal party in 1895 through a joint *Globe*/CPR news publicity arrangement. *Globe* editor J.S. Willison had travelled to the West that year and written a series of stories on the booming economic opportunities of the region. He trumpeted the huge potential for economic growth, the limitless agricultural possibilities, and the need for more immigration. Unusual for the time, the articles were richly illustrated with photographs. Viewing an advance copy, Van Horne informed Willison that the stories "were the best that had ever been seen on our Northwest." He offered to buy 100,000 copies of the paper (and possibly more) if Willison agreed to sign his own name to the article instead of using the Special Correspondent byline as originally planned. The reason for this was that "the value would be enormously increased, if it would appear definitely from the Editor-in-Chief of the *Globe*. As for special correspondent it would be open to suspicion of having been written for advertising purposes."[17] The series became a bestseller with the railway and federal government alike as the former eventually ordered 250,000 copies and the Interior department another 100,000.

The Willison connection became personal in 1896 when Van Horne, eager to make new Ottawa connections, invited him, along with Laurier's friends, J.D. Edgar and L.H. Davies, to travel with him on his luxurious private railcar. During that year Van Horne often wined and dined them and offered frequent trips to the West while assuring them of the CPR's political neutrality. As Willison himself recalled, "I had many evidences of his regard and goodwill."[18] It was probably no coincidence that the *Globe* launched a series of articles promoting the Crow's Nest Pass Railway on the very day Laurier was sworn in as prime minister and followed it up with a joint CPR/*Globe* campaign supporting the project.

The Crow's Nest promotion, however, was not solely the result of Van Horne's opulent hospitality. It was engineered in part by two major shareholders of the *Globe* – Robert Jaffray, the financier with a controlling interest in the paper, and George Cox, the leading Canadian insurance-banking mogul – both leading Liberal backers who later became senators. Jaffray and Cox instructed Willison to support the railway in editorials and in other coverage. In August 1896 the *Globe* sent its special correspondent, T.C. Irving, out west. He extolled the virtues of the region, reporting, among other things, that BC had room for a million miners.[19] Unknown to J.S. Willison, however, Jaffray and Cox were pursuing their own agenda in having these articles published: they were interested financially in a coal mining company that would be served by the proposed railway. This created quite a scandal when it became public, and to the end of his days Willison bitterly resented having been duped.

It is noteworthy that Jaffray wanted the CPR to pay its share of T.C. Irving's western expenses: "Although I agree with you that we should not be under too much obligation to the CPR still I said to Sir Wm [Van Horne] that we undertook it as a business enterprise and while it was in the interest of the paper it was also beneficial to them and I thought there should be a fair division of the expense, he quite agreed with the view."[20] Here is another example of the rising bias towards commercial information in news columns.

It was not the last time that the *Globe* was utilized to support the railway projects of its owners. On 3 August 1903, the paper declared that the Grand Trunk Pacific's proposal for a transatlantic route would "commend itself" to Canadians because it "symbolizes as well as promotes a realized nationality."[21] The proposal showed the extent to which economic necessity cut across party differences, and how newspapers were manipulated by interest groups. George Cox, for example, president of the Canadian Bank of Commerce, a minority owner of both the Toronto *Star* and the *Globe*, and a prominent Liberal, was also on the Grand Trunk Pacific board of directors and a prime mover of the project. Joseph Flavelle, a prominent capitalist and Conservative and owner of the Toronto *News*, was a fellow board member. The *News* was an enthusiastic supporter of the Grand Trunk Pacific proposal.

Perhaps the most blatant example of the nexus between railways, politicians, and newspapers was a murky 1904 plot that involved bringing Mackenzie and Mann's Great Northern Railway to Montreal, defeating the Laurier government by buying important Liberal or independent newspapers, initiating a smear campaign against Liberal cabinet ministers, buying off Liberal candidates in Quebec, and inducing an important Liberal politician to turn against Laurier. The purpose of the plot was to secure control of the government by using the newly purchased newspapers to initiate a campaign publicizing government scandals in order to force the government to nationalize bankrupt railways and secure fat contracts for government railway construction. Although the plot quickly derailed, part of it was realized with the one-million-dollar purchase of *La Presse* by J.N. Greenshields, who was backed by Mackenzie, Mann, and the Montreal *Star*'s Hugh Graham, and with the purchase of two important New Brunswick Liberal organs, the Saint John *Telegram* and *Evening Times*, by David Russell, a Montreal and Maritimes financial promoter.[22] (The threat from *La Presse* was immediately neutralized by Laurier, who secured a promise from Mackenzie and Mann that the paper was "not to be a Tory organ.")[23]

In 1909 a similar "conspiracy" was instigated by B.F. Pearson, owner of six Maritime newspapers and reputedly "the mainspring of the movement in the interests of Mackenzie and Mann."[24] The scheme also involved the takeover and offloading of a railway, this time the Inter-Colonial. Such machinations show that any major national scheme involving politics and the railways of necessity included newspapers as well.

From the foregoing it might be thought that the railways victimized the newspapers by manipulating or forcing them to do their bidding. In fact, the newspapers were often willing to give their support – for a price. In 1906, for example, the Ottawa *Citizen* published an editorial written by the CPR and entitled "New Railroad Policy," which opposed US railway magnate J.J. Hill's application for a branch line in the Northwest Territory. Such a line would drain the district trade through Hill's US main line. When the editorial was first brought in by veteran newspaper hack Ned Ferrar, the *Citizen* did not run it. Ferrar returned with the message that the then CPR president Charles Drinkwater himself requested that it be run as an editorial. Still the Southam brothers held back, claiming they had not studied the question adequately. This prompted a telephone call from Drinkwater in Montreal. The Southams offered to have it appear as a letter. Drinkwater reluctantly agreed but then changed his mind and asked them again to publish it as an editorial. As it turned out, the Southams were hesitating to run the editorial, not because they had not studied the question – indeed, they thought the article was a "very fine one" – but because they wanted something substantial in return. The CPR, they felt, had "not been treating THE MAIL JOB PRINTING COMPANY as nicely as they should have, and, secondly, we did not like the way the request was made, and thought it would do them good to be somewhat indifferent to their wishes."[25]

The matter was important enough for the CPR president to come to Ottawa and meet Wilson Southam at his club. Wilson told him that the Southams were always "pleased to accommodate the CPR as long as they showed any appreciation of it," but for the last few years, the Mail Job Printing Company had had nothing but "hard knocks" from the railway, which looked as if it no longer needed the Southams' friendship. Wilson then invoked the longstanding relationship between the two concerns and the support it had entailed: "Many years ago when the CPR was not the prosperous concern that it was at present, the Hamilton SPECTATOR stood by it through thick and thin, and, that by an arrangement we had with Mr Bunting of the MAIL, whose tenants we were, we often got the MAIL to take the same line on CPR questions that we did. I told him that we were very glad to do it, and, that the CPR showed their appreciation of our assistance by helping the job department along."[26] This relationship, Wilson complained, had now been broken by some new official who seemed inclined to cultivate people who "had done them no service in the past, and who could not do them anything like the same service the CITIZEN could do in the future":

The CITIZEN alone could do him ten times more good than the Montreal HERALD and Montreal GAZETTE together as far as reaching the members of Parliament with educational articles were concerned. He said GEORGE HAM had told him of our complaints, and, that he was going to look into them. I said I was sure that if he gave it his personal attention then we would have nothing to complain of in the future, and, if we had nothing to complain of, he would find that we would be very willing to, not only run articles that he might furnish us with, but get up articles of our own on lines which he might suggest.²⁷

Clearly, railways loomed large in the newspaper business, and other papers depended on their lucrative job printing contracts. Two-thirds of the Southam company's income in 1908 came from the Montreal and Toronto job printing plants, forty percent of whose work came from the railway business. Fred Southam watched like a hawk for any slurs against the railways in the Southam papers. When critical stories appeared in the *Spectator* and the Calgary *Herald* in 1908, he warned his brother Bill of the possible consequences, reminding him that the railway connection was far more important than the political one.²⁸ On the whole, the Southam papers handled railway issues with care; J.H. Woods pointed out to Fred Southam, "in all railway matters the *Herald* treats the CPR very liberally at all times" and it "boosts" the railway's "projects in our reading columns constantly."²⁹

Yet there was a limit to the kowtowing. The newspapers also had a public to think of, and given their self-appointed role as public guardian and spokesman, this occasionally meant criticizing the railways. Railways were the "most vital subject," Woods noted, and it was "practically impossible" for a paper not to discuss them. Since Southam Inc. did business with all three major railways and all three proposed branch lines, total abstention from criticism meant that "we might as well not publish newspapers at all."³⁰

The railways were influential in part because they were large advertisers. In the 1890s, the Grand Trunk exercised its advertising clout to ensure that advertising contracts could be legally voided if the papers "unfairly or unjustly criticized" the railway. The *CPP* urged publishers to unite against this attack on their editorial prerogatives.³¹

Adding to the railways' influence were the railway-owned telegraph companies, which controlled news agency franchises. Thus, after the CPR bought the *Free Press* in 1889, it financed the absorption of the rival *Sun* in part to deny its vital AP franchise to competitors. This was an effective move, as Duncan McIntyre of the newly established *Tribune* admitted, since the *Free Press* now had "exclusive use of the telegraph news collected by all [three] existing world news gathering associations, a connection with at least one of which is essential to the publication of a newspaper worthy of the name." His own paper found itself "out in the cold" and was driven to pirating outside dispatches from the *Free Press*, which answered by publishing a free evening bulletin.³²

In 1894 the CPR bought the exclusive AP franchise for $6,000 and used it thereafter to keep the western papers in line in a territory where it enjoyed a monopoly. The company maintained that it had charged a low flat rate "in the early days to build up papers in the new towns and cities, that settlers and others might have telegraphic news etc."[33] But the railway was losing about $40,000 a year on the service, and its losses must have become too much to bear when, in 1907, CP Telegraph told the three Winnipeg papers that they would receive their news service in a new form over a new route and at a new price, all to the papers' disadvantage. Formerly, the news came direct from Montreal in the form of an abbreviated AP report and a Canadian news summary. Now the service abandoned the composite report, and the AP report was sent from St Paul, Minnesota; the papers had to bring Canadian news from the East at their own expense. For this, they were charged double the old price of three hundred dollars, which was already high when compared to the fifteen dollars the Toronto *Globe* paid for the same service.

The three papers agreed to resist these changes together, declaring that the CPR was acting "in a manner prejudicial to newspaper responsibility to the public and that the principal of corporate control of news services is repugnant to the freedom of the press."[34] The papers cancelled their AP service and set up the cooperative news service that eventually became the Western Associated Press, discussed earlier. The CPR responded ruthlessly. For the same AP service it charged the Victoria *Colonist* $225 for use of its wires while demanding a prohibitive $1,800 from the Winnipeg-based WAP. WAP papers had to pay much higher press rates for their news dispatches to other western papers than the western papers that were still in the CPR franchise. And the WAP papers that operated within CP Tel's domain paid a heavy price. The Calgary *Herald*, for example, paid $166 a month for two thousand words a day, anything beyond that being charged at the full retail rate. The Edmonton *Journal*, on the other hand, was charged $170 a month for five thousand to seven thousand words a day over the CNR Telegraph line (a rate that the CPR had offered to match). Similarly, the WAP paper in Saskatoon was charged the higher word rate of $507 while its competitor, which subscribed to CP Tel's service, was charged a flat rate of $200.

Naturally, the WAP dailies screamed long and loud over discriminatory rates, and in December 1909 they induced the Railway Commission to hear their case. WAP charged that the telegraphs were a common carrier and had no right to discriminate between the different services carried over their lines; nor was it in the public interest for a railway corporation to engage in the news-distribution business. CPR countered that the telegraph service was a "chattel" and thus had a right to set discriminatory rates. It compared its exclusive provision of news and transmission to hauling coal from its own mine, claiming that it could charge whatever price it wanted for the haulage. Seizing on this point, the commissioners noted that "if this were permissible, railway companies owning coal mines could close up every mine except their own," and "in like manner telegraph companies could put out of business every news-gathering agency that dared to enter the field of competition with them."[35] The Railway Commission declared for WAP and ordered CPR to end discriminatory rate prices. Shortly after, CPR abandoned its AP franchise. But the details of this struggle show just how large a stick the railways had been wielding through their control of the telegraphic news services.

The railways also kept newspapers in line by providing free passes or substantially reduced fares to journalists. They offered the Canadian Press Association free passenger cars and special excursions – one of them to British Columbia and back – for its annual outing. In 1899 a proposed hike in rail fares for the press (from half a cent a mile to two cents) brought a howl of protest from the CPA, which reminded the railways that "they get an enormous amount of free advertising in return for low set rates for newspapermen."[36] In 1916 the railways were still subsidizing newspaper travel with a two-cent-a-mile charge on production of a press card.

The railways always made sure that they had important newspapers on their side. The largest Canadian corporation in Canada's financial capital had an informal alliance with the Montreal *Star* (in conjunction with the Bank of Montreal) and also directly controlled the Montreal *Gazette*, as Lord Beaverbrook discovered when he tried to buy the *Gazette* in 1911 only to be turned down by the railway, which had a veto over any proposed purchase.[37] Indeed, for E.F. Slack, the *Gazette*'s managing editor, criticizing the railway was equivalent to "firing on the Guards."[38]

While all three transcontinental railways had established strategic links with various newspapers, these links were maintained in secrecy wherever possible. As Van Horne had done with the Winnipeg *Free Press*, rumours of ownership by the railway were denied.

Other men with substantial financial and political interests also secretly owned or controlled newspapers, among them the rising number of businessmen who bought newspapers from the 1890s on. Like the railways, these entrepreneurs often used the newspapers to promote their various financial schemes and other outside interests. In 1895 the public was aware that well-known newsman E.E. Sheppard had taken control of the Toronto *Star*. What the public didn't know was that the bulk of the takeover money came from William Mackenzie, who then turned over his controlling share to Frederic Nicholls, utility baron and president of Canadian General Electric, to promote private utilities and Sunday streetcars. In 1903 the Ottawa *Free Press* was sold to newsman Alfred Wood, in reality the frontman for utility magnate Warren Y. Soper, a partner in the city's hydroelectric and street railway monopoly.

But so-called "secret" ownership or hidden control of newspapers made the public nervous, especially in an era of giant new corporations, monopolies (especially in street railways and public utilities), and amalgamation. Mackenzie King's anti-combines legislation was a response to public demands for curbs on corporate power. J.S. Willison spoke for many when he warned in 1901 that the "growing power of corporations and the influence of great aggregations of capital in few hands is most onerous and dangerous."[39]

Understandably, then, the public was suspicious of undue corporate influence on newspapers and the threat it posed to freedom of the press.[40] J.W. Flavelle's 1903 takeover of the Toronto *News* caused a public sensation as some observers alleged that the new venture would bear the taint of Flavelle's connection with various large corporations. Furthermore, they contended it was a "well-known fact that some daily papers are not altogether free from corporate influence."[41] Pointing to a leading Canadian newspaper proprietor who was offered a directorship in the Grand Trunk Pacific Railway, they judged that "as this gentleman has never been connected in any way with railways the inference is obvious."[42] The problem was serious enough for publishers at the 1905 CPA annual convention to worry about corporate influence and its effect on newspapers specifically and on political life in general.[43]

The October 1912 *Grain Grower's Guide* articulated rising public concern about corporate influence and control of the nation's press. It said that "nearly every paper in Canada is owned by a capitalist or politician and the news and views of that paper must measure up to the owner's selfish schemes." A great deal of capital was now required to publish a daily newspaper, which placed it out of the reach of ordinary journalists. Consequently, "the ownership of newspapers in Canada has become a side line with politicians and capitalists, and it is to suit the views of these people that the wells of truth have become defiled. The freedom of the press is gone completely. To-day the politician who aspires for power first secures control of a newspaper; public corporations, endeavouring to throttle the public do the same. Of course they keep the ownership of these papers in the background."[44] The *Guide* described the press as a "public utility" now unfortunately under the control of capital. It believed that "freedom of the press" would be restored if journalists were given back control of the newspapers. Such a change would lead to a popular revolution involving the abolition of special privileges. Clearly, the notion that newspapers had a public service function had persisted.

In 1907 the CPP commented on the high number of secretly owned papers in Canada and recommended that the public be told who the real owners were.[45] Again in 1914 the journal argued that the public had a "moral right to know the names of those who are directing their opinions in order that they may be in a position to judge the value of the advice given."[46] It revealed that the ownership of more than half of the Toronto *Star*'s stock capitalization of $200,000 was secretly held in trust, and that a big chunk of the total was owned by the T. Eaton Company and the estate of George Cox, which in turn was connected to bank, railway, trust, and insurance investments. In the case of the Toronto *News*, $135,000 out of a total capitalization of $500,000 was held in trust by "manufacturing and financial interests who do not wish to disclose their identity."[47] The CPP did not disclose the identity of these interests, but the stock in trust effectively represented control by federal minister of Mines and Railways Francis Cochrane and other Conservative businessmen. (*News* editor-in-chief J.S. Willison, who held the stock in trust, was outraged by these revelations, especially given his past warnings about corporate influence, and complained to CPP publisher J.B. Maclean that the article represented a bitter personal attack.)[48]

Disclosing newspaper ownership became a public issue. In 1917, MP J.A. Currie proposed amending the existing statutes so that all newspapers had to make public the names of those who controlled their stock or directed their policy. The public should be informed, he said, as to "the men and interests who control the public press. Then the bona fides of their policies will be better estimated."[49] The Progressive party also called for full disclosure of newspaper ownership. Nothing came of the amendment, and in the following year MP Rudolphe Lemieux moved a bill to force publication of the press's owners, editors, and stockholders.

The public was right in demanding to know who owned the papers since the outside interests of their owners occasionally dictated newspaper policy. This was the case with the Toronto *Globe*'s support of the Crow's Nest Pass and Grand Trunk Pacific railway schemes, and Interior minister Clifford Sifton had a political agenda of his own when he bought the Manitoba *Free Press* in 1898. Over the next few years, as he built up a large network of western Liberal party organs, the *Free Press* became the central dispensary of government propaganda, patronage, and outright cash subsidies. Sifton was so successful in keeping his ownership of the *Free Press* secret that only four men knew of it, and it wasn't until 1908 that a rumour surfaced that he might indeed be the owner. His first editor, A.J. Magurn, was kept in the dark and ironically complained to Sifton to intervene on his behalf with Sifton's frontman, John Mather, whom he thought was the owner.[50] Whenever Sifton wanted his paper to mount an attack on Ottawa, he supplied the necessary information but had his letters burned once the contents had been noted. It was necessary for Sifton to be secretive since, as he acknowledged, he was regarded as "too much for bonuses for railways and stood in with capitalists."[51]

The secrecy of newspaper owners was understandable given that so many of their outside interests had a political dimension. Papers were sometimes bought to influence public opinion on a specific issue, such as railway policy, and then sold once the need was over. But the railways did not really want or know how to manage papers, and their ownership, once suspected, could be a liability in itself since the public tended to shun papers controlled by the railways. It was financial loss that caused the CPR to sell the Montreal *Herald* and the Manitoba *Free Press* in 1884 and 1898: failing newspapers, as the Toronto *News* showed, could be an impressive money drain.

Once again the Toronto *Globe* serves as a particularly good example of how intimate the connection between newspapers and "vested interests" could be. In September 1905 the Toronto *World* under W.F. Maclean published an extraordinary exposé charging that Robert Jaffray and George Cox had used the *Globe* to further their big-business deals, and that the *Globe* had supported every one of Cox's schemes. Jaffray, in his role as Niagara Parks commissioner, made an "improvident and improper contract" when he gave a third franchise doubling the amount of Niagara River water it could use to the Electrical Development Co., of which Cox was a director (along with William Mackenzie, Henry Pellatt, Frederic Nicholls, and James Ross). Further, according to the *World*, although the Ontario government under James Whitney opposed the deal, a *Globe* editorial (12 May 1905) urged prompt action on final approval of the contract. The article also said that Cox was using trust money held by Canada Life (of which he was president) to support investments in other companies, and that the State of Michigan was investigating these possibly illegal activities. It was alleged the *Globe*, the *Star* (in which Cox was a major shareholder), and the *News* (through Cox's extensive business connections with publisher Joseph Flavelle) went out of their way to endorse everything in connection with Canada Life.[52] That Maclean's charges had hit the mark became apparent several years later, when *Globe* newsman M.O. Hammond was instructed by Jaffray to use "caution" in dealing with the Niagara power question and to interview Henry Pellatt, a backer of the scheme, for his side on the issue.[53]

It is unlikely that the public would have been shocked by the *World*'s revelations. Most papers, at one time or another, had been perceived as acting for a special interest, and quite often the suspicion was true. In the Ontario public power struggle, Premier Whitney thought the *News* was protecting "the pocket of Mr Flavelle."[54] The Ottawa *Citizen* was characterized as a "reliable advocate of the lumber and mineral industry of the Ottawa Valley"[55] – a fairly accurate description given that its owners had invested heavily in mining ventures (in partnership with the *Journal*'s P.D. Ross). Its sister paper, the Hamilton *Spectator*, was urged to follow the *Citizen*'s lead on the subject of mining concessions because the Southam brothers were in the midst of negotiations for mining concessions on Crown lands.[56] The Montreal *Gazette* was rumoured to be the mouthpiece of CPR-Bank of Montreal interests.[57] J.S. Willison of the *News* wrote to Toronto *Globe* editor Stewart Lyon, "You know as well as I do that the real estate element practically governs Toronto through the *Telegram*."[58] Melville Rossie, editor of the London *Advertiser*, admitted to feeling "the restraints of the big corporations through their influence on his boss T.H. Purdom."[59]

For special interests the stakes were large, especially in Canada's rapidly growing cities during the boom years under Laurier. A whole infrastructure of urban services – water, public transportation, and power – had to be built and run. It was efficient to operate most of these franchises as monopolies, and whoever possessed them stood to make large profits. That is why Ottawa Valley lumbermen, faced with the depletion of their resource, formed a syndicate that invested heavily in Ottawa's utilities during the late 1890s. Similarly, a group of Montreal venture capitalists wrested control of the street railway companies for its profits. And controlling or influencing newspapers was fundamental to the numerous late nineteenth and early twentieth century battles to win urban transportation and utility franchises.

It was absolutely necessary for the competing interests to win newspaper support because of the press's effectiveness in civic elections. One study of municipal reform noted that, since party lines were weaker at the municipal level than at the federal or provincial levels, voters were more influenced by local partisan institutions, notably the newspapers. Although the success rate of candidates endorsed by newspapers has not been studied, fragmentary evidence suggests that it was significant. For example, seven of eight candidates endorsed by the Calgary *Herald* were elected in the 1913 civic election.[60]

The press was influential locally in part because of its self-proclaimed role as city standard bearer and herald. Newspaper publishers tended to boost the growth and progress of their communities. They linked civic success with urban growth and the expansion of urban services, from power lines to tramways. Needless to say, their pro-growth propaganda and political sponsorship were often motivated by self-interest. In 1911, for example, developer J.J. McKittrick began to promote a hundred-acre suburban plot called Westlake in Hamilton. Westlake lacked urban services and McKittrick lacked the resources to develop them, so he linked up with local partners, among them the Southams, who acquired a major interest. In 1916, a "McKittrick man" ran for mayor with the strong backing of the Southam-controlled *Spectator*.[61] And it was no coincidence that W.F. Maclean, whose Toronto *World* was one of the loudest proponents of tramway expansion, owned a large amount of land in the Don Valley, whose development would be facilitated by the extra lines.

Newspapers served quite blatantly as fronts for "vested interests" during the 1896 Toronto controversy over Sunday streetcars. The issue had engrossed Toronto municipal politics throughout the 1890s. The Toronto *World* – which had been forbidden to publish its *Sunday World* on the Sabbath and so published as near to Saturday midnight as it could – took the lead in calling for Sunday public transportation in opposition to a coalition of clergymen and others. Predictably, the Toronto Railway Company, owned by railway promoter William Mackenzie and Montreal financier James Ross, actively supported the *World*'s campaign in the hope of winning extra business. Through veteran journalist E.E. Sheppard and Frederic Nicholls, Mackenzie and Ross purchased the Toronto *Star* to back the *World* in the fiercely contested 1896 plebiscite on the issue. One Sunday the *Star* sent its entire staff out to count the bicycling crowds in the country to prove that the masses were yearning for some way to get about on the Sabbath.[62] The streetcar company spent liberally to buy ads in the recalcitrant papers in the hope of turning them around. The *Globe*, which was neutral, eventually printed a pro-Sunday letter written by a company publicist and in all likelihood charged advertising rates for it.

The supportive papers were directly paid off; W.F. Maclean kept the *World* sound with a bank note cosigned by Sheppard, who also received $3,700 for services rendered at the *Star* and *Saturday Night*, which he also edited.[63] Sheppard had once written that a newspaper that "lends itself to a company or corporation and gives up its editorial space as freely as its advertising columns to a man who can give a cheque, is a much greater sinner than the man who merely sells his vote"[64] – an ironic contrast between public rhetoric and private morality. Incidentally, the *Star* campaign was quite revealing of its corporate ownership as it repeatedly argued that if Sunday cars were rejected, it would show that the city was not "safe for investment."[65]

Bribery, or, to put it more politely, economic patronage, also played a role in influencing other papers' policies. In 1907 an Ottawa syndicate headed by T. Lindsay, who also owned Ottawa's largest department store, tried to sell water power to the city. Although there were suspicious aspects to the deal, Lindsay's aldermanic minions attempted to rush the proposal through City Council, "relying on Mr Lindsay's large advertising contracts with the papers to keep the papers quiet."[66] Lindsay's advertising clout had an effect; the *Free Press* wholeheartedly supported the proposal while the *Citizen* rejected a request from Southam headquarters that it support public hydro for Ottawa because "we think the time inopportune to make such a suggestion, considering that our heaviest advertiser is endeavouring to sell his water power to the city."[67]

Bribery could take other forms too. Mindful of the strong public preference for public utility ownership, many private utilities kept the papers in line with loans and preferential rates on gas and electricity. In the early 1900s public cries for nationalization, fed by the *World* in the case of the telephone system, had resulted in a public inquiry led by Postmaster General William Mulock. During this period, a cautious telephone company refrained from charging the Ottawa *Citizen* for service.

The newspapers' heavy involvement in the Sunday streetcars campaign foreshadowed their role in the great issue of the early twentieth century – public ownership, or what Nelles and Armstrong term "civic populism."[68] Publishers were prominent on both sides of the question. Private syndicates that owned urban utilities and transportation often either controlled a newspaper or had a publisher as an ally in order to present their view. The public ownership side owed some of its success to the extensive press campaign that helped fuel the growing belief in public ownership as an anti-monopoly strategy. Inevitably, self-interest motivated both camps; even the proponents of public ownership had an agenda. Many of these businessmen-reformers ran Canada's young manufacturing plants and did not wish to pay exorbitant sums to the millionaires' syndicates that controlled the utilities. The campaign was a major one: by 1903, thirty-seven cities and towns in Ontario had taken control of their electric light plants, while seventy-eight others had assumed control of their waterworks.

Adam Beck, the man who led the public power fight and who was instrumental in creating the world's first publicly owned power company, Ontario Hydro, was successful in part because of his mastery of public relations. He won over the working newsmen of Ontario with a well-timed press conference in Toronto – one of the first such conferences in the province's journalistic history. Next, he organized a highly publicized demonstration in front of the Ontario legislature during which fifteen hundred irate taxpayers demanded public ownership of hydro.

The ensuing fight between rival groups of capitalists supporting public or private power intimately involved the newspapers and often turned traditional local politics upside down. Hydro politics, for example, divided Hamilton and caused the city's papers to abandon their usual party affiliation. Hamilton power was provided by the Cataract company, which was controlled by J.M. Gibson, the veteran Liberal capitalist who also owned the *Times*. The independent Liberal *Herald*, usually an ally of the *Times*, sided with Beck and Hydro, while the *Spectator*, long a *Times* rival, now supported the paper because owner William Southam was a director of Cataract. In fact, Hamilton Tories, who were angry at William Southam (a stalwart Conservative himself) for using the *Spectator* to "knife" Conservatives who fought the Cataract company, threatened to start a competing pro-Hydro Conservative daily. For some time, the terms "hydroelectric men" and "Cataract men" divided the politics of Hamilton more effectively than the traditional party labels. Indeed, the Liberal *Herald* promoted a Conservative mayoral candidate because of his support for Hydro.[69] Such politics occurred elsewhere; the strongly pro-Liberal Toronto *Star* consistently supported the provincial Conservatives until 1919 on the basis of their pro-Hydro stand.

Newspapers spearheaded public ownership fights in other cities, again representing the different warring capitalist factions. In London, for example, Adam Beck made his mark as a prosperous cigar manufacturer and also as mayor. Early on he allied himself with the *Free Press*, which championed his hydro fight. In 1914, with the establishment of Ontario Hydro under control of the Railway Commission, Beck moved to nationalize several street railway companies including the one in London which was controlled by the Purdom family. The battle that ensued on the issue was fought on the pages of the *Free Press*, which had Beck's backing, and the Purdom-owned *Advertiser*.[70]

In Ottawa, a syndicate that organized a utilities monopoly became the target of public opposition because of its poor service and high profits. Both sides were represented by newspapers. The side that wanted a public monopoly was represented by *Journal* publisher P.D. Ross. On the other side, syndicate member Warren Soper secretly bought the *Free Press* while another, T. Lindsay, exerted influence on the *Citizen*.[71]

That newspapers were indispensable components of these financial political alliances was evident in the rivalry between the Toronto *Telegram* and *Star*. Behind public and private proposals for the development of Toronto were different groups of capitalists and politicians, and the newspapers served as their advocates. John Ross Robertson of the *Telegram* vehemently opposed Sir William Mackenzie, who, with Donald Mann and Henry Pellatt, controlled Toronto's railway and street-lighting systems. The *Telegram*, in league with Adam Beck, finally broke Mackenzie's control when Toronto Hydro and Ontario Hydro were formed. In 1910 the *Telegram* proposed a downtown subway in the hope of damaging Mackenzie's streetcar monopoly. This was attacked by the *Star* and T.C. Hocken, who suggested an alternate subway plan and ran unsuccessfully for mayor against G.R. Geary, the *Telegram* candidate. Hocken was elected mayor in 1913 and quickly became embroiled in a struggle against Beck and Hydro. Hocken and the *Star* also opposed Beck's plan to cover Ontario with a network of electric railways known as radials. Although Beck proposed the idea in 1912, years of political obstruction in which Mackenzie's fine hand could be seen finally killed the idea in 1921. The *Telegram* attributed this to propaganda circulated by, among others, the *Star*.[72]

The Toronto tramway battles were repeated in other cities. In Montreal the fight began in 1911 when E.A. Robert, a Montreal financier and Quebec MNA, and industrialist J.W. McConnell took over the Montreal Tramways Company, which operated in metropolitan Montreal under thirty different contracts signed with fourteen different municipal corporations. Over the objections of the Montreal City Council, the provincial government passed legislation granting the company a forty-two-year lease for the entire region, provided it reached agreement with all the municipalities. An added incentive for the interested parties was to possess the undistributed tramway profits.[73]

In addition to civic reformers, who wished to have a public franchise and to use the profits to reduce route congestion, another syndicate led by rubber king D. Lorne McGibbon campaigned for the franchise as well. In early 1913 the Tramways ownership question was coming to a head. In quick succession, the *Witness* and the *Herald* changed ownership. The former, a critic of the current Tramways group, was secretly purchased by the *Star*'s Hugh Graham, partially on behalf of the Tramways group, whose aims he supported. It is also possible that Graham, who was involved in developing suburban Mount Royal, might have benefitted from tramway extensions. Following closely on the *Witness*'s sale was McGibbon's purchase of the Montreal *Herald*, which pursued a highly critical campaign against the Tramways group. This stopped in 1914 when Graham secretly bought the *Herald*. Eventually, the Robert-McConnell group won.[74]

Robert and McGibbon slugged it out again in Halifax between 1912 and 1914, once more over tramways and power. During this latest bout in what the *Monetary Times* dubbed "the war of the Montreal financiers," they employed the services of local newspaper publishers who were enmeshed in their affairs. Roberts led an alliance that included such Liberal luminaries as Sir Frederick Borden and B.F. Pearson, the Halifax *Chronicle* proprietor, against the *Herald*'s W.R. Dennis and McGibbon, who had bought one million dollar's worth of property in partnership with the publisher. Dennis did not hide his connection with McGibbon, whose virtues and concern for the "future of Halifax" were praised in the *Herald*. Nor did the *Herald* stint in its campaign on behalf of public ownership of the tramways as proposed in a bill introduced in City Council by Alderman Dennis; the bill was eventually adopted. Needless to say, Pearson's *Chronicle* did not hesitate to charge that the promoters of public ownership were hoping that the city-controlled utility would extend the street railway through land controlled by the Dennis-McGibbon syndicate.[75]

The increasing use of newspapers to present the views of various corporations, interests, and civic factions to the public showed how far the newspaper had shifted from its purely political role of the past. Where once they had represented political parties, newspapers increasingly spoke for businessmen and promoters in order to influence the governments that handed out subsidies, contracts, and franchises. In so doing, the press showed how completely it had become integrated into Canada's business world.

Conclusion

The years from 1890 to 1920 represent a transition period during which Canadian publishers turned their newspapers into a vital industry within the developing Canadian capitalist system. During the latter half of the nineteenth century, the press was perceived as a commercial venture; but unlike other businesses, it was also seen as having a social purpose. The public perception of the press as a social institution grew out of the political involvement of publishers (who were as much politicians as businessmen during that period), the consequent use of newspapers as propaganda adjuncts to the political parties, and the moralizing and educational messages of the editorial pages. Political patronage and subsidies helped shield newspapers from the full reality of the marketplace.

By the 1890s, however, newspapers had to face the full reality of a competitive market. The industrial transformation of the press into an industry resembling other developing Canadian industries accelerated significantly, especially after the onset of the industrial boom under Laurier. As business opportunities picked up in the rapidly expanding Canadian cities, entrepreneurs saw their chance and started newspapers. The rising number of papers and the increased capital costs of more expensive and complex printing presses, photo-engraving equipment, and the linotype intensified competition in the industry. Sharper competition forced publishers to adopt the latest business methods, such as "scientific management" and double-entry accounting, and to act like entrepreneurs, concentrating more on profit than political effect. In the process they redefined their relationship with the political parties: once cogs in the political machinery and subject to party discipline, they were becoming forces in their own right in the twentieth century, capable of acting against party and politician alike.

Conclusion

The new, popular "penny press," whose prototypes included the Montreal *Star* and Toronto *Telegram*, first appeared in the 1870s and 1880s, took off in the 1890s, and became the norm in the twentieth century. Publishers were now intent on providing entertainment in their papers at the expense of political content and purpose; they declared their papers to be "independent" rather than "party organs."

Underlying these changes was the development of advertising. It became the engine that drove the newspaper, providing the bulk of newspaper revenues, which grew from fifty percent to sixty-five percent in the late nineteenth century to seventy to eighty percent in the twentieth. In the push to meet the advertisers' needs, circulation growth displaced editorial appeal as the measure of a newspaper's success.

The pressure to increase circulation to attract advertisers transformed the content and appearance of newspapers. Publishers had to widen the scope of their papers to expand their audiences. To reach a greater portion of the growing urban audience, publishers made papers easier to read and added more human-interest features, such as women's pages, entertainment reviews, children's pages, sports, and so on. The press was increasingly forced to adopt advertising methods to promote and sell itself. The graphic appearance of the paper became important, and eye-catching devices such as blaring cross-column headlines, shorter paragraphs, illustrations and photographs, and more white space (introduced during the Boer War) became commonplace in the twentieth century, replacing the dense, type-heavy look of the nineteenth-century press. Content also changed with the introduction of descriptive headlines, subtitles, shorter sentences, and the replacement of the story model with the punchline at the end by the inverted pyramid style of article giving the most important news first.

Publishers adopted other advertising methods to promote and advertise their papers. They drew attention to their paper by sponsoring civic crusades, stunts, and charities, thus creating news events. They advertised their wares by promoting features in their pages and printing circulation statistics (showing their superiority) and also by advertising their papers on hustings and the sides of public transportation vehicles.

Dependence on advertising revenues caused publishers to turn news into a commodity designed to attract readers, who in turn were sold on advertisers' products, thus completing the commercialization of the press and turning it into an industry like any other. The new forms of technology adopted in the late nineteenth century meant that larger urban audiences could be reached faster than ever before. With the introduction of powerful rotary-web presses fed with rolls of woodpulp paper and typesetting by speedy linotypes, the average paper could be produced in the tens of thousands in a few hours. Papers grew dramatically in size from the typical four-page editions of the nineteenth century to the larger editions of eight and twelve pages or more that became common in the twentieth century. The impact of technology on newspaper production and the expansion of features and news coverage designed to attract ever-larger urban audiences necessitated an increase in staff. After 1900 it was common for the big-city dailies to employ over a hundred people.

Like other industries that had evolved from small-scale capitalist enterprises to large-scale corporate entities, newspapers underwent an administrative revolution in the twentieth century. Their growing size and complexity compelled owners to delegate daily operating responsibility to hired managers. Where the nineteenth-century owner had been part journalist and businessman, the twentieth-century owner oversaw and set policy but hired others to undertake the journalistic and commercial functions of his paper. The result was the administrative division of the newspaper into editorial and commercial offices.

As the commercial aspect grew, so did the power of the business manager, who played an increasingly important role in the twentieth-century paper. At the same time the political purpose of the newspaper waned. Its consignment to the now-secondary editorial pages signalled the diminishing importance of political patronage and subsidies.

In short, newspapers had become capital-intensive big businesses. Owning and, more importantly, maintaining a newspaper – especially given the saturated market conditions that were common to most cities in the early twentieth century – was largely confined to those with access to significant amounts of capital. The mounting cost of newspaper operations precluded the successful founding of newspapers by those working in the ranks – once a common practice. Instead, established papers tended to be purchased by monied outsiders. The price of these dailies rose dramatically in the twentieth century from tens of thousands of dollars in the smaller cities to hundreds of thousands in the major ones, thanks to the increased size and complexity of the newspapers as well as the rising real estate values of newspaper buildings and land. Hence, by the twentieth century successful publishers were financial entrepreneurs who built up their newspaper properties and became rich and powerful, or those, often representing syndicates, who bought into the press. Both kinds, however, needed capital to maintain and expand their press in order to meet intensifying competition in the marketplace. And money was available; for as men like Hugh Graham, John Ross Robertson, and William Southam proved, successful newspapers could be great generators of wealth.

Yet there was a political dimension to investing in newspapers. From the beginning, the development of the Canadian economy required the sponsorship of government, and this meant getting the ear of politicians by means of public opinion. This was not new. Newspapers represented the sole effective means of reaching the public and influencing government. The interests of promoters had been represented by papers since Confederation. Hugh Allan, for example, had taken control of the Montreal *Gazette* and other French journals to promote his railway schemes. The railways in general, as befitted the largest and most dynamic industrial aggregation in the country, were not slow to bend newspapers to their own ends. Other burgeoning industries did the same. Promoters who required government assistance or favours, most notably in the resource sector, or who wished to secure franchises in the developing public-sector enterprises (utilities, transportation, water, and construction), either bought into newspapers or secured publishers as allies in their promotional schemes.

The difference was that newspaper owners became significant players on the national scene. The Jaffray-Cox takeover of the Toronto *Globe* in 1882 was an important harbinger of the trend in the 1890s and early 1900s. P.D. Ross, Joseph Atkinson, Walter Nichol, and other newsmen who became wealthy and powerful in their own right did so because they had access to political connections, which meant connections were important because they linked to government financial resources. The successful newspaper entrepreneurs – the Southams, Sifton, Buchanan, Atkinson, Dennis, and Robertson – were all political as well as entrepreneurial. Newspaper ownership could lead to power, influence, and wealth.

The ethos of business pervaded and transformed the newspaper world through businessmen who bought into the press or newsmen who, upon becoming publishers, were forced by financial circumstances to behave like businessmen. The more industrialized publishing became, the more businesslike the publishers. Together they formed local, regional, and national associations to curb "ruinous" competition. The formation of the nationwide publishers' cooperative, the CPA (later CDNA) and the CP served to regulate the industry and reduce competition through pricefixing and other methods of collusion.

Like other industries in the twentieth century, the largest dailies came to dominate the field at the competition's expense. Their predatory and collusionary tactics in an increasingly saturated market, coupled with advertiser preference for the largest-circulation dailies, eventually shrank the overall number of titles. The straitened economic circumstances of World War I accelerated this trend as papers became bankrupt or merged with rivals. By war's end, the number of papers had dropped by approximately twenty-seven percent and many cities were reduced to monopolistic or oligarchical markets. Locales served by two or even one newspaper became increasingly commonplace as the downward trend continued.

Concentration increased first locally and then nationally. The success of the Southam Press, Canada's first newspaper chain, showed the way of the future in the early twentieth century. Its well-bankrolled penetration of an increasing number of Canadian cities – Ottawa, Calgary, Edmonton, Winnipeg, and Vancouver – from its Hamilton base introduced a national competitor to the local scene. Taking advantage of pooled resources, economies of scale, and superior access to the latest administrative and managerial strategies, the Southams proved to be formidable rivals – so formidable that by the 1920s other newspaper organizations were forced to meet the challenge by creating chains of their own. This "chain reaction" eventually resulted in an extreme concentration of press ownership that was at odds, as the Davey and Kent inquiries subsequently warned, with the public's right to information.

The growth in size and financial worth of the biggest dailies, which matched the explosive expansion of Canadian cities, enhanced the wealth, prestige, and power of the largest publishers, who became part of the financial and social élite of the country. Independent of the political parties by virtue of their financial prowess, they were able to influence the parties without being responsible to them.

Between 1890 and 1920, publishers weakened the overall political content and purpose of the newspaper in favour of entertainment, while at the same time concentrating political influence in themselves as they systematically took complete control of their newspapers. The papers became personal expressions of their enhanced status and power in society. Gradually, the publishers disengaged from direct political involvement and joined forces instead with their peers in the business world. They participated in the élitist civic reformism and non-partisan movements of businessmen in the late nineteenth and early twentieth centuries. Their attempts to place certain issues above politics (the naval question and Canadian involvement in the war, the formation of the Union government, and the introduction of conscription) further underlined their admission into Canada's ruling élite.

Despite these dramatic changes in the newspaper world, the public, conditioned by journalists and other social ideologues, retained its erstwhile view of the newspaper as a vehicle of free expression and a defender against oppression and wrongdoing: in short, as an institution with a public obligation. It was this unresolved social contradiction between public expectation and private purpose (the publisher's pursuit of profit) that led to the public inquiries of the last twenty years.

The shift from political advocate to interest advocate that occurred between 1890 and 1920 was indicative of a press that was functioning less and less as a public watchdog. The concept of press "freedom" was always based more on rhetoric than reality. Indeed, to paraphrase A.J. Liebling, freedom of the press was reserved for those who owned one.

Today, the privilege is reserved for the very rich. In 1992 Canada's last independent daily, the Kingston *Whig-Standard*, was bought by the Southam chain despite the public outcry against further concentration of media ownership. The process of consolidation begun in the early twentieth century has continued unabated, except that the predatory units are larger and more diverse conglomerates. The newspaper and other news media companies comprise smaller and smaller portions of these vast multinational corporations.

Now, such publishing giants as the Southam Corporation have been taken over by larger corporative predators, bringing to mind the cartoon in which each individual fish in a chain is threatened by the open mouth of a bigger fish behind. Communication concerns have gone global. But an important question remains: in all this global rationalization, where does the individual, whose voice needs to be represented and heard in society, fit in?

Notes

ABBREVIATIONS

CPP   *The Canadian Printer and Publisher*, vols. 1–26
HD   Hammond Diary (M.O. Hammond Papers, Archives of Ontario)
NA   National Archives of Canada
PAM   Public Archives of Manitoba
QUA   Queen's University Archives
SA   Southam Inc. Archives
SP   Clifford Sifton Papers; NA, MG 27 IID15
WP   J.S. Willison Papers, NA, MG 30 D29

INTRODUCTION

1 Royal Commission on Newspapers, *Report*, 1, 14. In 1946 American publishers established the Hutchins Commission to investigate the state of the American press. It condemned the concentration of press ownership in the hands of a few representatives of "big business" and criticized the "exaggerated drives for power and profit" as leading towards monopoly and a "common bias" of the large investors and employers. For a discussion of the significance of the commission see Altschull, *Agents of Power*, 179–83. For a brief summary of the three British commissions held in 1947–49, 1961–62, and 1975, see Boyce, "The Fourth Estate," 39–40.
2 Senate Special Committee on the Mass Media, *Report*, 1:3; Davey, *The Uncertain Mirror*, 3; Royal Commission on Newspapers, *The Newspaper as Business*, 4.
3 Dafoe, "Early Winnipeg Newspapers," 17.
4 Quoted in De Bonville, *La presse québécoise*, 139.

5 Waite, *Life and Times of Confederation*, 6.
6 Rutherford, *A Victorian Authority*, 49. Circulation figures for the nation's other leading papers were as follows: Montreal *Witness*, 10,500; Toronto *Mail*, 7,500; Montreal *Star*, 5,600.
7 *McKim's Newspaper Directory, 1899*, 176.
8 McGregor, "Adventures of Vancouver Newspapers," 89.
9 "Cheaper Newspapers," 11–12.
10 Ibid.
11 For Raymond Williams ("The Press and Popular Culture," 47), this mechanization meant that "leadership in the press from this period was inherently associated with access to ever-rising amounts of capital."
12 In his classic study *Press*, 78–9, Harold Innis noted that the low prices of newspapers covered only a small percentage of the costs of their production, so the publishers changed their newspapers' content to attract the largest number of purchasers. As a consequence, the business office assumed a dominant position and "news became a commodity, and was sold in competition like any other commodity."
13 The trend towards high capitalization, fewer newspapers, and collusion followed the general tendencies in the Canadian economy as described by Warskett, "The Information Economy," 184–5. The emerging newspaper industry began to experience "the tremendous concentration of capital ... the high capital-labour ratio, changing products and production techniques, durability of leading firms in industry, [and the] absence of price competition."
14 Lee, *Origins of the Daily Newspaper*, 168.
15 Rutherford, *Making of the Canadian Media*, 52.
16 Bliss, *Northern Enterprise*, 362.
17 Schudson, *Discovering the News*, 63.
18 Curran and Seaton, *Power without Responsibility*, 19.
19 Boyce, "The Fourth Estate," 79. Developments of British newspaper publishing mirrored the changes experienced by the industry in Canada; see also Lee.
20 Douglas McCalla has suggested that the rise of entrepreneurship is crucial to the understanding of Canadian economic development and change during this period, ("Introduction," 53).
21 For a description of the new kind of entrepreneur, see Bliss, *Living Profit*; Weaver, "Elitism and the Corporate Ideal"; Artibise, *Winnipeg*.
22 Porter, *Vertical Mosaic*, 483.
23 McNaught, *Canada Gets the News*, 20.
24 See Villard, *The Disappearing Daily*.
25 Baldasty's *Commercialization of the News*. His extensive bibliography reveals that these aspects of newspaper history have attracted little scholarly attention. He cites Lee's *The Daily Newspaper in America*, published

in 1937, as still the best study of newspaper industry concentration, saturation, and collusion in the United States. In the 1930s Lee explained how newspapers, once simply adjuncts to printing plants, political parties, and powerful individuals, were moving in the direction of concentration, chain ownership, and "management structures resembling more and more those of other large manufacturing establishments," although he only devoted one short chapter (7) to this topic. And the Emerys' widely used recent textbook *The Press and America* confines its discussion of press concentration and related issues to a mere one page (206).
26 McNaught, *Canada Gets the News*, 16–17.
27 Typical examples of this genre are Bilkey, *Persons, Papers and Things*; Charlesworth, *Candid Chronicles*; and Cranston, *Ink on My Fingers*.
28 Kesterton, *History of Journalism in Canada*; Harkness, *Atkinson;* and Poulton, *The Paper Tyrant*.
29 See for example, Rhodes, "*The Star*"; Spalding, "The Toronto Daily Star"; and Clippingdale, "Willison."
30 This situation has been somewhat rectified of late with the pioneering work of Paul Rutherford, Thomas Walkom's study of the industrialization of the Toronto and Ottawa press from 1871 to 1911 and Jean de Bonville's detailed description of the Quebec popular press from 1884 to 1914.

CHAPTER ONE

1 Bone et al., *History of Canadian Journalism*, 4.
2 Ibid., 83.
3 Ibid., 92.
4 C.P. Scott, "On Journalism," in *C.P. Scott 1846–1832*, 161.
5 Mackay, "Journalism," 4.
6 Colquhoun, "Canadian Universities and the Press," 23.
7 "The Canadian Publishers' Association Annual Meeting," 27.
8 "Does Capital Threaten Liberty of the Press," Toronto *Star*, 26 August 1905.
9 House of Commons, *Debates*, 13 May 1898, 5543, 5550. A similar view was expressed by the Vancouver *Province*'s W.C. Nichols, who wrote in the daily's first issue (26 March 1898) that "whatever its merit and demerits be, there is this to be said for the paper, and that it is first and last a business enterprise."
10 Black, "Canadian Journalism," 434–5.
11 The essays in *Journalism and the University* had been submitted to a prize essay competition sponsored by Queen's University on the question "How can Canadian universities best benefit the profession of

Journalism, as a means of moulding and elevating public opinion?"
12 QUA, Joseph Flavelle Papers, case 1, J.W. Flavelle to J.S. Willison, 8 April 1903.
13 "The News and Its Promoters," 5.
14 Willison, "A Lecture on Journalism," 4.
15 HD, 25 October 1904.
16 *CPP* (September 1910): 27.
17 Smith, *The Journal Men*, 60–1.
18 Archives of Ontario, C.H.J. Snider Papers, 1934.
19 *CPP* (July 1896): 2.
20 Quoted in Oxley, "What the University Can Do for the Journalist," 90–1.
21 Bone et al., *History of Canadian Journalism*, 293.
22 Chippingdale, "Willison," 408.
23 Dafoe, "The Press Blamed for National Paralysis," 39.
24 "The Largest in Canada," Toronto *Star*, 26 August 1905, 2.
25 NA, MG 30, D45, J.W. Dafoe Papers, reel M-74, George Iles to Dafoe, 22 December 1924.
26 F.A. Acland, "Beacon of Light," Toronto *Globe*, 5 March 1919.
27 "The Relation of the Press to National Life," 42.
28 "Is the Editorial Page Necessary?" 32.
29 Donnelly, *Dafoe*, 50.
30 Lyon, "Shall the Editor or the Business Manager Reign?" 17–18. According to de Bonville (*La presse québécoise*, 232), a similar diminution of political content had occurred in Montreal's *La Presse*, which began as a political organ under William Blumhart in 1884 but later developed as a sensationalist operation under Treffle Berthiaume. De Bonville found that while editorials and political commentary and news about politics fell from 14.0 and 37.4 percent respectively in 1885 to 3.4 and 28.5 percent in 1914, sports and leisure content rose 5.1 percent in 1885 to 15.4 percent in 1914.
31 *CPP* (March 1893): 7.
32 Schudson, *Discovering the News*, 95.
33 Altschull, *Agents of Power*, 66.
34 The following newspapers were examined: Manitoba *Free Press*; Montreal *Star*; Ottawa *Journal*; Regina *Leader*; Toronto *Empire*, *Globe*, *Mail*, *News*, *Star*, *Telegraph*, and *World*; and Vancouver *Province*.
35 As in other areas of Canadian life, Americans had an enormous influence on Canadian journalism. Large numbers of Canadian journalists went to the United States to work for newspapers and in many cases later returned to Canada, bringing back American techniques. Others attended American industry meetings. P.D. Ross, for instance, was a CPA delegate to the Eighth Annual Convention of the National

Editorial Association (see *CPP* [May 1892]: 11). Canadian publishers belonged to the American Newspaper Publishers' Association and attended its conventions (see for example "Annual Meeting of the American Newspaper Publishers' Association," 29). At CPA conventions members delivered talks on the latest American methods; J.S. Brierley, for example, read tips on how to make newspapers more profitable from *Newspaperdom*. The *CPP* often reprinted articles from the American trade journals; see for instance *CPP* (July 1897): 10, and ibid. (October 1898): 6.

36 Miller, *A Century of Western Ontario*, 244.
37 *CPP* (December 1902): 6.
38 Dafoe, "Where the Best News Should Be," 10.
39 Latta, "A Clean Front Page," 23.
40 HD, 9 October 1907.
41 *CPP* (July 1894): 7. The editor of the Collingwood *Bulletin* asserted that "yellow journalism in this country is practically an unknown quantity" (ibid. [April 1909]: 2). Agnes Laut, in an address on "The Newspaper of the Present Day" delivered to the literature section of the Women's Congress in Toronto in 1909, also claimed that yellow journalism did not exist in Canada (HD, 29 June 1909). See also *CPP* (2 May 1909): 2. The term "yellow journalism" originated during the circulation battle between Hearst's New York *Journal* and Pulitzer's New York *World* in the late 1890s. Both men published wildly exaggerated and even fabricated stories to increase readership and indulged in other forms of sensationalism. See Schudson, *Discovering the News*, chapter 3.
42 Cameron, "University Chairs in Journalism," 214.
43 See Spalding, "The Toronto Daily Star," 15. The *Star*, for instance, devoted a week to detailed coverage of New York's lurid Thaw murder trial in 1906. The newspaper justified its often sensationalistic coverage by claiming the case was "illustrative of the morbid mentality of a prominent section of American society" (26 June 1906).
44 March, *Red Line*, 68. An 1899 study of American newspaper content found an almost steady increase in the amount of space devoted to illustrations, stories about crime and vice, and medicinal and "help wanted" advertisements at the expense of political news, editorials, letters to the editor, and political advertisements: Innis, *The Press*, 21–2.
45 *CPP* (November 1894): 20.
46 Ibid. (April 1906): 26.
47 See front page of Vancouver *Province*, 11 March 1900.
48 Just as the Spanish-American War encouraged sensationalist reporting by the New York *Journal* and New York *World*, the Boer War brought out the worst in the Canadian press. At the outbreak of the

war, the Toronto and Montreal English-language press played a major role in whipping up patriotic hysteria and support for imperial intervention and in forcing a reluctant Laurier government to send troops to South Africa (Stevens, "Laurier," 205–7; Page, "Impact of the Boer War," 43–4). The stories that appeared in the press were often inflammatory, exaggerated, and sometimes utterly false. The Toronto *Globe* (21 September 1899) resorted to rumour mongering in a headline that screamed "Poisoning Streams – Incredible Story That the Boers are Planning a Peculiarly Dastardly Campaign." The Hamilton *Spectator* (13 October 1899) reported that the Boers had dynamited a train, killing three hundred British women and children; this incident never happened (Page, "Canadian Response," 312). The Montreal *Star* (13 October 1899), which broke the train-dynamiting story on 13 October 1899, used the incident to denounce the Laurier government for not sending troops to South Africa. Heated accusations of French Canadian cowardice in the English press and counter-charges in the French press led to three days of rioting in Montreal.

49 CPP (July 1894): 7.
50 Miller, *A Century of Western Ontario*, 248. For discussion of the morality and economics of comic strips, see "Is the Coloured Comic Supplement a Desirable Feature for Canadian Newspapers?" 4. See also Poulton, *The Paper Tyrant*, 183.
51 NA, MG 30, D98, P.D. Ross Papers, vol. 1/1, undated editorial (c. 1910). Cranston (*Ink on My Fingers*, 77) observed that the "importance of the comic strip in attracting readership had assumed proportions that no publisher could ignore."
52 White, "Newspapers of the Past and Present," 10.
53 Darby, "The Comic Supplement," 20.
54 Cranston, *Ink on My Fingers*, 61.
55 "City Edition Net for News," Toronto *Star*, 26 August 1905, 11.
56 Hewitt, *Down the Stretch*, 37.
57 QUA, Flavelle Papers, case 1, Chas. B. Clarke to Flavelle, 21 June 1906.
58 Ibid., Flavelle to Chas. B. Clarke, 25 June 1906.

CHAPTER TWO

1 McNaught, *Canada Gets the News*, 18.
2 Walkom, "Daily Newspaper Industry," 26. He figured that by 1906 there were 2.6 newspapers per English family in Ottawa (p. 309). In Toronto the figure was 2.53 in 1898, 2.55 in 1902, and 2.21 in 1906 (p. 24).
3 de Bonville, *La presse québécoise*, 271.
4 Cranston, *Ink on My Fingers*, 47.

5 WP, vol. 5, J.S. Brierley to J.S. Willison, 17 December 1896.
6 "A Snare and a Delusion," 68.
7 Bladen, *Introduction to Political Economy*, 178.
8 Rutherford, *A Victorian Authority*, 81. A turn-of-the-century CPP symposium elicited numerous publisher comments on "heavier expenses" and increased machinery costs, CPP (April 1900): 1, 4.
9 CPP (September 1892): 20.
10 Ibid. (May 1893): 10.
11 Ross, *Retrospects of a Newspaper Person*, chapter 21.
12 De Bonville, *La presse québécoise*, 105.
13 The letters of W.H. Woods of the Calgary *Herald* to W.J. Southam are filled with pleas, especially during the early days of the *Herald*, for extra money to meet payments. The following is typical: "Principal creditors included in statement [of the *Herald*] – Toronto Type Foundry, payable Jan. $680, Apr. $526, July $533, Oct. $541 ... Balance yet to be arranged. $2,000 is overdue; Canadian Linotype, $150 is overdue and $150 due Jan. 16th, remainder payable $150 every 3 months, Stovel Co., $400 overdue, remainder $150 due Jan. 16th, remainder payable $150 every 3 months ... and Imperial Bank, notes at 2 and 3 months ... $1,500 (SA, vol. 105, J.H. Woods to Wilson Southam, 5 October 1908 and 3 April 1909).
14 Schudson, *Discovering the News*, 95; CPP (November 1894): 14.
15 The rising importance of illustrations was evident in the growth of the Montreal *Star*'s illustration department from one to five full-time artists in 1900. A CPP article entitled "Profile of R.C. Matthews" (June 1900: 12; July 1900: 1) observed that illustrated portfolios greatly helped to increase circulation during the South African war.
16 Harkness, *Atkinson*, 52.
17 Fry, "Half-tone Cuts for Newspapers," 4.
18 De Bonville, *La presse québécoise*, 113.
19 Walkom, "Daily Newspaper Industry," 248; CPP (February 1905): 15.
20 De Bonville, *La presse québécoise*, 113.
21 SA, reel 105, Herald Publishing Co. Ltd statement for month of July 1909.
22 Rutherford, *A Victorian Authority*, 89: De Bonville, *La presse québécoise*, 113.
23 Ewan, "War Correspondence," 10.
24 WP, vol. 18, C.F. Hamilton to J.S. Willison, 11 November 1899.
25 CPP (September 1900): 8.
26 The war prompted the *Globe* to print spectacular headlines every day. The drama of Canada's first overseas military adventure carried the newspaper's editors away in a rush of enthusiasm, and the public responded by buying the *Globe* to learn what was happening to the men at the front. At the beginning of the war in October 1899 the

newspaper's average circulation was 36,975, but it hit highs of 63,600 and 71,200 during scoops and spectacular news (Clippingdale, "Willison," 319). Other newspapers enjoyed similar gains. The Toronto *Mail and Empire* soared from an average of 23,167 copies to 41,181 because of the war (*Mail and Empire*, 26 January 1898 and 2 January 1900).

27 QUA, Joseph Flavelle Papers, case 1, Clarkson and Cross Chartered Accountants to Flavelle, 23 December 1902.
28 "City Edition Net for News," Toronto *Star*, 26 August 1905.
29 Archives of Ontario, C.H.J. Snider Papers, Toronto *Telegram* Employment Lists, 18 May 1891; 1 November 1901; 13 April 1908.
30 SA, reel 116, List of Special Features, 12 July 1907; List of Special and Saturday Features, October 1912.
31 SA, reel 116, W.M. Southam to F.N. Southam, 22 December 1915.
32 Cranston, *Ink on My Fingers*, 76.
33 Rutherford, *A Victorian Authority*, 53; Poulton, *The Paper Tyrant*, 74.
34 SA, reel 105, W.H. Woods to W.J. Southam, 17 October 1911.
35 *CPP* (April 1904): 8; ibid. (November 1914): 46; ibid. (September 1919): 28.
36 Kealey, "Work Control," 75–101.
37 QUA, Flavelle Papers, case 51, Report of the News Publishing Company, 20 January 1908. Vancouver *Province* publisher Walter Nichol cited the growing costs of labour, especially the salaries of the machinists running the Mergenthaler linotype machines, as the reason why the "majority of papers barely keep their heads above water" "The Newspaper Business," (Vancouver *Province*, 18 November 1898, 4).
38 SP, vol. 165, E.H. Macklin to Sifton, 10 May 1904.
39 "A Snare and a Delusion," 67.
40 Avern Pardoe, "Salutations from the Old Boys," Toronto *Globe*, 2 July 1904, 5.
41 Walkom, "Daily Newspaper Industry," 89.
42 See NA, MG 30, D98, P.D. Ross Papers, vol. 2/2, P.S. Ross to P.D. Ross, 22 February 1892; SA, reel 128, W.J. Southam Memorandum, "The Hamilton Spectator Story," 17 September 1952, 4; and Spalding, "The Toronto Daily Star," 5.
43 Walkom, "Daily Newspaper Industry," 308.
44 Spalding, "The Toronto Daily Star," 5; Harkness, *Atkinson*, 63.
45 *CPP* (February 1902): 9.
46 "Does Capital Threaten the Liberty of the Press?" Toronto *Star*, 26 August 1905.
47 QUA, Flavelle Papers, case 1, Flavelle to J.S. Willison, 3 December 1902.
48 Bliss, *A Canadian Millionaire*, 183.
49 QUA, Flavelle Papers, case 1, Flavelle to J.S. Willison, 1 December

1902. Initial inquiries by Flavelle showed that the *Mail and Empire*'s price was $1 million, but he thought it could be had for $500,000. The latter price was regarded as too high by half, according to C.A. Gregg (WP, vol. 17, C.A. Gregg to Willison, 18 December 1902). Walkom ("Daily Newspaper Industry," 106) notes that Flavelle was rumoured to have offered $350,000 for the Toronto *World*; Flavelle estimated that the real value of the newspaper was about $50,000, the balance being "good will." Nevertheless, the point remains that profitable big-city dailies were expensive big-business propositions at the beginning of the twentieth century.

50 HD, 1 April 1913.
51 "Origins of the Star," Toronto *Star*, 26 August 1905.
52 De Bonville, *La presse québécoise*, 18.
53 Poulton, *The Paper Tyrant*, 176.
54 SA, reel 107, J.H. Woods to William Southam, 22 December 1909; CPP (September 1909): 36 and (March 1909): 36.
55 Bruce, *News and the Southams*, 181; SA, reel 133, W.S. Southam to W.J. Southam, 7 April 1914.
56 SA, reel 133, 15 May 1912, J.H. Woods to W.M. Southam.
57 CPP (April 1895): 8.
58 Colquhoun, "The Man Who Made the Montreal Star," 7.
59 Poulton, *Paper Tyrant*, 118.
60 CPP (October 1895): 1; ibid. (March 1897): 4.
61 Pense, "Character and Position," 912.
62 SP, vol. 145, E.H. Macklin to Sifton, 16 November 1903.
63 Smith, *The Journal Men*, 90.
64 SA, reel 133, "The Citizen Building," 21 February 1906; Harkness, *Atkinson*, 62.
65 CPP (January 1909): 39.
66 Ibid. (March 1912): 90.
67 Ibid. (February 1913): 38; ibid. (April 1913): 48.
68 SA, reel 133, "The Citizen Building," 21 December 1906.
69 Bruce, *News and the Southams*, 152.
70 SA, reel 105, W.J. Watson to W.J. Southam, 11 June 1914.
71 Bruce, *News and the Southams*, 66.
72 Walkom, "Daily Newspaper Industry," 61.
73 "The Newspaper Business," The Vancouver *Province*, 18 November 1898, 4.
74 For example, Southam Ltd was adversely affected by the poor business climate and tighter credit that prevailed during the period leading up to 1914 and during the early part of World War I (Bruce, *News and the Southams*, 33). M.O. Hammond commented that the Toronto *Globe* was forced to make cutbacks because of the business depression

of 1913–14 (HD, 9 August 1914). Senator Robert Jaffray, the *Globe*'s owner, remarked in September 1914 that "if we were paying our way, it would not be so bad, but we are running behind" (ibid. 9 September 1914).
75 Walkom, "Daily Newspaper Industry," 328.
76 Hall, *Sifton*, 2: 146.
77 Walkom, "Daily Newspaper Industry," 61; Burton, *A Sense of Urgency*, 70. The losses suffered by Flavelle's *News* did not stop when the newspaper acquired new owners in 1917, a Tory consortium led by provincial and, later, federal cabinet minister Francis Cochrane. See, for instance, the reference to "heavy losses" in WP, vol. 9, Willison to Francis Cochrane, 11 May 1915.
78 Rogers, *Newspaper Building*, chapter 6.
79 NA, MG 29, C39, Dougall Family Papers, vol. 3, R.C. Smith to J.R. Dougall, 16 July 1909. By the 1890s the *Witness* had ceased to be profitable, a circumstance that was worsened by the *Herald*'s switch to afternoon publication and the Laurier government's massive patronage. Only J.R. Dougall's independent means kept the paper alive (ibid., vol. 3/2 [c. 1912] Unsigned [probably F.R. Dougall] to Wilfrid Laurier). The *Herald* chronically ran a loss, which is why publisher Brierley persistently proposed a "fusion" between the two papers (see ibid., J.S. Brierley to J.R. Dougall, 29 June 1897 and 15 July 1908.
80 de Bonville, *La presse québécois*, 125.
81 Miller, *A Century of Western Ontario*, 75.
82 Bruce, *News and the Southams*, 226.
83 March, *Red Line*, 79.
84 SA, reel 107, J.H. Woods to W.J. Southam, 12 May 1908.
85 The *Herald* made its first profit in 1910 and afterwards remained profitable (SA, reel 107, J.H. Woods to William Southam, 25 September 1910); The *Journal* started to becoming profitable in 1911 (ibid., J.H. Woods to W.J. Southam, 13 December 1911).
86 In 1911 the *News* lost $2,500, and in 1912 $10,000 (SA, reel 107, J.H. Woods to W.J. Southam, 30 December 1912). It was shut down in 1913.
87 NA, MG 26, G, Wilfrid Laurier Papers, vol. 250, J.S. Brierley to Wilfrid Laurier, 28 January 1908.
88 Ross, *Retrospects*, 34–7.
89 Smith, *The Journal Men*, 96.
90 March, *Red Line*, 96. The Hamilton *Post* went bankrupt in 1910 after six months because "the longer the paper lived, the tougher it was to get money. After the first six weeks, the Post had no bank credit," according to Cranston, *Ink on My Fingers*, 23–4.
91 Fischer, "'An Engine yet Moderate,'" 103.

92 Steele, *Prairie Editor*, 53.
93 SA, reel 105, J.H. Woods to W.J. Southam, 22 February 1908.
94 NA, MG 30, D 98, P.D. Ross Papers, Ross Diary, 28 October, 28 December 1891, 1 January 1893, 23 February 1894; 23 September 1895; Ross, *Retrospects*, 34–7.
95 HD, 1 April 1913.
96 NA, MG 30 D 98, Ross Papers, vol. 9/9, William Ross to P.D. Ross, 30 January 1904. .
97 McGregor, "Adventures of Vancouver Newspapers," 102.
98 Cranston, *Ink on My Fingers*, 52.
99 March, *Red Line*, 104.
100 SP, vol. 83, E.H. Macklin to John Mather, 27 December 1900.
101 "This plant is imperatively demanded if we are to publish the newspaper required by competitive conditions" PAM, W. Sanford Evans Papers, box 13/23, internal memorandum, n.d., probably 1903).
102 SA, reel 133, H.N. Southam to W.J. Southam, 30 December 1913.
103 The *Globe* passed out of the hands of the Brown family because it was starved for capital (Walkom, "Daily Newspaper Industry," 37).
104 CPP (February 1895): 7. See also chapter 8 of this book, which describes outside business involvement in the ownership of newspapers.
105 CPP (December 1899): 30 contained six mentions of outside groups of financiers taking over newspapers. A partial list of newspapers taken over by businessmen between 1890 and World War I includes, in addition to those just mentioned, the Montreal *Herald*, Kingston *News*, Sherbrooke *Pioneer*, Fort William *Journal*, Alberta *Tribune*, Halifax *Morning Chronicle* and *Evening Echo*, St John *Sun Times* and *Telegraph*, Prince Rupert *Optimist*, and Chatham *Banner*.

CHAPTER THREE

1 Rutherford, *Victorian Authority*, 28; *Canada Year Book*, 1911, 101–2.
2 Braverman, *Labor and Monopoly Capital*, chapter 4.
3 Bliss, *Northern Enterprise*, 354. For a discussion of Taylorism and scientific management in Canada see Heron, "Crisis of the Craftsman," 77–113; Palmer, "Class, Conception and Conflict," 31–49.
4 Bliss, *A Canadian Millionaire*, 119–20.
5 Chandler, *The Visible Hand*, 230–1.
6 Lowe, "Administrative Revolution in the Canadian Office," 122–3.
7 Cranston, *Ink on My Fingers*, 60.
8 Bone et al., *History of Canadian Journalism*, 116. According to the CPA's official history, many publishers were hurt financially because of "the competition begotten of many journals issued in a limited field." The growth of advertising agencies in Canada involved payment

of commissions on advertising. The lowering of subscription rates, in many cases below the profit point, added to the distress. These problems, moreover, were compounded by a "time of national commercial depression" (see p. 115).

9 CPP (December 1894): 2.
10 Bone et al., *History of Canadian Journalism*, 118. The 1900 CPA convention, for example, offered sessions on efficient typesetting, newspaper delivery systems, advertising rates, and advertising sales techniques: CPP (January 1900): 3.
11 CPP (July 1895): 2. For a while, CPP ran a regular business advice column entitled "The Business Department." A typical column, published in December 1898, advised publishers on how to keep orderly books.
12 Cranston, *Ink on My Fingers*, 60. Imrie's message was that "a cost system will conduce to greater efficiency by showing up the leaks in the various departments, for showing through a comparative record of the output and cost of each man and machine that are more suited for the work which they are expected to perform: and by compelling the proprietor to adequately equip his plant through showing him the increased cost of doing business with inadequate equipment." He also said that "the knowledge that a record of every hour for which they are paid is seen the following morning by the employer has a good moral effect on the employees. It leads to punctuality in commencing work, and to system and speed in performing it": CPP (July 1911): 56. See also ibid. (July 1910): 28–39 and (June 1911): 55.
13 Smith, "The Business Management of a Newspaper," 56.
14 Cranston, *Ink on My Fingers*, 23–4.
15 SA, reel 107, Report submitted by Allan Haynes Ltd on the reorganization of the Edmonton Journal, 16 September 1911, 2.
16 Ibid., 6.
17 Ibid., 7.
18 Bruce, *News and the Southams*, 138.
19 SA, reel 105, J.H. Woods to W.M. Southam, January 25, 1915.
20 Rutherford, *A Victorian Authority*, 51.
21 CPP (April 1897): 4. According to March, *Red Line*, 59, Dennis was forced to make these changes when the federal Conservatives withdrew their patronage following the Liberal election victory of 1896. Dennis's newspaper had made it apparent that the loss of political patronage had been a "blessing in disguise" because it had forced him to rely on his own talents and abilities to keep the *Herald* going.
22 Cranston, *Ink on My Fingers*, 52.
23 NA, MG 26, G, Wilfrid Laurier Papers, 29 November 1899, vol. 132, J.E. Atkinson to Wilfrid Laurier.
24 Cranston, *Ink on My Fingers*, 57. At the Ottawa *Citizen*, business

concerns gradually took up more and more of Harry and Wilson Southam's time, so much so that by 1910 they were barely able to write one editorial a month (Bruce, *News and the Southams*, 120).

25 Rogers, *Newspaper Building*, 305; Hewitt, *Down the Stretch*, 35.
26 Bliss, *A Canadian Millionaire*, 120; Cranston, *Ink on My Fingers*, 47; Harkness, *J.E. Atkinson*, 51.
27 Nelson, "The Tomb of the Profits," 29.
28 Rutherford, *A Victorian Authority*, 54.
29 Charlesworth, *Candid Chronicles*, 131–2.
30 Dafoe ("Review: Press, Politics and People," 60) wrote: "Nothing could more clearly reveal the relationship which existed between parties and party journals than the fact that the appointment of Willison as editor was submitted to the party leader for approval."
31 NA, MG 29, C34, Dougall Family Papers, vol. 2, J.R. Dougall to J.E.B. McCauley, 30 January 1896. .
32 NA, MG 30, D98, P.D. Ross Papers, vol. 2/2, 19 April 1903, P.D. Ross to P.S. Ross.
33 Dafoe, *Sifton*, xxiii. Dafoe claimed that Sifton practised a "self-denying ordinance" in which he committed himself to a "voluntary renouncement of power." For commentary on Sifton's active and forceful direction of the Manitoba *Free Press* see Hall, *Sifton*, 1: 248; 2: 23. Donnelly (*Dafoe*, 123) quotes Sifton telling Dafoe that "I positively will not allow the *Free Press* to lead such a movement [establishing a permanent income tax]." In a letter written to Dafoe in 1917 Sifton was very clear in asserting his authority: "I wish to have a very serious talk with you about the policy of the paper ... I think you therefore make arrangements to come down here so that we can get settled on the points I have in mind. It is quite impossible for me to say on paper what I wish to say, but as there is the possibility of the F.P. being put in a false position I want to make sure we understand each other.

"I think it would be just as well for you to come at once and then take two weeks holiday wherever you prefer to go. In fact, it would be well for both of you and the paper to have a sort of interregnum" (NA, MG 30, D45, J.W. Dafoe Papers, box 4/4, Clifford Sifton to Dafoe, 15 October 1917).
34 Rhodes, "The Star," vi. Rhodes also describes Atkinson as a "staunch individualist" who "brooked no interference with the policies of his paper" (chapter 3).
35 Poulton, *The Paper Tyrant*, 215.
36 Ibid.
37 CPP (February 1910): 57.
38 SP, vol. 65, A.J. Magurn to Sifton, 3 June, 5 June, 5 July, and 18 July 1899.

39 WP, vol. 37, Clifford Sifton to J.S. Willison, 21 February 1908. Macklin's tenure at the *Free Press* clearly demonstrated the benefits of hiring a capable and energetic business manager. In December 1901, when Macklin had been at the newspaper for seven months, the month's advertising revenues totalled $8,114 on a daily circulation of 14,000. In December 1902 it was $10,332 on a circulation of 16,500, and in December 1903 $15,000 on a circulation of 20,400. Thus, while circulation increased over the period by forty-one percent, advertising revenues jumped eighty-five percent. While improved economic conditions may have contributed to some extent to the rise in revenues, Macklin's innovative and modern business methods clearly helped: see SP, vol. 83, E.H. Macklin to Sifton, 16 July 1900; ibid., vol. 145, "Circulation Statement," January 1903; ibid., vol. 145, E.H. Macklin to Clifford Sifton, 14 December 1903.
40 CPP (April 1903): 4.
41 C.H.J. Snider Papers, Toronto *Telegram* employment lists, 18 May 1891, 1 November 1901, and 13 April 1908. By 1908 the *Telegram* had added an art department, which had two employees.
42 "Six Years of Progress in the *Star* Office," Toronto *Star*, 26 August 1905, 9.
43 NA, MG 30, D98. P.D. Ross Papers, vol. 1/1, Salaries Expenditures, 1884.
44 Ibid., 1899.
45 QUA, Joseph Flavelle Papers, case 1, Clarkson and Cross, Chartered Accountants, to Flavelle, 23 December 1902; Archives of Ontario, C.H.J. Snider Papers, Toronto *Telegram* Employment List, 13 April 1908; SA, reel 105, The Herald Publishing Company Limited, Revenue and Expenses for three months ending 30 April 1908; reel 105, The Herald Publishing Company Limited, Profit and Loss Account as at 30th June 1915.
46 NA, MG 30, D98, P.D. Ross Papers, vol. 1/1, Salaries Expenditures, 1884, 1889.
47 SA, reel 105, The Herald Publishing Company Limited, Profit and Loss Account as at December 1913.
48 Somerville, "Future of the Reporter," 17.
49 WP, vol. 19, C.F. Hamilton to Willison, 31 March 1911.
50 HD, 7 December 1908.
51 Ibid. 30 September 1908.
52 Ibid. 3 August 1910.
53 Ibid. 3 March, 13 March, 15 July, 22 October 1913.
54 CPP (December 1900): 9.
55 Ibid. (July 1902): 4.
56 McNaught, *Canada Gets the News*, 235.
57 HD, 13 August 1919; CPP (February 1919) 43.

58 "E.F. Slack's Views on Newspaper Publishing," 50. P.D. Ross insisted that his editor honour preferred positions. He also stipulated that no alcohol advertisements appear the same page as a temperance articles (NA, MG 30, D98, vol. 1/6, "Instructions for City Editor and Telegraph Editor for 1907").
59 SP, vol. 193, J.W. Dafoe to Sifton, 4 January 1910.
60 HD, 23 May 1907.
61 Bruce, *News and the Southams*, 24.
62 Breed, "Social Control in the Newsroom," 326–35, describes the overt and subtle ways in which publishers direct their newspapers' policies.
63 Flavelle Papers, case 1, Flavelle to J.S. Willison 25 November 1903, 6 February 1906.
64 Hall (*Sifton*, 2: 23) concludes that a man such as Sifton would not have stood for Dafoe's claim of Sifton's so-called "self-denying ordinance" had he and Dafoe not seen eye to eye on most major policy issues.
65 HD, 5 February 1908.
66 WP, vol. 8, Francis Cochrane to Willison, 3 December 1907.
67 This was especially true of Brenton A. Macnab. See NA, MG 26, H, R.L. Borden Papers, vol. 327, B.A. Macnab to Hugh Graham, 9 July 1907; B.A. Macnab to Borden, 18 September 1907.
68 CPP (September 1905): 17.
69 White, "Newspapers of the Past and Present," 9.

CHAPTER FOUR

1 Sandwell, "The Star," 11.
2 Quoted in Altschull, *Agents of Power*, 66.
3 *McKim's Newspaper Directory*, 1892, 243–4.
4 See the "ears," the space on either side of the masthead, on the following publishers' letterheads: WP, vol. 34, 30 September 1905, T.H. Preston to Willison ibid., vol. 5, 22 February 1896, J.S. Brierley to Willison; ibid., vol. 6, 27 February 1902, John Cameron to Willison.
5 CPP (December 1906): 22; ibid. (August 1907): 36.
6 Ibid. (May 1911): 54.
7 NA, MG 21, D106, E.N. Smith Papers, folder 1, "The Ottawa Newspaper Field," typewritten manuscript, 23 March 1923.
8 CPP (November 1906): 17.
9 WP, vol. 9, J.S. Willison to Francis Cochrane, 15 April 1915.
10 "Standardizing Circulation Records," 61.
11 SA, reel 116, W.J. Southam to William Southam, 6 March 1916.
12 "A.B.C. in Canada," 32.
13 "The Circulation Manager," 15; "Circulation Managers Gather in Montreal," 59.
14 "Canada Has Now a Circulation Managers' Association," 21.

15 Hall, *Sifton*, 1: 288.
16 Harkness, *Atkinson*, 57.
17 SA, reel 133, W.J. Southam to W.M. Southam, 6 February 1906.
18 HD, 15 September 1910; "A Unique Statement of City Circulation," 66–7; see also Sutherland, "How Our Circulation Doubled in Twelve Months," 33.
19 SA, reel 105, J.H. Woods to W.J. Southam, 21 October 1913.
20 WP, vol. 23, Vernon Knowles to Willison, 27 December 1919.
21 Walkom, "The Daily Newspaper Industry," 297.
22 QUA, Flavelle Papers, "Report of the News Publishing Company," case 1, 20 January 1908, 3, 5.
23 "Vast Improvement in Newspaper Advertising," Toronto *Star*, 26 August 1905, 5.
24 The figures are from Walkom, "Daily Newspaper Industry," 375. This is an average, the rates varied in 1885 from a low of 32.1 percent (*Mail*) to a high of 57.8 percent ((*Telegram*). In 1898 the range varied from 65 percent to 80 percent. In 1906, the six dailies' individual percentages of advertising revenue went from 65 percent of total income to 73 percent.
25 CPP (April 1895): 5.
26 Ibid. (October 1902): 16. Stephenson et al. (*The Story of Advertising*, 67) point out that the "week-in week-out Salada campaign of name display which resulted in mounting Salada sales effectively convinced formerly sceptical retailers and producers of the effectiveness of newspaper advertising."
27 Walkom, "Daily Newspaper Industry," 359.
28 "F. Murray Abraham Puts Newspaper Advertising First," 56.
29 Walkom, "Daily Newspaper Industry," 357.
30 NA, MG 30, D 98, Ross Papers, Diary, 24 January 1893.
31 SA, reel 105, J.H. Woods to W.J. Southam, 16 August 1913.
32 Hall, *Sifton*, 2: 323.
33 SA, reel 105, J.H. Woods to W.J. Southam, 16 August 1913; the fourteen percent figure was arrived at by compiling local advertising revenues in SA, reel 105, The Herald Publishing Co. Ltd Profit and Loss Account. Feb. to Dec. 1913; Walkom, "Daily Newspaper Industry," 348, found that by 1906 three or four department stores accounted for, on average, 31.8 percent of the display advertising space of the three leading Toronto dailies.
34 CPP (March 1913): 38; "Ways Canadian Publishers Use to Sell Space," 33; "A Shopping Festival that Proved Big Success," 68.
35 "The Function of the Promotion Dept.," 63.
36 "Increasing the Value of Advertising Space," 12.
37 Walkom, "Daily Newspaper Industry," 375.

38 Taylor, "Advertising the Real Backbone of the Business," 13.
39 The percentages for 1891 and 1892, figured on the ratio between advertisement and subscription sales revenues, are taken from NA, MG 30, D 98, Ross Papers, vol. 1/7, "Statement of assets and liabilities of P.D. Ross ..." for 1891 and 1892. Five-month averages in 1895 and 1896 show the same approximately sixty percent figure (ibid., P.D. Ross Diary, vol.9, f.9). The 1920 figures are taken from ibid., Ross Papers, vol. 1/7, "Ottawa Journal Balance Sheet Dated December 31, 1920."
40 Only once before 1890 had a Canadian newspaper taken in more than $100,000 in advertising: the Toronto *Globe* received $115,000 in 1874. In 1877, however, its advertising revenues dropped to $76,000, and in 1883 to $64,000. It is only in the latter 1890s that revenue began to climb significantly. In Toronto, for example, the *Mail*'s ad income rose from $73,000 in 1892 to $155,000 in 1898, and in the same period the *Telegram*'s climbed from $55,000 to $116,000, the *News*'s from $34,000 to $76,000, the *World*'s from $40,000 to $106,000, and the *Globe*'s from $83,000 to a whopping $309,000. By 1906, advertising revenue was over $150,000 for four of the six Toronto dailies (Walkom, "Daily Newspaper Industry," 375).
41 CPP (February 1896): 9; "To What Extent Is a Newspaper Responsible for the Publication of Fraudulent and Objectionable Advertising?" 64–5.
42 SA, reel 133, H.S. Southam to William Southam, 9 November 1906.
43 HD, 2 February 1911.
44 Channell, "The Moral Tone and Ideas of Newspapers," 6; CPP (June 1913): 75.
45 SA, reel 133, H.S. Southam to William Southam, 9 November 1906.
46 CPP (October 1893): 4; ibid. (September 1898): 3.
47 Ibid. (November 1900): 6.
48 SA, reel 105, W.J. Watson to W.J. Southam, 20 September 1908.
49 WP, vol. 18, C.F. Hamilton to Willison, 22 December 1905.
50 HD, 16 October 1909.
51 SA, reel 105, W.H. Woods to W.J. Southam, 16 November 1908; W.J. Southam assured his father, William Southam, that "of course, we take jolly good care not to offend any of Southam Ltd's customers in Toronto or Montreal." In 1915, Richard Southam protested that the *Citizen*'s editorial policies were "against the interests of our printing business" (SA, reel 116, W.M. Southam to W.J. Southam, 25 November 1915).
52 CPP, (February 1899): 12.
53 Steele, *Prairie Editor*, 47–8.
54 CPP (April 1912): 78.
55 "All the News: or Only Some? A Newspaper Problem," 56.
56 "The Local Paper as a Factor in the Development of the Town," 17.

57 CPP (April 1892): 18.
58 Ibid. (June 1913): 75.
59 Harkness, *Atkinson*, 62; HD, 9 March 1908; ibid., 1 May 1909.
60 "This month's advertising is light, but our special will pull it up." (SA, reel 105, J.H. Woods to W.J. Southam, 19 February 1908).
61 "Publishers East and West Gather in the Money," 29.
62 "W.C.P.A. Holds Annual Meeting at Head of Great Lakes," 49.
63 For a description of the development of the Canadian advertising agencies, see Stephenson, *The Story of Advertising*, 18–35.
64 McConnell, "The Business of Advertising," 206. For several examples of early conceptual home product advertisements, see Stephenson, *The Story of Advertising*, 50.

CHAPTER FIVE

1 Bliss, *A Living Profit*, especially chapter 2,
2 Bliss, *Northern Enterprises*, 361.
3 Mackay, "Journalism," 4.
4 "A Farce: the Toronto Daily News," 7.
5 Rutherford, *A Victorian Authority*, 76.
6 CPP (October 1908): 33.
7 Ibid. (July 1911): 97.
8 Ibid. (November 1894): 7.
9 Ibid. (September 1898): 9.
10 Ibid. (February 1904): 14.
11 WP, vol. 12, W.S. Dingman to J.S. Willison, 29 July 1905.
12 "The Canadian Publishers' Association," Hamilton *Spectator*, 27 September 1862. The CPA always had a permanent postal committee because of the importance of the postal rate to the publishers. For a survey on rates, newspapers charges, and post office deficits, see Currie, "The Post Office since 1867," 241–5. Free postage lasted until Confederation, when a nominal fee was imposed (a quarter cent per pound). In 1882 the government again allowed newspapers to be sent through the mails without charge.
13 House of Commons, Debates, 1898, 5526.
14 Ibid., 5543.
15 Ibid., 5550.
16 "The Dollar Daily," 63.
17 CPP (October 1902): 4.
18 Ibid. (May 1901): 41.
19 "Split Developing in Canadian Press Association," 31.
20 "Superiority of Local Papers Over Big City Dailies," 63.
21 *McKim's Newspaper Directory, 1913*, 41–3.

22 Walkom, "Daily Newspaper Industry," 72. The *Citizen*'s Wilson Southam admitted that by 1911 the *Star* had "some considerable circulation" and revealed that its circulation of one thousand subscribers in Ottawa proper was matched by another one thousand readers in the surrounding rural area.
23 CPP (February 1904): 14.
24 "The Efficient Remedy for Dollar Daily Competition," 58.
25 "The 'Dollar Dailies' Are Seeking to Becloud the Real Issue," 58; "The Dollar Daily Contravenes the Postal Regulations," 68.
26 "Postmaster-General Admits Post Office Department Is Seriously Considering Increase in Rate on Newspapers," 58; "Signs of Success of Campaign Against 'Dollar Dailies'," 26. It is no wonder the few large dollar dailies fought so vigorously against any plan that would have raised their rates. For the Montreal *Star*, for example, an increase of three-quarters a cent per pound in the postal rate would have quadrupled its mailing costs from $15,000 at the quarter-cent rate to $60,000 a year.
27 Colquhoun, "The Man Who Made the Montreal Star," 6.
28 Ibid., 26.
29 "Cheaper Newspapers," 11–12.
30 NA, MG 29, C34, Dougall Family Papers, vol. 3, J.S. Brierley to J.R. Dougall, 29 June 1897 and 15 July 1908. Apparently, the merger talks between the *Witness* and *Herald* in 1908 broke down over the question whether the editorial office would be subordinate to the business office in the question of "objectionable" advertising (ibid., vol. 3, R.C. Smith to J.R. Dougall, 16 July 1912?).
31 Ibid., vol. 5, TMS, n.p., n.d.
32 Ibid.
33 Ibid., vol. 3, F.E. Dougall to Sydney Fisher, 16 March 1911.
34 Ibid., Unsigned (most likely F.E. Dougall) to Wilfrid Laurier, n.d. (1912?).
35 *McKim's Newspaper Directory, 1891*, 14; ibid. *1905*, 153.
36 Nichols, (CP): *The Story of the Canadian Press*, 285. Nicholls had first-hand information as he had been publisher of the ill-fated Montreal *Mail* and *News*, which collapsed in 1917 because of Graham's ruthless competition.
37 D. Lorne McGibbon bought the *Herald* on 26 June 1913 (CPP [June 1913]: 75). On 14 January 1914, he sold his *Herald* shares to Hugh Graham, who then merged the *Witness* (which had been renamed the *Telegraph*) with the *Herald*, dropping the former name ("Settlement Made in the Montreal Herald Case," 31).
38 Roberts, *These Be Your Gods*, 201.
39 In 1904 there were already assertions that Graham was involved in

the paper industry and that he wanted to raise prices so that there would be fewer competitors (*CPP* [February 1904]: 14). The *Gazette* accused Graham of hastening the end of the *Witness* and *Herald* by cornering the available newsprint supply (Cooper, *A Short History of Montreal*, 119).

40 "The Basis of a Newspaper's Life and Favour," 24.
41 "Mr Patullo's Success," 7; Cranston, *Ink on My Fingers*, 22.
42 SA, reel 107, J.H. Woods to W.J. Southam, 18 July 1911.
43 Ibid., 4 August 1909.
44 Ibid., reel 105, J.H. Woods to W.J. Southam, 10 February 1915.
45 *CPP* (October 1901): 8.
46 Ibid. (March 1901): 42.
47 Ibid. (January 1906): 3.
48 In 1914, the August *CPP* (p.61) had an editorial titled "No More Papers Needed."
49 *CPP* (January 1906): 3.
50 "Important Merger at Galt," 54.
51 "McInnis Papers Bought by Regina 'Province'," 53.
52 Craick, *A History of Canadian Journalism*, 2: 105.
53 SA, reel 105, W.H. Woods to W.J. Southam, 14 August 1914.
54 WP, vol. 9, J.S. Willison to Francis Cochrane, 11 May 1915.
55 "Rossland Miner Says Farewell," 27.
56 "Fewer Papers – Better Service," 37; see also, "No More Papers Needed," 43.
57 "The Amalgamation in St Thomas," 31.
58 "Newspaper Amalgamation," 28.
59 "Niagara Falls Paper Explains Why Amalgamation Came About," 18. Similar reasons were advanced for the merger of the newly formed Kitchener *News-Record* in that "the amalgamation is deemed advisable in view of the increasing cost of producing a newspaper. It is expected to reduce the overhead expenses" (*CPP* [November 1919]). Brantford became a one-newspaper town in 1919 when it was "decided that there was not room for two papers to live in Brantford and make money in the proposition" (The Brantford Courier Ceases Publication," 21).
60 "Closing of The Vancouver *News-Advertiser*," 27.
61 Harkness, *Joseph Atkinson*, 205.
62 "The Basis of a Newspaper's Life and Favor," 24.
63 *CPP* (March 1912): 89.
64 "The Amalgamation in St Thomas," 31.
65 Colquhoun, *Press, Politics and People*, 134, suggests that the *News*'s failure was caused in part when the "great stores either lessened or withdrew their advertising."

66 For example, Nova Scotia financier and politician B.F. Pearson owned six Maritime dailies in the early 1900s: see "B.F. Pearson, MPP," 34, and Morgan, *Canadian Men and Women*, 895.
67 Bruce, *News and the Southams*, 64–5.
68 Harry Southam proposed selling the Alberta dailies in 1913 (SA, reel 133, H.N. Southam to W.J. Southam, 30 December 1913).
69 SA, reel 105, J.H. Woods to W.J. Southam, 3 April 1909; the Southams took control of the Edmonton *Journal* and the Lethbridge *Herald* after assuming some of the debts of the overextended W.H. Woods, who had undertaken to acquire control of the two papers. By translating these debts into stocks, they obtained overall control of the umbrella structure, Canadian Newspapers Ltd, which controlled all three Alberta dailies (ibid., reel 133, W.M. Southam to William Southam, 29 December 1911).
70 Ibid., reel 107, J.H. Woods to W.J. Southam, 19 July 1911.
71 Ibid., reel 133, W.M. Southam to William Southam, 16 May 1907.
72 Ibid., reel 107, J.H. Woods to W.J. Southam, 12 June 1911; ibid., "Canadian Newspapers Limited," 1 June 1911. The proposal by Allan Haynes Ltd. Organization was accepted and later incorporated, see Ibid., 12, 14.
73 Ibid., reel 133, W.M. Southam to William Southam, 26 June 1911.
74 Ibid., 9 June 1911.
75 Ibid., reel 116, W.M. Southam to F.N. Southam, 1 February 1915; ibid., reel 105, W.H. Woods to W.J. Southam, 25 January 1915.
76 Ibid., reel 116, W.M. Southam to W.J. Southam, 26 May 1915.
77 Bruce, *News and Southams*, 99. The Ottawa arrangements between the three papers showed how unimportant political differences between the publishers had become by World War I. The Ottawa Southams initially were Conservative party supporters, P.D. Ross started out as an independent Tory, and E.N. Smith was an ardent Liberal. By 1916 the Southams supported the Liberals as much as the Tories, prompting complaints from Fred Southam that the *Citizen*'s editorial policies were hurting patronage from the Borden government. As for Ross and Smith, their political differences did not prevent the merger; indeed, they liked each other.
78 Kesterton, *History of Journalism in Canada*, 77.

CHAPTER SIX

1 Bladen, *Political Economy*, 215–16.
2 Bliss, *Northern Enterprise*, 338. See also ibid., *Living Profit*, especially chapter 2.
3 Rutherford, *A Victorian Authority*, 84; "The Canadian Publishers'

Association," Hamilton *Spectator,* 27 September 1862.
4 Ross, "Co-operation among Local Publishers," 4; Walkom, "Daily Newspaper Industry," 306.
5 CPP (April 1900): 2.
6 Ibid.
7 SA, reel 116, P.D. Ross to H.S. Southam, 14 May 1934.
8 NA, MG 31, D106, E.N. Smith Papers, folder 2, "The Ottawa Newspaper Field"; Bruce, *News and the Southams,* 274.
9 SA, reel 105, W.J. Watson to W.J. Southam, 22 September 1908.
10 Ibid., reel 116, H.S. Southam to W.J. Southam, 31 May 1914.
11 Ibid., J.H. Woods to W.J. Southam, 14 January 1915.
12 Ibid., reel 105, F.N. Southam to W.H. Woods, 5 August 1912.
13 Ibid., W.J. Watson to W.J. Southam, 12 January 1912.
14 Ibid., J.H. Woods to W.J. Southam, 3 May 1918. The weekly subscription price rose from ten cents to fifteen cents and the yearly rate from five dollars to seven dollars.
15 Ibid., 5 May 1918.
16 Ibid., F.N. Southam to W.H. Woods, 5 August 1912.
17 NA, MG 30, D45, J.W. Dafoe Papers, J.W. Dafoe to Clifford Sifton, 12 February 1917.
18 Hall, *Sifton,* 2: 269.
19 NA, MG 27 III, C9, W.J. Maclean Papers, vol. 1, H.J. Maclean to H.H. Harris, 11 February 1916.
20 CPP (February 1907): 10. The smaller dailies agitated among themselves to lower the advertising rate commission to fifteen percent from twenty-five percent as the big dailies had done (ibid. [February 1905]: 20). At the 1906 CPA convention, one publisher complained that other publishers were breaking the CPA agreement on "foreign" (out-of-town) advertising rates by going below the rate agreement (ibid. [February 1906]: 25).
21 Ibid. (March 1907): 17.
22 Craik, *Canadian Journalism,* 2: 8.
23 CPP (February 1907): 11.
24 "Agreement between Newspaper Publishers and the Canadian Press Association as Represented by Its Advertising Committee," 43.
25 WP, vol. 35, P.D. Ross to J.S. Willison, 13 May 1917. Similarly, Wilson Southam wrote to his brother William: "I hope you will take the matter of an increased subscription rate up with your contemporaries at the earliest possible moment. The London papers are selling at $3.00, the Toronto papers seem willing to go to $3.00 with the exception of the *News,* which I hope I can get in line, and the Montreal *Star* has written that if I get the Toronto papers in line they think they will come in line also" (SA, reel 116, 11 May 1917).

26 SA, reel 105, W.H. Woods to W.J. Southam, 3 May 1918.
27 Cooper, *History of Montreal*, 119–20.
28 Nichols, (CP), 96.
29 *CPP* (April 1917): 10; ibid. (September 1911): 65.
30 Nichols, (CP), 175.
31 Nichols, (CP), 175–7, chapter 24. There were three gaps in news wire service in Canada: Calgary-Vancouver; Fort William-Winnipeg; and St John-Montreal. Sparse populations in these areas made the eastern publishers reluctant to subsidize their western and Atlantic Canadian colleagues. See "Canada's National News Service Inaugurated," 25; and "Why Western Canada Wants Better News Service," 29.
32 For an overview of Canadian anti-trust policy and legislation from 1889 to 1927, see Traves, *The State and Enterprise*, 79–81.
33 Finance minister W.S. Fielding, a former Halifax *Chronicle* editor, urged publishers to establish a Canadian-British cable service. He offered $15,000 if publishers matched it (NA, MG 29, C34, Dougall Family Papers, vol. 2, J.S. Brierley to J.R. Dougall, 30 June 1903). See also *CPP* (March 1908): 47; a reduced subsidy lasted for at least five years (Craick, *History of Journalism*, 2: 21). See also Poulton, *Paper Tyrant*, 194–6.
34 See note 31, above. See also Nichols, (CP), chapter 24.
35 Nichols, (CP), 159.
36 Kealey, *Toronto Workers*, 129–31. See chapter 8 for a discussion of the nine-hour movement. Brown's common front of newspapers and job master printers was not complete, for Edward Beatty's *Leader* supported the pressmen, according to Careless, *Brown of the Globe*, 292–3.
37 *CPP* (December 1892): 11; ibid. (May 1902): 1.
38 "Value of Publishers' Union," 22; Walkom, "Daily Newspaper Industry," 65.
39 Craick, *Canadian Journalism*, 2: 7; SA, reel 105, W.H. Woods to W.J. Southam, 20 November 1915.
40 Among the parliamentary supporters were William Templeman of the Victoria *Colonist* and Joseph Tarte of *La Patrie*. See Bone et al. *History of Canadian Journalism*, 128; and *CPP* (February 1902): 9. During the inquiry it was revealed that the papermakers' association had a fixed schedule of prices that featured no discounts or rebates for customers. Members had to deposit $500 and could be fined the same amount for infractions (*CPP* [June 1901]: 11).
41 CPA president H.P. Acton, 1903, cited in Bone et al. *History of Canadian Journalism*, 121.
42 Ibid., 94.
43 *CPP* (June 1900): 2.
44 Ibid., (March 1905): 6.

45 Beck, "Canadian Press and Franchise Rights," 27.
46 Ibid.
47 Bladen, *History of Political Economy*, 176.

CHAPTER SEVEN

1 Stewart, *The Origins of Canadian Politics*, 71.
2 Smith, "Patronage in Britain and Canada," 40-4. According to Stewart (*The Origins of Canadian Politics*, 74) once in office Laurier followed Macdonald's line on patronage. He himself paid attention to details – even down to the appointment of station masters and porters and the hiring of temporary Christmas personnel at the post office. He tried to make sure that only dedicated party workers received posts in the public service.
3 Quoted in English, *The Decline of Politics*, 9.
4 Colquhoun, *Willison*, 12.
5 Quoted in Waite, *The Life and Times of Confederation 1864-1867*, 8.
6 Hill, "A Note on Newspaper Patronage," 44.
7 Ward, "The Press and Patronage," 3.
8 Rutherford, "The People's Press," 169-91.
9 Beaven, "Press," 325.
10 See Harkness, *Joseph Atkinson*, 19-24; and WP, vol. 37, Clifford Sifton to J.S. Willison, 7 February 1901.
11 CPP (August 1899): 16.
12 Ibid. (July 1908): 33.
13 Ibid. (January 1909): 32.
14 SA, reel 108, H.M. Evans to W.M. Southam; CPP (March 1909): 22; ibid. (March 1910): 34; ibid. (December 1911), and ibid. (September 1911): 65.
15 WP, vol.19, C.H. Hamilton to J.S. Willison, 17 May 1908. See also Colquhoun, *Willison*, 150.
16 Ward, "The Press and Patronage," 9.
17 March, *Red Line*, 49.
18 Beaven, "Press," 328.
19 From 31 January to 31 July 1904, the *Free Press* billed the Interior ministry $5,468 for printing advertisings and other jobs (SP, vol. 165, bill in E.H. Macklin file); C.H. Beddoe, the Dominion accountant, assured Clifford Sifton that many Interior pamphlets and mining regulations printing contracts were awarded to the *Free Press* (ibid., C.H. Beddoe to Clifford Sifton). See also ibid., E.H. Macklin to Clifford Sifton, 10 May 1904.
20 WP, vol. 12, 2 October 1902, W.H. Dickson to J.S. Willison; NA, MG 26, G, Wilfrid Laurier Papers, vol. 250, 28 January 1903, J.S. Brierley to

Wilfrid Laurier; *CPP* (February 1902): 9.
21 Robin, *The Rush for Spoils*, 135.
22 SP, vol. 83, A.J. Magurn to James Sutherland, 17 March 1900; Hall, *Sifton*, 2: 148.
23 WP, vol. 37, 29 January 1901, J.S. Willison to Clifford Sifton; ibid., vol. 18, 15 November 1905, C.F. Hamilton to J.S. Willison; Hall, *Sifton*, 1: 290; ibid., 2: 146–50. See also Donnelly, *Dafoe*, 146–7.
24 Willison, *Reminiscences*, 122.
25 March, *Red Line*, 52.
26 Ford, *As the World Wags On*, 43.
27 HD, 10 October 1911.
28 SP, vol. 127, A.J. Magurn to Clifford Sifton, 2 May 1902.
29 NA, MG 26, H, R.L. Borden Papers, vol. 132, R.L. Borden to J.S. Willison, 14 December 1912.
30 J.S. Willison, *Reminiscences*, 215.
31 Ford, *As the World Wags On*, 225–6.
32 See NA, MG 30, D45, J.W. Dafoe Papers, reel M-73, Wilfrid Laurier to Dafoe, 5 November 1901, 14 August 1903, 28 April 1903, 6 May 1903, and 28 February 1906.
33 WP, vol. 12, 5 December 1910, W.H. Dickson to J.S. Willison.
34 Ibid., vol. 19, 9 June 1908, C.F. Hamilton to J.S. Willison.
35 NA, MG26, H, R.L. Borden Papers, vol. 132, 12 December 1912, J.S. Willison to R.L. Borden, emphasis added.
36 WP, vol. 6, John Cameron to J.S. Willison, 5 April 1898.
37 NA, MG26, G, Wilfrid Laurier Papers, vol. 506, 21 February 1908, J.E. Atkinson to Wilfrid Laurier.
38 Ford, *As the World Wags On*, 42–3.
39 SP, vol. 91, 27 July 1900, Clifford Sifton to J.S. Willison.
40 Pense, "Characters and Position," 213.
41 Rutherford, *A Victorian Authority*, 213.
42 Poulton, *The Paper Tyrant*, 27.
43 SA, reel 128, 21 May 1950, P.S. Fisher to Pierre Berton (*Maclean's Magazine* background interview).
44 Winnipeg *Tribune*, 26 January 1890.
45 Winnipeg *Tribune*, 4 August 1897.
46 "An index for the City Council will be provided so that week by week the votes of the aldermen, or a particular act for or against the public interest, may be recorded so that at the end the value of each representative can be added up" (Archives of Ontario, C.H.J. Snider Papers, John Ross Robertson, "Memoranda regarding the staff," 1 January 1902).
47 Dafoe, "Review," 62.
48 Ibid., 63.

49 SA, reel 107, "Memorandum to *Citizen* correspondents," 16 May 1907, emphasis added.
50 "E.F. Slack's Views on Newspaper Publishing," 50.
51 Cranston, *Ink on My Fingers*, 65.
52 Nichol, "Newspapers from a Business Point of View," 10–11.
53 NA, MG31, D106, Smith Papers, folder 2, "The Ottawa Newspaper Field" (26 March 1923).
54 SA, reel 105, 22 December 1919, J.H. Woods to William Southam.
55 CPP (March 1906): 20.
56 "Winnipeg Free Press Out of Politics," 29.
57 Graham, "Meighen and the Montreal Tycoons," 450.
58 Ibid., *Arthur Meighen*, 2: 242–4.
59 Taunton, "The Man Behind the Halifax Herald," 38.
60 Ibid.
61 "Charles C. Blackadar," 38.
62 SA, reel 133, 5 February 1914, W.M. Southam to Richard Southam.
63 Francis Frost, a Smith Falls manufacturer of farm equipment, wrote to Laurier (NA, MG26, G, Wilfrid Laurier Papers, vol. 63, 24 January 1898) that "I find through this section of the country a good deal of dissatisfaction existing among our newspapermen because of a lack of printing or advertising patronage ... For about a year these papers have dropped all reference to the Government." Milton *Reformer* White complained to Laurier (Wilfrid Laurier Papers, vol. 791b, 29 March 1898) that "dozens of advertisements have been sent out from the Department [Public Works and Railways and Canals] and given only to a few favoured ones."
64 Beaven, "Partisanship, Patronage and the Press," 329.
65 Charlesworth, *Candid Chronicles*, 147–9.
66 Ibid.
67 NA, MG26, G, Wilfrid Laurier Papers, vol. 132, 1 December 1899, J.E. Atkinson to Wilfrid Laurier.
68 WP, vol. 37, 29 January 1901, J.S. Willison to Clifford Sifton.
69 Ibid., vol.18, C.F. Hamilton to J.S. Willison, 7 February 1906.
70 Ibid.
71 HD, 3 May 1906.
72 WP, vol. 19, 10 November 1908, C.F. Hamilton to J.S. Willison.
73 Ibid., 30 October 1908, C.F. Hamilton to J.S. Willison.
74 Donnelly, *Dafoe*, 122.
75 HD, 2 March 1905.

CHAPTER EIGHT

1 Rutherford, *A Victorian Authority*, 5.
2 Skelton, *Sir Wilfrid Laurier*, 2: 270–1.

3 Beaven, *Partisanship, Patronage and the Press,* 338–9.
4 Ibid.
5 The extent to which the political and business interests of Charles Magee and George Perley were intertwined is noteworthy. Magee was president of the local Conservative association, an alderman and an organizer of the Bank of Ottawa. Lumberman and manufacturer Perley was a director of the same bank and also a Conservative MP. See Morgan, *Men and Women in Canada 1912,* 723, 897.
6 Gillis, "Big Business," 105.
7 Bone et al., *A History of Canadian Journalism,* 182.
8 Ibid.
9 *CPP* (August 1902): 4.
10 Ibid. (April 1897): 12.
11 McGregor 97–102, 105, 132–3; Cooke, "The House That Nichol Built," 5.
12 NA, MG30, D98, P.D. Ross Papers, "Instructions to City-Editor and Telegram Editor for 1906," vol. 1, folder 6.
13 *CPP* (July 1905): 22; Morgan, *1912,* 1194.
14 PAM, W. Sanford Evans Papers, box 3, 15 September and 8 November 1902, Edward Gurney to W.S. Evans.
15 Ibid., 19 September 1900, W.S. Evans to J. Macdonald Oxley.
16 Throughout his lifetime Evans was an avid club joiner. He founded the Canadian Clubs in Hamilton (1893), Toronto (1897), and Winnipeg (1905) and was a member of many others including the Zetland Club and the Business Association for the Advancement of Science.
17 PAM, W. Sanford Evans Papers, box 3, 21 November 1900, W.S. Evans to R.T. Riley.
18 Ibid., 27 November 1900, R.T. Riley to W.S. Evans.
19 Ibid., 7 January 1901, W.S. Evans to C.R. McCullough.
20 Ibid., 19 December 1900, W.S. Evans to Irene Evans.
21 Ibid., 2 February 1901, W.S. Evans to Irene Evans.
22 Ibid., 26 February 1901, W.S. Evans to Irene Evans.
23 Ibid., 28 February 1901, W.S. Evans to Irene Evans.
24 Ibid., box 4, 4 November 1904, Edward Gurney to W.S. Evans.
25 Ibid., 4 July and 11 August 1905, Harry Evans to W.S. Evans.
26 Ibid., 23 November 1905, R.L. Borden to W.S. Evans.
27 "Very privately, there is a strong movement amongst leading Conservatives and Liberals in this city to secure a united public opinion in favour of prompt and adequate action for naval defence. Two or three meetings have been held with J.A. Macdonald, Jaffray and J.E. Atkinson in attendance and I am in hopes that the *Globe* and the *Star* will yet fall into line. I will let you know more about this movement later. Meantime, *keep it very quiet,* telling no one" (WP, vol. 19, 12 August 1912, F.D.L. Smith to C.F. Hamilton; see also ibid., August

1912, author unknown to M.W.M. Grigg, and NA, MG30, D465, J.W. Dafoe Papers, reel M-73, 19 August 1912, J.E. Atkinson to J.W. Dafoe.
28 Acheson, *The Canadian Industrial Elite*, 167.
29 Morgan, *Canadian Men and Women*, 1898, 1912; CPP (various); various biographies.
30 Maclean had been read out of the Conservative party in 1905, in part for his strong pro-nationization stance. See Craven, *Ink on My Fingers*, 282. See also Charlesworth, *Candid Chronicles*, 131.
31 Walkom, "Daily Newspaper Industry," 226, 244–5, 251, 256.
32 Rhodes, "The *Star* and the New Radicalism," 4, 63–4.
33 QUA, Flavelle Papers, case 1, 8 April 1903, Joseph Flavelle to J.S. Willison.
34 Colquhoun, *Press, Politics and People*, 236.

CHAPTER NINE

1 Armstrong and Nelles, "Private Property in Peril."
2 Nelles, *The Politics of Development*, 491.
3 English, *The Decline of Politics*, 491.
4 Armstrong and Nelles, "Private Property in Peril," 22.
5 Armstrong, "The Empire Taken Over," 17.
6 Easterbrook and Aitken, *Canadian Economic History*, chapters 14–18 *passim*. See also Craven and Traves, "Canadian Railways as Manufacturers, 1850–1880," 29–53.
7 SA, reel 108, 2 March 1908, W.H. Woods to W.J. Southam.
8 Young, *Promotions and Politicians*, 12.
9 Ibid., 42–4.
10 Quoted in English, *The Decline of Politics*, 23.
11 SA, reel 105, 2 November 1908, W.H. Woods to W.J. Southam.
12 Ibid., reel 128, 21 May 1950, Pierre Berton interview with P.S. Fisher.
13 Hall, *Clifford Sifton*, 1: 213.
14 CPP (October 1893): 11.
15 Hall *Clifford Sifton* 1: 214.
16 Ibid., 210.
17 Clippingdale, "J.S. Willison," 260.
18 Willison, *Reminiscences*, 221.
19 Clippingdale, "J.S. Willison," 196.
20 WP, vol. 22, 1 August 1896, Robert Jaffray to J.S. Willison.
21 Editorial, Toronto *Globe*, 3 August 1904.
22 NA, MG26, H, R.L. Borden Papers, vol. 327, 17 September 1903, B.A. Macnab to A.E. Blount and 24 September 1903, B.A. Macnab to R.L. Borden; Cooper, *A Short History of Montreal*, 117. For a detailed look at the plot see Skelton, *Sir Wilfrid Laurier*, 2: 203–17.
23 Skelton, *Sir Wilfrid Laurier*, 2: 209.

24 HD, 5 March 1910.
25 SA, reel 133, 11 May 1906, W.M Southam to Richard Southam.
26 Ibid.
27 Ibid.
28 Ibid., reel 133, 5 November 1908, F.N. Southam to W.J. Southam.
29 Ibid., reel 105, 5 October 1909, W.H. Woods to F.N. Southam.
30 Ibid., reel 105, 18 November 1908, W.H. Woods to W.J. Southam.
31 CPP (April 1899): 14.
32 Hall, *Clifford Sifton* I, 214.
33 Canada, House of Commons, Sessional Paper 20c, 1911, Board of Railway Commissioners for Canada, *Fifth Report*, 274.
34 Nichols, (CP): 24.
35 Canada, House of Commons, Sessional Paper 20c, 1911, Board of Railway Commissioners for Canada, *Fifth Report*, 275.
36 CPP (February 1899): 4.
37 Beaverbrook, *My Early Life*, 163. The Bank of Montreal also had veto power over a change of ownership.
38 Nichols, (CP), 93.
39 CPP (February 1901): 22.
40 "Does Capital Threaten the Liberty of the Press?" (Toronto *Star*, 26 August 1905). A.H.U. Colquhoun warned that "the growth of huge trusts in commerce has suggested the idea of a newspaper trust which might be organized by persons with large selfish ends to serve in gaining the ear of the public. Newspapers thus manipulated could, it is thought, provide the necessary impetus of an apparent popular opinion in favour of class legislation. The danger is not imaginary" (Bone et al., *A History of Canadian Journalism*, 23). John Bone, the 1912 CPA president, recognized the danger of the press being under the control of large capital: "It is axiomatic that no newspaper can rise higher than its proprietor, and that the salvation of our press depends on the its control remaining in the hands of high-minded, public-spirited citizens" (Craick, *A History of Canadian Journalism*, 2: 59).
41 "The News and Its Promoters," 6.
42 Ibid.
43 CPP (January 1905): 5.
44 "Poisoned Wells of Truth," 10.
45 CPP (January 1907): 13.
46 "Who Owns the Press of Canada?" 32.
47 Ibid.
48 WP, vol. 27, 1 April 1914, J.B. Maclean to J.S. Willison.
49 "Who Owns the Newspapers," 36.
50 See SP, vol. 104, 23 January 1901, 17 March 1901, A.J. Magurn to Clifford Sifton.
51 WP, vol. 37, 7 February 1901, Clifford Sifton to J.S. Willison.

52 W.F. Maclean, "Jaffray-Cox Alliance," Toronto *World*, 26 September 1905, 1.
53 HD, 18 August 1908.
54 Bliss, *A Canadian Millionaire*, 175.
55 A.H.D. Ross, *Ottawa: Past and Present*, 146.
56 SA, reel 133, 19 April 1906 and 4 December 1907, W.M. Southam to William Southam.
57 Graham, "Tycoons," 450.
58 WP, vol.26, J.S. Willison to Stewart Lyon, 6 May 1919.
59 HD, 21 November 1905.
60 Anderson, "The Municipal Reform Government in Western Canada," 96.
61 Weaver, "From Land Assembly," 215.
62 Bilkey, *Persons, Papers and Things*, 32–3.
63 Armstrong and Nelles, *Revenge of the Methodist Bicycle Company*, 161, 168.
64 CPP (March 1895): 32.
65 Armstrong and Nelles, *Revenge of the Methodist Bicycle Company*, 160.
66 SA, reel 133, 4 December 1907, W.M. Southam to William Southam.
67 Ibid.
68 Armstrong, *Monopoly*, 141–3.
69 Bruce, *News and the Southams*, 41–3.
70 Avery, "A Speculative View," 10.
71 Gillis, "Big Business," 61; Ross, *Retrospects*, 246–50; Walkom, "Daily Newspaper Industry," 298; and SA, reel 133, 4 December 1907, W.M. Southam to William Southam.
72 Poulton, *Paper Tyrant*, 116.
73 Armstrong, *Monopoly*, 249.
74 Rumilly, *Histoire de Montréal*, 455–6; CPP (May 1913): 74; "Merger of Montreal Herald and Telegraph," 61; CPP (June 1913, 75; "Montreal Herald Transferred," 24; "Settlement Made in Montreal Herald Case," 26; Armstrong, *Monopoly*, 251.
75 March, *Red Line*, 113–14.

Bibliography

UNPUBLISHED MANUSCRIPTS

NATIONAL ARCHIVES OF CANADA
  R.L. Borden Papers, MG 26, H
  Wilfrid Laurier Papers, MG 26, G
  Dougall Family Papers, MG 29, C34
  J.W. Dafoe Papers, MG 30, D45
  W.F. Maclean Papers, MG 27 IIIC9
  P.D. Ross Papers, MG 30, D98
  E.N. Smith Papers, MG 31, D106
  Clifford Sifton Papers, MG 27, IID15
  J.S. Willison Papers, MG 30, D29

ARCHIVES OF ONTARIO
  R.S. Dimock Papers
  M.O. Hammond Papers
  C.H.J. Snider Papers
  J.S. Willison Papers

PROVINCIAL ARCHIVES OF MANITOBA
  W. Sanford Evans Papers

QUEEN'S UNIVERSITY ARCHIVES
  Joseph Flavelle Papers

UNIVERSITY OF MANITOBA ARCHIVES
  J.W. Dafoe Papers

SOUTHAM INC. ARCHIVES

SECONDARY SOURCES

"A.B.C. in Canada." *CPP* (July 1917): 32.
Acheson, T.W. "The Social Origins of the Canadian Industrial Elite, 1880–1885." In *Canadian Business History: Selected Studies, 1497–1971*, edited by David S. Macmillan. Toronto: McClelland and Stewart, 1972.
– "Changing Social Origins of the Canadian Industrial Elite, 1880–1910." In *Enterprise and National Development: Essays in Canadian Business and Economic History*, edited by Glenn Porter and Robert D. Cuff, 51–79. Toronto: Hakkert, 1973.
"Advertising Advertising." *CPP* (February 1910): 60.
"Advertising Advertising Throughout Canada." *CPP* (February 1912): 37.
"The Advertising Negotiations." *CPP* (April 1907): 37–8.
"Agreement between Newspaper Publishers and the Canadian Press Association as Represented by Its Advertising Committee." *CPP* (August 1914): 43.
Aitken, Hugh G.J., ed. *Explorations in Enterprise*. Cambridge, MA: Harvard University Press, 1965.
"All the News: or Only Some? A Newspaper Problem." *CPP* (January 1911, 56).
Altschull, J. Herbert. *Agents of Power: The Role of the News Media in Human Affairs*. New York: Longman, 1984.
"The Amalgamation in St Thomas." *CPP* (July 1918): 31.
"Amalgamation of Circulations of Twin Cities Dailies." *CPP* (April 1910): 31.
Anderson, James D. "The Municipal Reform Government in Western Canada." In *The Usable Urban Past: Planning and Politics in the Modern Canadian City*, edited by Alan F.J. Artibise and Gilbert A. Stelter. Toronto: Macmillan, 1979.
"Annual Meeting of the American Newspaper Publishers' Association." *CPP* (May 1910): 29
Archer, William L. *Joe Atkinson's Toronto Star: The Genius of Crooked Lane*. Montreal: N.p., n.d.
Armstrong, Christopher, and H.V. Nelles. "The Rise of Civic Populism in Toronto 1870–1920." In *Forging a Consensus: Historical Essays on Toronto*, edited by Victor L. Russell, 192–237. Toronto: University of Toronto Press, 1984.
– *Monopoly's Moment: The Organization and Regulation of Canadian Utilities, 1830–1930*. Philadelphia: Temple University Press, 1986.
– "Private Property in Peril: Ontario Businessmen and the Federal System." In *Enterprise and National Development: Essays in Canadian Business and Economic History*, edited by Glenn Porter and Robert D. Cuff, 20–38. Toronto: Hakkert, 1973.
– *The Revenge of the Methodist Bicycle Company: Sunday Streetcars and Municipal Reform in Toronto, 1888–1897*. Toronto: Peter Martin Associates, 1977.

Artibise, Alan F.J. *Winnipeg: A Social History of Urban Growth, 1874–1914* Montreal: McGill-Queen's University Press, 1975.

Artibise, Alan F.J., and Gilbert A. Stelter, eds. *The Usable Urban Past: Planning and Politics in the Modern Canadian City.* Toronto: Macmillan, 1979.

Atcheson, James H., ed. *The Political Process in Canada.* Toronto: University of Toronto Press, 1963.

Avery, Lydia. "Evolution of the Canadian Daily Newspaper Industry." Master's research paper, University of Western Ontario, 1981.

Avery, T.E. "A Speculative View of the Decline and Fall of a Competitive Daily, the London *Advertiser* 1863–1936." Honours research paper, Carleton University, 1977.

Baldasty, Gerald J. *The Commercialization of News in the Nineteenth Century.* Madison: University of Wisconsin Press, 1992.

"The Basis of a Newspaper's Life and Favor." CPP (November 1917): 24.

Beaven, Brian. "'Anxious, Vexed, or Harassed': Philip Dansken Ross 'Making It' as a Working Journalist in the 1880's." Paper presented at the Canadian Historical Association conference, University of Windsor, June 1988.

– "Partisanship, Patronage and the Press in Ontario, 1880–1914: Myths and Realities." *Canadian Historical Review* 44 (September 1983): 317–51.

Beaverbrook, Lord. *My Early Life.* Fredericton, NB: Brunswick Press, 1965.

Beck, Edward. "Canadian Press and Franchise Rights." CPP (September 1918): 27.

– "Should the Business Office be Abolished?" CPP (November 1916): 30.

Bercuson, David. *Confrontation at Winnipeg: Labour, Industrial Relations, and the General Strike.* Montreal: McGill-Queen's University Press, 1974.

Bertram, Gordon W. "Economic Growth in Canadian Industry, 1870–1915: The Staple Model and the Take-off Hypothesis." *Canadian Journal of Economics and Political Science* 29 (1963): 159–84.

"B.F. Pearson, MPP" CPP (March 1906): 34.

Bilkey, Paul. *Persons, Papers and Things: Being the Casual Recollections of a Journalist with Some Flounderings in Philosophy.* Toronto: Ryerson Press, 1940.

Black, Robson. "Canadian Journalism." *The Canadian Magazine* 32, no. 5 (March 1909): 434–40.

Bladen, V.W. *An Introduction to Political Economy.* Toronto: University of Toronto Press, 1956.

Bliss, Michael. *A Canadian Millionaire: The Life and Business Times of Sir Joseph Flavelle, Bart. 1858–1939.* Toronto: Macmillan, 1978.

– *Northern Enterprise: Five Centuries of Canadian Business.* Toronto: McClelland and Stewart, 1987.

– *A Living Profit: Studies in the Social History of Canadian Business, 1883–1911.* Toronto: McClelland and Stewart, 1974.

Bocking, D.H. "Premier Walter Scott: A Study of His Rise to Political Power."

MA thesis, University of Saskatchewan, 1959.
Bone, John R., ed. *Journalism and the University.* Toronto: Copp Clark, 1903.
Bone, John R., Joseph T. Clark, A.H.U. Colquhoun, and John F. Mackay. *A History of Canadian Journalism in the Several Portions of the Dominion with a Sketch of the Canadian Press Association 1859–1908.* New York, NY: AMS Press, 1976.
Bonville, Jean de. *La presse québécoise de 1884 à 1914: Genèse d'un média de masse.* Québec: Les presses de l'Université Laval, 1988.
Boyce, George. "The Fourth Estate: The Reappraisal of a Concept." In *Newspaper History from the Seventeenth Century to the Present Day,* edited by George Boyce et al., 19–40. Beverly Hills, CA: Sage Publications, 1978.
Boyce, George, James Durran, and Pauline Wingate, eds. *Newspaper History from the Seventeenth Century to the Present Day.* Beverly Hills, CA: Sage Publications, 1978.
"The Brantford Courier Ceases Publication." *CPP* (January 1919): 21.
Braverman, Harry. *Labor and Monopoly Capital: The Degradation of Work in the Twentieth Century.* New York: Monthly Review Press, 1974.
Bray, Robert Matthew. "The Role of Sir Clifford Sifton in the Formulation of the Editorial Policy of the *Manitoba Free Press*, 1916–1921." MA thesis, University of Manitoba, 1921.
Breed, Warren. "Social Control in the Newsroom: A Functional Analysis." *Social Forces* 32 (1955): 326–35.
Brown, Lorne Alvin. "Progressivism and the Press in Saskatchewan, 1916–1926." MA thesis, University of Saskatchewan, 1966.
Bruce, Charles. *News and the Southams.* Toronto: Macmillan, 1968.
Buckley, Kenneth. *Capital Formation in Canada, 1896–1930.* Toronto: McClelland and Stewart, 1974.
Burton, C.L. *A Sense of Urgency: Memoirs of a Canadian Merchant.* Toronto: Clarke, Irwin, 1952.
"The Business Management of a Newspaper." *CPP* (September 1911): 56.
Campbell, Burt R. "From Hand-set Type to Linotype: Reminiscences of Fifty Years in the Printing Trade." *British Columbia Historical Quarterly* 10 (1946): 253–72.
Cameron, John. "University Chairs in Journalism," In *Journalism and the University,* edited by John R. Bone. Toronto: Copp Clark, 1903.
Canada. House of Commons. *Debates 1898.* vol. 2, Ottawa: Queen's Printer, 1898.
– Sessional Paper 20 C. Board of Railway Commissioners. *Report.* Ottawa: King's Printer, 1911.
– Royal Commission on Corporate Concentration. *Report.* Ottawa: Supply and Services Canada, 1978.
– Royal Commission on Newspapers. *Report.* Prepared by Chairman Tom Kent et al. Ottawa: Supply and Services Canada, 1981.

– Senate Special Committee on the Mass Media. Vol. 1: *The Uncertain Mirror.* Prepared by Keith Davey et al. Ottawa: Information Canada, 1970.
"Canada Has Now a Circulation Managers' Association." CPP (November 1917): 21.
"Canada's National News Service Inaugurated." CPP (September 1917): 25.
"A Canadian Associated Press Organized." CPP (November 1910): 39.
"Canadian Newspapermen in Parliament." CPP (November 1908): 20–3.
Canadian Printer and Publisher (CPP), vols. 1–26. (November 1884): 20; (April 1892): 18; (May 1892): 11; (September 1892): 20; (December 1892): 11; (March 1893): 7; (May 1893): 10; (October 1893): 4, 11; (July 1894): 7; (November 1894): 7, 14; (December 1894): 2; (February 1895): 7; (March 1895): 32; (April 1895): 5, 8; (July 1895): 2; (October 1895): 1; (February 1896): 9; (July 1896): 2; (March 1897): 4; (April 1897): 10; (July 1897): 10; (September 1989): 1, 3; (October 1898): 6; (February 1899): 4, 12; (April 1899): 14; (August 1899): 16; (December 1899): 30; (January 1900): 3; (April 1900): 1, 2; (June 1900): 2; (September 1900): 8; (November 1900): 6; (December 1900): 9; (February 1901): 22; (March 1901): 42; (June 1901): 11; (October 1901): 8; (February 1902): 9; (May 1902): 1; (July 1902): 4; (August 1902): 4; (October 1902): 4, 16; (December 1902): 6; (February 1904): 14; (April 1904): 8; (January 1905): 5; (February 1905): 15, 20; (March 1905): 6; (July 1905): 22; (September 1905): 17; (January 1906): 3; (February 1906): 25; (March 1906): 20; (April 1906): 26; (November 1906): 17; (December 1906): 22; (January 1907): 13; (February 1907): 10, 11; (March 1907): 47; (August 1907): 36; (March 1908): 47; (July 1908): 33; (October 1908): 33; (January 1909): 32, 39; (March 1909): 22, 36; (April 1909): 2; (May 1909): 2; (September 1909): 36; (February 1910): 57; (March 1910): 34; (July 1910): 28–39; (September 1910): 27; (May 1911): 54; (June 1911): 55; (July 1911): 56, 97; (September 1911): 65; (March 1912): 89, 90; (April 1912): 78; (February 1913): 38; (March 1913): 38; (April 1913): 48; (May 1913): 74; (June 1913): 75; (November 1914): 46; (April 1917): 10; (February 1919): 43; (September 1919): 28; (November 1919): n.p.
"The Canadian Publishers' Association Annual Meeting," 27.
"Canadian War Correspondents for the South African War." CPP (November 1899): 6.
Careless, J.M.S. *Brown of The Globe,* Vol. 1: *The Voice of Upper Canada 1818–1859,* Vol. 2: *Statesman of Confederation 1860–1880.* Toronto: Macmillan, 1959, 1963.
Carruthers, George. *Paper in the Making.* Toronto: Garden City, 1947.
Chandler, Alfred D., Jr. *The Visible Hand: The Managerial Revolution in American Business.* Cambridge, MA: Harvard University Press, 1977.
Channell, L.S. "The Moral Tone and Ideas of Newspapers." CPP (September 1898): 3.

Charlesworth, Hector. *Candid Chronicles: Leaves from the Notebook of a Canadian Journalist.* Toronto: Macmillan, 1925.
– *More Candid Chronicles: Further Leaves from the Notebook of a Canadian Journalist.* Toronto: Ryerson Press, 1950.
"Changed Conditions in Canadian Publishing." *CPP* (December 1898): 8.
"Changes in Ownership." *CPP* (April 1910): 30.
"Charles C. Blackadar." *CPP* (February 1917): 38.
"Cheaper Newspapers," *CPP* (November 1894): 11–12.
"Circulation Contests." *CPP* (April 1911): 59.
"The Circulation Manager." *CPP* (July 1904. 15.
"Circulation Managers Gather in Montreal." *CPP* (June 1910): 59.
Clark, Joe T. "The Daily Newspaper." *The Canadian Magazine.* 7, no. 2 (June 1896): 101–4.
Clippingdale, Richard T. "J.S. Willison, Political Journalist: From Liberalism to Independence." Ph.D dissertation, University of Toronto, 1970.
"Closing of the Vancouver *News-Advertiser.*" *CPP* (October 1917): 27.
Cole, Arthur F. *Business Enterprise in Its Social Setting.* Cambridge, MA: Harvard University Press, 1959.
Colquhoun, A.H.U. "Canadian Universities and the Press." In *Journalism and the University*, edited by John R. Bone. Toronto: Copp Clark, 1903.
– "The Man Who Made the Montreal Star." *CPP* (January 1895): 7.
– *Press, Politics and People: The Life and Letters of Sir John Willison, Journalist and Correspondent of* The Times. Toronto: Macmillan, 1935.
Cook, Ramsay. *The Politics of John W. Dafoe and the Free Press.* Toronto: University of Toronto Press, 1963.
– *The Dafoe-Sifton Correspondence 1919–1927.* Altona, Man.: D.W. Friesen and Sons, 1966.
Cooke, Britton B. "The Paper Nichol Built: The Story of the Vancouver *Province.*" *Canadian Courier* 20 (15 July 1916): 5–6.
Cooper, J.A. "The Editors of the Leading Canadian Dailies". *The Canadian Magazine* 12, no. 4 (February 1899): 349–50.
Cooper, J.I. *Montreal: A Brief History.* Montreal: McGill-Queen's University Press, 1969.
"Co-operation between the Publisher and the Advertiser." *CPP* (February 1912): 49.
Cowan, Ruth Schwartz. *More Work for Mother: The Ironies of Household Technology from the Open Hearth to the Microwave.* New York: Basic Books, 1983.
Craick, W.A. *A History of Canadian Journalism II.* Toronto: Ontario Publishing Company, 1959.
Cranston, J.H. *Ink on My Fingers.* Toronto: Ryerson Press, 1953.
Craven, Paul, and Tom Traves. "Canadian Railways as Manufacturers, 1850–1880." In *A History of Ontario: Selected Readings*, edited by Michael J. Piva, 29–54. Toronto: Copp Clark Pitman, 1988.

Cross, Michael S., and Gregory S. Kealey, eds. *The Consolidation of Capitalism: 1896–1929.*
Curran, James. "The Press as an Agency of Social Control: An Historical Perspective." In *Newspaper History from the Seventeenth Century to the Present Day*, edited by George Boyce et al., 51–75. Beverly Hills, CA: Gage Publications, 1978.
Curran, James, Michael Gurevitch, and Janet Woollacott. "The Study of the Media: Theoretical Approaches." In *Culture, Society and the Media*, edited by Michael Gurevitch et al., 11–29. London: Methuen, 1982.
Curran, James, and Jean Seaton. *Power without Responsibility: The Press and Broadcasting in Britain.* Glasgow: Fontana, 1981.
Currie, A.W. "The Post Office since 1867." *Canadian Journal of Economics and Political Science* 24, no.2 (May 1958): 241–50.
Dafoe, John W. "Where the Best News Should Be." CPP (December 1895): 10.
– "The Press Blamed for National Paralysis," CPP (July 1917): 39.
– *Clifford Sifton in Relation to His Times.* Toronto: Macmillan, 1931.
– "Review: Press, Politics and People." *Canadian Historical Review* 17 (March 1936): 59–64.
– *Sixty Years in Journalism.* Address to Winnipeg Press Club, 16 October 1943.
– "Early Winnipeg Newspapers." *Historical and Scientific Society of Manitoba.* 3 (1947). 14–24.
"Daily Newspaper Advertising Regulation." CPP (April 1907): 12–13.
Darby, W.J. "The Comic Supplement." CPP, June 1906): 20.
Donnelly, Murray. *Dafoe of the Free Press.* Toronto: Macmillan, 1968.
"The 'Dollar Dailies' Are Seeking to Becloud the Real Issue." CPP (December 1913): 58.
"The Dollar Daily." CPP (January 1912): 63.
"The Dollar Daily Contravenes the Postal Regulation." CPP (May 1913): 68.
Drake, E.G. "Pioneer Journalism in Saskatchewan, 1878–89." *Saskatchewan History* 5, (1952): 17–27, 41–54.
Dudek, Louis. *Literature and the Press: A History of Printed Media, and Their Relation to Literature.* Toronto: Ryerson and Contact, 1960.
Eaman, Ross A. *The Media Society: Basic Issues and Controversies.* Toronto: Butterworths, 1987.
"The Efficient Remedy for Dollar Daily Competition." CPP (May 1913): 67.
"E.F. Slack"s Views on Newspaper Publishing." CPP (February 1915): 50.
"An Eight-Hour Day for The Star's Reporters." CPP (February 1919): 43.
Emery, Michael, and Edwin Emery. *The Press and America: An Interpretative History of the Mass Media.* Englewood Cliffs, NJ: Prentice Hall, 1992.
"The Empire Taken Over by a Syndicate." CPP (November 1894): 17.
English, John. *The Decline of Politics: The Conservatives and the Party System 1901–1920.* Toronto: University of Toronto Press, 1977.
"Enlargening the Journalistic Graveyard." CPP (January 1919): 29.

Ewan, J.A. "War Correspondence. " CPP (March 1901): 10
Ewen, Stuart. *Captains of Consciousness: Advertising and the Social Roots of the Common Culture.* New York: McGraw-Hill, 1976.
"A Farce: The Toronto Daily News." CPP (December 1894): 14.
Ferguson, Ted. *Kit Coleman: Queen of Hearts.* Toronto: Doubleday Canada, 1978.
"Fewer Papers – Better Service." CPP (February 1915): 37.
Fischer, Lewis R. "'An Engine Yet Moderate': James Peake, Entrepreneurial Behaviour and the Shipping Industry of Nineteenth Century Prince Edward Island," in *The Enterprising Canadian: Entrepreneurs and Economic Developments in Eastern Canada, 1820–1914,* edited by Lewis R. Fischer and Eric W. Sager. St John's NFLD: Memorial University, 1979. 99–118.
"F. Murray Abraham Puts Newspaper Advertising First." CPP ((May 1913): 56.
"Flat Rates for Press Messages are Abolished." CPP (March 1910): 45.
Ford, Arthur. *As the World Wags On.* Toronto: Ryerson Press, 1947.
Fry, W.A. "Half-tone Cuts for Newspapers." CPP (June 1910): 4.
"The Function of the Promotion Dept." CPP (August 1914): 63.
Gillis, Peter. "Big Business and the Origins of the Conservative Reform Movement in Ottawa, 1890–1912." *Journal of Canadian Studies* 15, no. 1 (Spring 1980): 93–109.
Goheen, Peter G. *Victorian Toronto, 1850 to 1900.* Chicago: University of Chicago Press, 1970.
"The Growth of the Toronto Mail." CPP (November 1895): 6
Graham, W.R. "Meighen and the Montreal Tycoons: Railway Policy in the Election of 1921." In *Canadian History since Confederation: Essays and Interpretations,"* edited by Bruce Hodgins and Robert Page, 447–64. Georgetown, Ont.: Irwin-Dorsey, 1972.
– *Arthur Meighen: A Biography.* Vol. 2: *And Fortune Fled.* Toronto: Clarke, Irwin, 1963.
Gurevitch, Michael, Tony Bennett, James Curran, and Janet Woollacott, eds. *Culture, Society and the Media.* London: Methuen, 1982.
Hall, David. *Clifford Sifton.* Vol. 1: *The Young Napoleon 1861–1900.* Vol. 2: *A Lonely Eminence 1901–1929.* Vancouver: University of British Columbia Press, 1981, 1985.
– "The Political Career of Clifford Sifton, 1896–1905." Ph.D thesis, University of Toronto, 1973.
Hallman, Eugene. *The Newspaper as Business.* Prepared for the Royal Commission on Newspapers. Research Publications, vol. 4, 1–16. Ottawa: Supply and Services Canada, 1981.
Ham, George. *Reminiscences of a Raconteur.* Toronto: Musson, 1921.
Hamelin, Jean, and André Beaulieu. "Aperçu du journalisme québécois d'expression française." *Recherches Sociographiques* 7 (September-December

1966): 305–48.
Hamilton, Charles Frederick. "Canadian Journalism." *The University Magazine* 16 no. 1 (February 1917): 17–40
Hammond, M.O. "Ninety Years of the Globe." Unpublished manuscript, Archives of Ontario, n.d. (193?).
– "The Parliamentary Press Gallery." *The Westminster* 10.no.4 (April 1907): 224–30.
Harkness, L.C. "The Western Press Grievances before the Railway Commission." CPP (December 1909): 44.
Harkness, Ross. *J.E. Atkinson of the Star*. Toronto, University of Toronto Press, 1963.
Harris, James G. "The *News* and Canadian Politics, 1903–1914." MA thesis, University of Toronto, 1952.
"W.F. Herman Buys Windsor Record." CPP (August 1918): 25.
Heron, Craig. "The Crisis of the Craftsman: Hamilton's Metal Workers in the Early Twentieth Century." In *The Consolidation of Capitalism: 1896–1929*, edited by Michael S. Cross and Gregory S. Kealey, 77–113. Toronto: McClelland and Stewart, 1983.
Heron, Craig, and Robert Storey, eds. *On the Job: Confronting the Labour Process in Canada*. Montreal and Kingston: McGill-Queen's University Press, 1986.
Hewitt, W.A. *Down the Stretch: Recollections of a Pioneer Sportsman and Journalist*. Toronto: Ryerson Press, 1958.
Hill, R.A. "A Note on Newspaper Patronage in Canada during the Late 1850s and Early 1860s." *Canadian Historical Review* 49, no. 1 (March 1968): 44–59.
Hodgins, Bruce, and Robert Paye, eds. *Canadian History Since Confederation: Essays and Interpretations*. Georgetown, Ont.: Irwin-Dorsey, 1972.
Hopkins, J. Castell. "Historical Sketch of the Montreal Star." *The Canadian Annual Review of Public Affairs, Special Historical Supplement*, 1910. Toronto: The Canadian Review Co, 1911.
– "A Review of Canadian Journalism." In *Canada: An Encyclopaedia of the Country*, edited by J. Castell Hopkins, 220–34. Toronto: Linscott Publishing, 1899.
Hopkins, J. Castell, ed. *Canada: An Encyclopaedia of the Country*. Toronto: Linscott Publishing, 1899.
– *Empire Club Speeches*. Toronto: William Briggs, 1906.
"How Toronto Dailies Handle Agency Commissions." CPP (January 1913): 64.
Humphries, C.W. "The Sources of Ontario 'Progressive' Conservatives, 1900–1914." *Canadian Historical Association Reports 1967*, 119–21.
Hutt, Allen. *The Changing Newspaper: Typographic Trends in Britain and America 1622–1972*. London: Gordon Fraser, 1973.
"Important Merger at Galt." CPP (August 1912): 54.

"Increasing the Value of Advertising Space." *CPP* (January 1909): 12.

Innis, Harold. *The Bias of Communication.* Toronto: University of Toronto Press, 1973.

- *The Press, A Neglected Factor in the Economic History of the Twentieth Century.* New York: AMS Press, 1949.

"Is the Coloured Comic Supplement a Desirable Feature for Canadian Newspapers?" *CPP* (July 1914): 4.

"Is the Editorial Page Necessary?" *CPP* (May 1909): 32.

Jackel, Susan. "First Days, Fighting Days: Prairie Presswomen and Suffrage Activism, 1906–1916." In *First Days, Fighting Days: Women in Manitoba History,* edited by Mary Kinnear, 53–75. Regina: Canadian Plains Research Centre, University of Regina, 1987.

Kealey, Gregory. *Toronto Workers Respond to Industrial Capitalism 1867–1892.* Toronto: Toronto: University of Toronto Press, 1980.

- "Work Control, the Labour Process, and Nineteenth Century Printers." In *On the Job: Confronting the Labour Process in Canada,* edited by Craig Heron and Robert Storey, 75–101. Montreal and Kingston: McGill-Queen's University Press, 1986.

Kealey, Gregory S., and Peter Warrian, eds. *Essays in Working Class History.* Toronto: McClelland and Stewart, 1976.

Kesterton, W.H. *History of Journalism in Canada.* Toronto: Macmillan, 1978.

Kinnear, Mary, ed. *First Days, Fighting Days: Women in Manitoba History.* Regina: Canadian Plains Research Centre, University of Regina, 1987.

Lamb, Bessie. "From 'Tickler' to 'Telegram': Notes on Early Vancouver Newspapers." *British Columbia Historical Quarterly.* 9 (1945): 174–99.

Latta, Sam J., "A Clean Front Page." *CPP* (February 1910): 23.

Lee, Alfred M. *The Daily Newspaper in America: The Evolution of a Social Instrument.* New York: Macmillan, 1937.

Lee, Alan J. *The Origins of the Popular Press 1855–1914.* London: Croom Helm, 1980.

"Let All Join Hands." *CPP* (July 1912): 60.

"The Local Paper as a Factor in the Development of the Town." *CPP* (September 1909): 17.

Livesay, J.F.B. *The Making of a Canadian.* Toronto: Ryerson Press, 1947.

Loveridge, D.M. *A Historical Directory of Manitoba Newspapers 1858–1978.* Winnipeg: University of Manitoba Press, 1981.

Lowe, Graham S. "The Administrative Revolution in the Canadian Office: An Overview." In *Essays in Canadian Business History,* edited by Tom Traves, 114–33. Toronto: McClelland and Stewart, 1984. Lyon, Stewart. "Shall the Editor or the Business Manager Reign?" *CPP,* July 1916): 17–18.

McCalla, Douglas. "An Introduction to the Nineteenth-Century Business World." In *Essays in Canadian Business History,* edited by Tom Traves, 13–23. Toronto: McClelland and Stewart, 1984.

McClelland, C.P. "Press Memories of Halifax," *Dalhousie Review* 23 (January 1944): 426–27.

Macdonald, Christine. *Historical Directory of Saskatchewan Newspapers 1878–1950*. Saskatoon: Office of the University Archives, University of Saskatchewan, 1951.

McDougall, Gordon M. "Canadian Manufactured Commodity Output, 1870–1915." *Canadian Journal of Economics* 4 (1971): 21–36.

"McInnis Papers Bought by Regina 'Province.'" CPP (January 1914): 53.

McGregor, D.A. "Adventures of Vancouver Newspapers: 1892–1926." *British Columbia Historical Quarterly* 10 (April 1946): 89–142.

Mackay, J.F. "Journalism," CPP 12 April 1903, 4.

McNaught, Carlton. *Canada Gets the News*. Toronto: Ryerson Press, 1940.

March, William. *Red Line: The Chronicle-Herald and The Mail-Star 1875–1954*. Halifax: Chebucto Agencies, 1986.

"Merger of Montreal Herald and Telegraph." CPP (June 1913): 75.

Miliband, Ralph. *The State in Capitalist Society: The Analysis of the Western System of Power*. London: Quartet Books, 1973.

Miller, Orlo. *A Century of Western Ontario: The Story of London, "The Free Press," and Western Ontario, 1849–1949*. Westport, CT: Greenwood Press, 1949.

"Montreal Herald Reorganized – 'News' Out." CPP (June 1914): 55.

"Montreal Herald Transferred." CPP (November 1917): 24.

"Montreal Newspaper War on Again." CPP (April 1914): 65.

The Montreal Star: One Hundred Years of Growth, Turmoil and Change, 1869–1969. Montreal: Montreal Star, 16 January 1969.

Morgan, Henry James, ed. *The Canadian Men and Women of the Times: A Handbook of Canadian Biography*. Toronto: William Briggs, 1898.

– *Canadian Men and Women of the Time*. Toronto: William Briggs, 1912.

"Mr Pattullo's Success." CPP (November 1898): 7.

Murray, John. *A Story of the Telegraph*. Montreal: Lovell, 1905.

Naylor, Tom. *The History of Canadian Business 1867–1914*. Vol. 2: *Industrial Development*. Toronto: James Lorimer, 1975.

Nelles, H.V. *The Politics of Development: Forests, Mines and Hydro-Electric Power in Ontario, 1849–1941*. Toronto: Macmillan, 1974.

Nelson, John. "The Tomb of the Profits." CPP (July 1911): 29.

"The News and Its Promoters," CPP (January 1903): 5

"Newspaper Amalgamation." CPP (January 1917): 28.

"The Newspaper Situation in Canada as Affected by Shortage of Paper, High Prices and Postage Rates." CPP (May 1900): 1–3.

"Newspapermen Elected to Municipal Offices." CPP (February 1914): 68.

Nichol, W.C. "Newspapers from a Business Point of View." CPP (December 1901): 10–11.

Nichols, M.E. (CP): *The Story of the Canadian Press*. Toronto: Ryerson Press, 1948.

"Niagara Falls Paper Explains Why Amalgamation Came About." *CPP* (May 1918): 18.
"No More Newspapers Needed." *CPP* (August 1914): 61.
"N.W. Ayer & Son's Directory." *CPP* (June 1918): 30.
"Organization and the Labor Question." *CPP* (May 1912): 47.
Oxley, J. Macdonald. "What the University Can Do for the Journalist." In *Journalism and the University*, edited by John R. Bone. Toronto: Copp Clark, 1903.
Page, Robert J.D. "Canada and the Imperial Idea in the Boer War Years." *Journal of Canadian Studies* 5, no. 1 (1970): 33–49.
– "The Canadian Response to the 'Imperial' Idea during the Boer War Years." In *Canadian History Since Confederation: Essays and Interpretations*, edited by Bruce Hodgins and Robert Page, 291–333. Georgetown, Ont.: Irwin-Dorsey, 1972.
– "The Impact of the Boer War on the Canadian General Election of 1900 in Ontario." MA thesis, Queen's University, 1964.
Palmer, Bryan. "Class, Conception and Conflict: The Thirst for Efficiency, Managerial Views of Labor and the Working Class Rebellion, 1903–1922." *Review of Radical Political Economics* 7 (1975). 31–49.
Parker, C.W., ed. *Who's Who in Western Canada*. Vancouver: Canadian Press Association, 1911.
Pelletier, Jean-Guy. "La presse canadienne-française et la guerre des Boers." *Recherches sociographiques* 4, no. 3 (1963): 337–50.
Pense, E.J.B. "Character and Position of the Canadian Press." In *Canada: An Encyclopaedia of the Country*, edited by J. Castell Hopkins, vol. 5, 191–5. Toronto: Linscott Publishing, 1899.
– "Journalism in Canada." In *Empire Club Speeches*, edited by J. Castell Hopkins, 213–18. Toronto: William Briggs, 1906.
Piva, Michael J., ed. *A History of Ontario: Selected Readings*. Toronto: Copp Clark Pitman, 1988.
"Poisoned Wells of Truth." *The Grain Grower's Guide* (12 October 1912): 10.
"The Powers Behind the Press." *CPP* (May 1918): 33.
Porter, Glenn, and Robert D. Cuff, eds. *Enterprise and National Development: Essays in Canadian Business and Economic History*. Toronto: Hakkert, 1973.
Porter, John. *The Vertical Mosaic: An Analysis of Social Class and Power in Canada*. Toronto: University of Toronto Press, 1965.
"Postmaster-General Admits Post Office Department Is Seriously Considering Increase in Rate on Newspapers." *CPP* (May 1913): 67.
Poulton, Ron. *The Paper Tyrant: John Ross Robertson of the Toronto Telegram*. Toronto: Clarke, Irwin, 1971.
Presbrey, Frank. *The History and Development of Advertising*. Garden City, NJ: Doubleday, 1929.
"Press Independence." *CPP* (August 1917): 34.

Preston, W.T.R. *My Generation of Politics and Politicians.* Toronto: D.A. Rose, 1937.
"Profile of R.C. Matthews." *CPP* (June 1910): 12; (July 1910): 1.
"Publishers East and West Gather in the Money," *CPP* (May 1916): 29.
Rawlyk, G.A. "Nova Scotia Regional Protest, 1867–1967." In *Canadian History Since Confederation: Essays and Interpretations,* edited by Bruce Hodgins and Robert Page, 209–24. Georgetown, Ont.: Irwin-Dorset, 1972.
"The Relation of the Press to National Life." *CPP* (December 1909): 42.
Rhodes, David Berkeley. "*The Star* and the New Radicalism." MA thesis, University of Toronto, 1955.
Roberts, Leslie. *These Be Your Gods.* Toronto: Musson, 1929.
Roberts, Wayne. "The Last Artisans: Toronto Printers, 1896–1914." In *Essays in Working Class History,* edited by Gregory S. Kealey and Peter Warrian, 125–42. Toronto: McClelland and Stewart, 1976.
Robin, Martin. *The Rush for Spoils: The Company Province 1871–1933* Toronto: McClelland and Stewart, 1972.
Rogers, Jason. *Newspaper Building: Application to Efficiency to Editing, to Mechanical Production, to Circulation and Advertising With Cost Finding Methods Office Forms and Systems.* New York: Harper and Brothers, 1918.
Ross, A.H.D. *Ottawa: Past and Present.* Toronto: Musson, 1927.
Ross, P.D. "Cooperation among Local Publishers." *CPP* (April 1895): 4.
– "Increasing Prices under Heavier Expenses." *CPP* (May 1900): 12.
– *Retrospects of a Newspaper Person.* Toronto: Oxford University Press, 1931.
"Rossland Miner Says Farewell." *CPP* (December 1918): 27.
Rumilly, Robert. *Histoire de Montréal.* Vol. 3. Montréal: Fides, 1972.
Russell, Victor L., ed. *Forging a Consensus: Historical Essays on Toronto.* Toronto: University of Toronto Press, 1984.
Rutherford, Paul. *A Victorian Authority: The Daily Press in Late Nineteenth-Century Canada.* Toronto: University of Toronto Press, 1982.
– "Introduction." In *Saving the Canadian City: The First Phase 1820–1920,* edited by Paul Rutherford. Toronto: University of Toronto Press, 1974.
– *The Making of the Canadian Media.* Toronto: McGraw-Hill Ryerson, 1978.
– "The People's Press: The Emergence of the New Journalism in Canada, 1869–99." *Canadian Historical Review.* 56 (June 1975): 169–91.
– "The Western Press and Regionalism 1870–1896." *Canadian Historical Review* 52 (September 1971): 287–305.
– "Tomorrow's Metropolis: The Urban Reform Movement in Canada, 1880–1920." In *The Canadian City: Essays in Urban History,* edited by Gilbert A. Stelter and Alan F.J. Artibise. Toronto: McClelland and Stewart, 1977.
Rutherford, Paul, ed. *Saving the Canadian City: The First Phase 1820–1920.* Toronto: University of Toronto Press, 1974.
Salter, Liora, ed. *Communication Studies in Canada.* Toronto: Butterworths, 1981.

Sandwell, B.K. "Why Newspapers Are Unreadable." *The University Magazine* (1916): 171–82.
- "The Millionaires Did Not Love the Publisher of the *Star.*" *Saturday Night* 63, no. 32 (15 May 1948): 19.
Schofield, F.H. *The Story of Manitoba*. Vols. 2, 3. Winnipeg: N.p. 1913.
Scott, C.P., "On Journalism," in *C.P. Scott 1846–1932: The Making of the "Manchester Guardian."* London: Frederick Muller Ltd., 1941. 160–1.
Schudson, Michael. *Discovering the News: A Social History of American Newspapers*. New York: Basic Books, 1978.
"Settlement Made in the Montreal *Herald* Case." CPP (February 1919): 31.
"A Shopping Festival that Proved a Big Success." CPP (January 1914): 68.
Siebert, Fred S., Theodore Peterson, and Wilbur Schramm. *Four Theories of the Press*. Urbana, IL: University of Illinois Press, 1956.
"Signs of Success of Campaign Against 'Dollar Dailies.'" CPP (January 1916): 26.
Simpson, Jeffrey. *Spoils of Power: The Politics of Patronage*. Toronto: Harper and Collins, 1988.
Skelton, Oscar Douglas. *Life and Letters of Sir Wilfrid Laurier*. Vol. 2. Toronto: Oxford University Press, 1921.
Smith, D. "The Business Management of a Newspaper." CPP (September 1911): 56.
Smith, I. Norman. *The Journal Men: P.D. Ross, E. Norman Smith and Grattan O'Leary of The Ottawa Journal: Three Great Canadian Newspapermen and the Tradition They Created*. Toronto: McClelland and Stewart, 1974.
"A Snare and a Delusion." CPP (May 1913): 68.
Somerville, R.S. "The Future of the Reporter." CPP (May 1918, 17.
Spalding, G.L. "The Toronto Daily Star as a Liberal advocate, 1899–1911." MA thesis, University of Toronto, 1954.
"Split Developing in Canadian Press Association." CPP (July 1916): 31.
Stainsby, Donald. "British Columbia: Journalistic Graveyard." *British Columbia Library Quarterly* 22 (January 1959): 3–11.
"Standard Contracts for Recognized Agents." CPP (April 1914): 69.
"Standardizing Circulation Records." CPP (July 1914): 61.
Steele, C. Frank. *Prairie Editor: The Life and Times of Buchanan of Lethbridge*. Toronto: Ryerson Press, 1961.
Stelter, Gilbert A., and Alan F.J. Artibise, eds. *The Canadian City: Essays in Urban History*. Toronto: McClelland and Stewart, 1977.
Stephenson, Harry Edward, and Carlton McNaught. *The Story of Advertising in Canada: A Chronicle of Fifty Years*. Toronto: Ryerson Press, 1940.
Stevens, Paul Douglas. "Laurier and the Liberal Party in Ontario, 1887–1911." MA thesis, University of Toronto, 1966.
Stevens, Paul, and J.T. Saywell, eds. *The 1911 General Election: A Study in*

Canadian Politics. Toronto: Copp Clark, 1970.
Stewart, Gordon T. *The Origins of Canadian Politics: A Comparative Approach*. Vancouver: University of British Columbia, 1986.
Strasser, Susan. *Satisfaction Guaranteed: The Making of the American Mass Market*. New York: Pantheon Books, 1989.
Strathern, Gloria. *Alberta Newspapers 1880–1908: An Historical Directory*, edmonton: University of Alberta Press, 1988.
"Superiority of Local Papers over Big City Dailies." *CPP* (March 1914): 63.
"Survey of the Field." *CPP* (June 1913): 57.
Sutherland, Robb. "How Our Circulation Doubled in Twelve Months." *CPP* (February 1910): 33.
Taunton, W.D. "The Man Behind the Halifax Herald." *CPP* (November 1911): 38.
Taylor, L.D. "Advertising the Real Backbone of the Business." *CPP* (June 1918): 13.
Thomas, L.H. *The Liberal Party in Alberta*. Toronto: University of Toronto Press, 1959.
Thompson, John Herd. *The Harvest of War: The Prairie West 1914–1918*. Toronto: McClelland and Stewart, 1978.
"To What Extent Is a Newspaper Responsible for the Publication of Fraudulent and Objectionable Advertising?'" *CPP* (August 1913): 64–5.
"Toronto Publishers and the A.C.A. War – to a Finish." *CPP* (March 1917): 31.
"Toronto's Evening Papers." *CPP* (April 1903): 4.
Traves, Tom. *The State and Enterprise: Canadian Manufacturers and the Federal Government, 1917–1931*. Toronto: University of Toronto Press, c. 1979.
Traves, Tom, ed. *Essays in Canadian Business History*. Toronto: McClelland and Stewart, 1984.
"A Unique Statement of City Circulation." *CPP* (July 1914): 66–7.
"Uneconomic Publishing." *CPP* (September 1916): 43.
"Value of a Publisher's Union." *CPP* (June 1901): 22.
Villard, Oscar Garrison. *The Disappearing Daily: Chapters in American Newspaper Evolution*. Frankfurt, NY: Books for Libraries Press, 1969.
Waddell, W.S. "Frank Oliver and the Bulletin." *Alberta Historical Review* (Summer 1957): 7–12.
Waite, P.B. *The Life and Times of Confederation 1864–1867: Politics, Newspaper, and the Union of British North America*. Toronto: University of Toronto Press, 1967.
Walkom, Thomas Laurence. "The Daily Newspaper Industry in Ontario's Developing Capitalist Industry 1871–1911." Ph.D thesis, University of Toronto, 1983.
Wallace, W.S. "The Journalist in Canadian Politics: A Retrospective." *The*

Canadian Historical Review 22 (March 1941): 14–24
Ward, Norman. "Davin and the Founding of the Leader." *Saskatchewan History* 6 (1953): 13–16.
– "The Press and Patronage: an Exploratory Operation." In *The Political Process in Canada*, edited by James H. Atchison, 3–16. Toronto: University of Toronto Press, 1963.
Warskett, George. "The Information Economy in Late Capitalism". In *Communication Studies in Canada*, edited by Liora Salter, 178–95. Toronto: Butterworths, 1981.
– "Elitism and the Corporate Ideal: Businessmen and Boosters in Canadian Civic Reform, 1890–1920." In *The Consolidation of Capitalism 1896–1929*, edited by Michael S. Cross and Gregory S. Kealey, 143–66. Toronto: McClelland and Stewart, 1983.
– "From Land Assembly to Social Maturity: The Suburban Life of Westdale (Hamilton), Ontario, 1911–1951." In *A History of Ontario: Selected Readings*, edited by Michael J. Piva, 214–41. Toronto: Copp Clark Pitman, 1988.
"Ways Canadian Publishers Use to Sell Space." *CPP* (September 1915): 33.
"W.C.P.A. Holds Annual Meeting at Head of Great Lakes." *CPP* (September 1913): 49.
"What C.P. News Costs." *CPP* (April 1917): 10.
White, R.S., "Newspapers of the Past and Present." *CPP* (June 1905): 10.
"Who Owns the Newspapers" *CPP* (August 1917): 36.
"Who Owns the Press of Canada?" *CPP* (February 1914): 32.
"Why Western Canada Wants Better News Service." *CPP* (April 1917): 23–7.
Williams, Edward. "Review of Newspaper Changes in Vancouver." *CPP* (May 1915): 33.
Williams, Raymond. "The Press and Popular Culture: An Historical Perspective." In *Newspaper History: From the Seventeenth Century to the Present Day*, edited by George Boyce et al. London: Constable, 1978.
Willison, John S. "Journalism and Public Life in Canada." *The Canadian Magazine* 5 (October 1905): 554–8.
– "A Lecture on Journalism." *CPP* (January 1900): 4.
– *Reminiscences Personal and Political.* Toronto: McClelland and Stewart, 1919.
"Winnipeg Free Press Out of Politics." *CPP* (October 1917): 29.
"Winnipeg 'Free Press' Replies to 'Tell-Tale Figures' Editorial." *CPP* (April 1913): 4.
Woods, Shirley E. *Ottawa: The Capital of Canada.* Toronto: Doubleday, 1980.
"The Year 1918 in Review." *CPP* (March 1919): 31.
Young, Brian J. *George-Etienne Cartier: Montreal Bourgeois.* Kingston: McGill-Queen's University Press, 1981.
– *Promoters and Politicians: The North-Shore Railways in the History of Quebec 1854–85.* Toronto: University of Toronto Press, 1978.

Young, Scott, and Astrid Young. *Silent Frank Cochrane: The North's First Great Politician.* Toronto: Macmillan, 1973.

Zerker, Sally. *The Rise and Fall of the Toronto Typographical Union 1832–1972: A Case Study of Foreign Domination.* Toronto: University of Toronto Press, 1982.

"The Zone System Alone Inadequate." *CPP* (May 1913): 67.

Index

Acadian Recorder, 120
Acland, F.A., 15, 46
advertising, 5–7, 10, 14, 16, 52–69, 78, 83–4, 86, 88, 120, 157–8, 160; ad agencies, 61, 68, 94, 97–9; brand- name, 58, 60; as bribery, 152; and business/political coalitions, 125; Canadian Newspapers Ltd, 90; circulation and, 28, 56, 57; civic boosterism and, 65–7; and "clubbing," 72, 73; coloured, 27; and comic strips, 20; concept, 68–9; CPA and, 40–1; decline in, 77, 85, 119; display, introduction of, 59; editorial and, 11–12, 21, 47–8, 62, 63–5; features and, 29; fraudulent or questionable, 62–3, 79; listing of, 18; mail-order, 70, 72, 75; and out-of-town markets, 70; patronage, 108, 109, 110, 121; positioning of, 16–17, 18, 48, 49–50, 63; postal rates and, 74, 77; production of, 25–6; promotion department, 61; railway, 144; rates, 57, 59–60,

71, 93–7; revenues, 30, 57–8, 62, 123; shopping festivals, 61; special editions, 67–8
advice column, 16
Albertan, 36, 95–6
alcohol. See liquor
Allan, Hugh, 138, 159
amalgamations. See chains, concentration
Anson McKim and Co., 68, 94, 97–8. See also McKim, Anson, McKim's Newspaper Directory
anti-combines issue, 79, 100, 147. See also combines
anti-tariff issue, 79
anti-trust policies, 101
Associated Press (AP): biased, 101; controlled by CP, 100; and CPR, 130, 144–6
Association of Canadian Advertisers, 54
Association of Canadian Advertising Agencies, 61
Atkinson, Joseph, 45, 88, 126, 135; businessman, 7–8, 36–7, 43–4, 132; cheque-book journalism, 28; connections of, 126, 159; and "dumping," 73; and Liberal party, 114, 119; London

Advertiser, 91; organized labour and, 102; politically independent, 122; promotional products, 55–6; reporter, 127; Star Weekly, 29; technological innovations, 27; Toronto Star, 14, 20, 114, 117; advertising, 52, 60; circulation, 53
Atkinson family, 8
Audit Bureau of Circulation (ABC), 54

Bank of Montreal, 146, 150
Bank of Nova Scotia, 37
Bank of Ottawa, 35, 36
Bassett family, 8
Beaverbrook, Lord, 146
Beck, Adam, 153, 154
Beck, Edward, 104
Bell Telephone, 64
Bengough, J.W., 26, 50
Berthiaume, Treffle, 7–8
Bilkey, Paul, 113
Black, Robson, 12–13
Blackadar, Charles, 120
Board of Commerce, 101
Boer War, 16–17, 19, 28, 78, 124; and establishment of CAP, 101
Bone, John R., 14, 43
boosterism, 65–8, 151

Booth, J.R., 90
Borden, Frederick, 155
Borden, Robert, 112, 113, 123, 130
Borden government, 77, 111, 120
Bostock, Hewitt, 36, 127
Bowell, Mackenzie, 107, 111
Brantford: newspaper market, 24, 91–2
Brantford *Courier*, 87
Brantford *Expositor*, 32, 53
bribery, 146, 152. *See also* patronage
Brierley, James S., 14; *Herald*, 44, 78, 80; Hugh Graham and, 81; launching French-language daily, 35; merger with *Witness*, 79; patronage contracts, 110
Britain. *See* Great Britain
Brown, George, 7, 108; editorials of, 4; ideals of, 10–11, 50–1; legacy of, 49; and organized labour, 102
Buchanan, W.A., 35–6, 45, 65; appointed to Senate, 111; connections of, 159; MP, 107
Buckingham, William, 126
Bunting, Mr, 143
business manager, rise of, 39–51, 55, 158
business news, 17, 80
"Buster Brown" comic strip, 20

Cahan, C.H., 111
Calgary: Canadian Newspapers Ltd, 90; censorship of news in, 66; and John J. Young, 128; newspaper market, 24, 32, 83–4; pricefixing, 95–6, 99; and Southams, 33–4, 160. *See also* separate newspaper entries

Calgary *Herald*, 83–4; administration of, 27, 35, 42–3, 47–8; advertising, 60, 61, 64; circulation, 29–30, 56, 95–6; and Conservative party, 113; and CP Tel, 145; editorial position and influence, 64–5, 118, 151; J.H. Woods, 36, 128; John J. Young, 128; railways, 138, 144; and real estate market, 33–4; Southam publication, 42, 64–5, 89, 90, 91; special edition, 67
Calgary *News*, 35, 36, 83
Calgary *News-Advertiser*, 83, 84, 87
Calgary *News-Telegram*, 67, 83, 95–6
Cameron, John, 19, 114
Cameron, William, 10
Canada Atlantic railway, 72
Canada Life, 149
Canada Permanent, 130
Canadian (Calgary *News-Advertiser*), 84
Canadian Associated Press (CAP), 78, 101
Canadian Bank of Commerce, 142
Canadian Daily Newspaper Association (CDNA), 103, 159
Canadian General Electric, 37, 147
Canadian Manufacturer's Association (CMA), 54
Canadian National Exhibition, 63–4
Canadian Newspapers Ltd, 89, 90
Canadian Pacific Railway (CPR), 149; AP franchise, 130; Calgary *Herald*, 61; *Globe*, 108; Montreal *Gazette*, 150; newspaper circulation by, 56, 72, 75, 82; political power of, 138–46; Vancouver *Province*, 36, 127
Canadian Pacific Railway Telegraph Company (CPR Tel), 100
Canadian Press (CP), 82, 99–102, 104, 122–3, 159
Canadian Press Association, 146
Canadian Printer and Publisher (*CPP*), 41, 66, 67; concerns of: advertising, 62, 63, 64, 75, 144; chains, 91–2; circulation, 54, 55, 56; CPA, 65, 104; journalism, 19–20, 50–1; political appointments, 112; railways, 144; role of newspaper, 13; vested interests, 132, 148; volume of newspapers, 84–6
Canadian Publishers' Association (CPA), 10, 103–4, 159; advertising, 61, 62–3; annual conventions: 54, 65, 72–4, 76, 147; CDNA formed, 103, 159; changed focus of, 40–1; corporate influence, 147; dailies and, 73–4, 75; daily publishers and, 98; "dumping," 72–3; editorial page, 15; and Montreal *Star*, 76; pricefixing, 93; subscription rates, 99; wartime economy, 85
Carey, William, 89
Carrell, Frank, 132
cartels: advertising, 93; news, 99–104
cartoons, 26, 55. *See also* comics
Cataract company, 153
chains, newspaper, 6, 88–91, 160. *See also* Southam Press

Channell, L.S., 76
Charlesworth, Hector, 44, 122
Chatham *Evening Banner*, 53
cheque-book journalism, 28
children's features, 29, 39, 157
circulation, 36, 47-8; Boer War coverage and, 28; contests, 56-7, 79, 83, 104; dollar dailies and, 70-6; features and, 28-9; figures, 5, 52-7; government/party subscriptions, 125; home delivery, 63; increased by necessity, 26, 30; market saturation, 24; political independence and, 120; pricefixing and, 96; promoting, 16, 18, 29-30, 52-7, 78-9, 157, 160; special editions, 67; wars, 75, 78-9, 79-80, 83-4. See also subscriptions
city desk men, 8
civic boosterism, 65-8, 151
"civic populism," 10, 152
civil service patronage appointments, 111-12, 125
Clark, Gregory, 45
Clarke, Charles, 21-2
"clubbing," 72
CNR Telegraph, 145
coalitions, business/political, 125-31
Cochrane, Francis (Frank), 133; politician, 50, 107, 132; Toronto *News*, 50, 108, 148; Tory takeover, 109
Cody, Canon, 13
collusion, 70-92
Colquhoun, A.H.U., 11, 78
combines, 94, 103, 104; anti-combines issue, 79, 100, 147
comics, 16, 20, 29, 77. See

also cartoons
competition and collusion, 70-92
composing room. *See* typesetting
concentration, newspaper, 93-105; amalgamations, 84-7, 147; chains, 6, 88-91, 160
conscription debate, 88, 114
Conservative party, 115-16; Arthur Meighen, 119; bribery by, 123; and CPR, 138; "dumping" by, 73; Hugh Graham, 50; and hydro issue, 153; influence of, 44, 112-14; newspaper interests of, 81, 109, 125, 139, 142; organs of, 86, 135, Calgary *Herald*, 118, Hamilton *Spectator*, 117, *Mail and Empire*, 123, Ottawa *Citizen*, 117, Ottawa *Journal*, 126, Toronto *Empire*, 38, 122, Toronto *News*, 109, Winnipeg *Free Press*, 140, Winnipeg *Telegram*, 128-9, 130; patronage, 109, 110, 120-1; press bureau, 111; railway issue, 130; Southams, 119; syndicate, 38, 137, and *Globe*, 108; W. Sanford Evans, 128, 130; William Dennis, 119-20
contests, circulation-boosting. *See* circulation
copy editor, 8
copywriting, 68. *See also* advertising
corporatization of press, 6
cost-accounting, 41
Cox, George: and CPR, 141; estate of, 148; financial interests of, 133, 142, 149; Toronto

Star, 43-4, *Globe* takeover, 37, 108, 126, 159, Liberal syndicate of, 137
CP Telegraph, 145
Cranston, J.H., 20, 24, 41
crime, sensationalized, 16, 19
Crockett, J.H., 114
Crow's Nest Pass Coal Company, 67
Crow's Nest Pass Railway, 140, 141, 148
Currie, J.A., 148
customs duties, 103

Dafoe, John W., 4, 131; and CAP cartel, 101; and Clifford Sifton, 50; influence of Laurier, 113; Manitoba *Free Press* under, 45, 46, 66, 97, 135; policies and opinions of, 13, 15, 18, 49, 68, 116; tax issue, 124
Darby, W.J., 20, 55
Dartmouth *Patriot*, 109
Davey Committee (Senate Special Committee on the Mass Media), 3, 160
Davies, L.H., 138, 141
demographics, readership, 54
Dennis, William R., 135; business interests of, 36-7, 133; and Halifax *Herald*, 19, 43, 155; political connections of, 119-20, 159
department stores, 59, 60, 64, 70, 75, 88, 148
Dickson, W.H., 113
Dingman, W.S., 73
Dingman family, 84-5
dollar dailies, 25, 70-6, 77, 78, 80
double-entry accounting, 6, 156
Dougall, John R., 7, 45, 79
Douglas, W.J., 99
drama section, 17; theatre

advertising, 63, 79. *See also* entertainment coverage
Drinkwater, Charles, 143
Duluth-Minnesota railway, 140
"dumping," 72–3
Dunnville *Chronicle*, 27
Dunsmuir, Robert, 133

Eastern Townships Press Association, 98
Eaton, John, 60
Eaton, Timothy, 27, 43–4, 60, 133
Eaton's. *See* T. Eaton Company
E.B. Eddy, 60
E.D. Smith, 128
Edgar, J.D., 138, 141
editor, 8, 49, 50, 107, 127; copy editor, 8. *See also* journalists
Editor and Publisher, 18
editorial, 21–2, 50, 90, 150–1; advertising and, 60, 62, 63–5; decline of, 11, 15, 47–51, 157. *See also* journalism, journalists
Edmonton, 108; collusion among publishers in, 97; newspaper market, 24, 99, 160. *See also* separate newspaper entries
Edmonton *Bulletin*, 97
Edmonton *Journal*: and *Bulletin*, 97; and Calgary *Herald*, 95; CNR Telegraph services, 145; financial state of, 35, 109; and Southams, 42, 89; subscriptions, 99
educator, newspaper as, 10–11, 12–13, 20, 62, 74
Electrical Development Co., 149
élite, newspapers part of, 125–35
engraving processes, 27, 28, 59, 156. *See also* illustrations, photographs, printing press, production
entertainment coverage, 11, 14, 20, 21, 157; children's, 29, 39, 157; features, 10, 39, 125; sections, 17, 28; theatre advertising, 63, 79. *See also* sports news, women's features
Evans, W. Sanford, 127, 128–31, 140
expansionism, 6

"fair trade practices," 93
Family Compact, 11
features, 31, 48–9, 60, 83, 125; pioneered by Hugh Graham, 78. *See also* entertainment coverage; sports news; women's features
Ferrar, Ned, 143
festivals, shopping, 61
Fielding, W.S., 107
financial news, 17, 80
fires, coverage of, 19
Fisher, P.S., 138
Flavelle, Joseph W., 108, 126, 131, 135; business interests, 133, 142, 149, 150; Conservative connections, 114, 135; and Toronto *News*, 13, 21–2, 31, 37, 50, 53, 109, 114, 147
"Flying Post," 71–2
Ford, Arthur, 111, 113, 114
Forget, Rodolphe, 136
Fort William, 41, 85, 118
Fort William *Evening Herald*, 118
Fort William *Times-Journal*, 41
"Fourth Estate," 11
Fredericton *Daily Mail*, 109
Fredericton *Herald*, 111
freedom of press: Senate Special Committee on the Mass Media, 3
French-language dailies, 24–5, 35
Fry, W.A., 27

Galbraith, J.F., 84
Galt *Reformer*, 85
Galt *Reporter*, 85
gambling, 79
Gaven (Saskatchewan) *Prairie News*, 18
Geary, G.R., 154
Gentleman Usher of the Black Rod, 112
George, Henry, 123
Gibson, J.M., 133, 134, 153
Gooderham, George, 109, 133
Gordonsmith, Charles, 81
Graham, G.P., 107
Graham, Hugh, 31, 77–8, 80–1, 127, 135; business interests, 132; CAP, 101; competitive edge of, 159; Conservative ties, 50, 113, 114; editorial page, 15; knighted, 111, 123; and *La Presse*, 142; Montreal *Star*, 29, 32, 34, 43, 52, 76; political scheming, 119; publisher-entrepreneur, 7–8; tramways issue, 154–5
Grain Grower's Guide, 147–8
Grand Trunk Pacific Railway, 137; advertising clout of, 144; and Calgary *Herald*, 65; collusion with newspapers, 141–2, 147; "Flying Post" service, 71–2; and *Globe*, 148
Great Britain, 3, 25, 98; CAP established in London, 101
Great Northern Railway, 142
Great North-Western train service, 82
Greenshields, J.N., 142
Greenway, Thomas, 140

215   Index

Grits. *See* Liberal party
Guelph *Sentinel-Review*, 118–19
Gurney, Edward, 128, 130
Gurney, Irene, 128

Halifax: newspaper market, 23, 24, 32; tramway and hydro issue, 155. *See also* separate newspaper entries
Halifax *Chronicle*, 19, 133, 155
Halifax *Echo*, 133
Halifax *Herald*, 43, 119–20; and Conservative party, 111; financial state of, 34, 35, 37; and J.J. Stewart, 133; patronage contracts, 109; rivalling *Chronicle*, 19
Halifax *Mail*, 34, 37, 119–20
Ham, George, 143
Hamilton: hydro politics in, 153; labour, 102; newspaper market, 23, 24, 99; publishers' agreements, 95; Southams, 88, 160. *See also* separate newspaper entries
Hamilton, C.F., 48, 112, 113, 123
Hamilton *Herald*, 102, 117, 153
Hamilton *Post*, 41–2, 84
Hamilton *Spectator*, 32, 34; circulation figures, 54; city editor John Wodell, 50; competition from Toronto, 71, 102; and CPR, 143; editorial positions of, 63, 117, 124, 153; labour at, 27, 102; political independence of, 116; and railways, 144; Southam newspaper, 64–5, 89–90, 91, 118, 150, 151
Hamilton *Times*: bought by Southams, 91; demise of, 87; J.M. Gibson, 133, 153; labour and, 102; Liberal bias of, 117
Hammond, M.O., 48, 49–50, 111, 113, 123, 150
Haynes, Albert, 42
Hazen, Douglas, 114
headlines, 16–17, 19, 20, 157
Hearst, William Randolph, 18, 21
Hearst newspaper chain, 88
Herman, W.F., 104
Hewitt, W.A., 21
Hill, J.J., 142–3
Hindmarsh family, 8
Hocken, Horatio, 100
Hocken, T.C., 154
home delivery, 63
Howe, Joseph, 11
Hudson's Bay Company, 60, 84, 96, 97
human interest stories, 14–15, 16, 21
Hunter, Sam, 26, 55
hydroelectricity, 126, 147; public ownership issue, 152–4. *See also* utilities

illustrations, 17, 25, 26–7, 29, 157; cutting of illustrated sections, 48–9. *See also* engraving processes, photographs
Imrie, John, 41
information patronage, 111. *See also* patronage
interest politics, 126–7, 136–55
International Typographers' Union (ITU), 49
International Union, 102
inverted pyramid writing, 17, 21, 157
Irving, T.C., 141

Jaffray, Robert, 108, 119, 135, 149; appointed to Senate, 111; CPR and, 141; *Globe*, 37, 49, 67, 108, 126, 159, editorial positions, 50, 124; and Liberal party, 46, 123, 137; parks commissioner, 149, 150
Jennings, Bob, 99
journalism, 14, 47, 50–1, 79, 127; cheque-book, 28; and politics, 107, 126–8; yellow, 18–20. *See also* journalists
Journalism and the University, 13
journalists, 8, 13; becoming editors, 127; bribing of, 146; correspondents, 31, 78; demoralization of, 47–9; partisan newspapers and, 121–2; pensioning of, 108; politicization of, 125; power of, 147–8; unionization of, 49. *See also* editor, journalism

Kemp, A.E., 109, 133
Kent Commission (Royal Commission on Newspapers), 3, 160
King, Mackenzie, 100, 147
King, W.L.M., 107
Kingston, 24. *See also* separate newspaper entries
Kingston *British Whig*, 67–8, 76
Kingston *Standard*, 76
Kingston *Whig*, 94, 115
Kingston *Whig-Standard*, 161
knighthood, as reward, 111

labour: cost of, 26, 27–8, 30, 82; and CPA, 103; salaries, 47–8, 85, 94; and "scientific management," 39–40; shortage,

82, 85, 86; unions, 30, 49, 102, 103, 104, 127
Lanigan, George, 43
Larkin, Peter, 58, 108, 133
Laurier, Wilfrid: and Clifford Sifton, 45, 46, 139; and Conservative press, 114; and CPR, 138, 141; and Hugh Graham, 111; influence of, 4, 113; and Joseph Atkinson, 122; Manitoba *Free Press*, 110; Montreal *Herald*, 80; patronage, 106-7, 110, 120, 121; publisher, 107; separate schools issue, 124; smear campaign against, 142, *Globe*, 113, Toronto *Star*, 110, 117. *See also* Laurier government
Laurier government: and advertising revenues, 58; boom period, 58, 135, 150, 156; and Clifford Sifton, 46; defeat of, 142; *Globe*, 111; Montreal *Herald*, 31, 78, 125; Ottawa *Free Press*, 118, 125; patronage, 31, 78, 109, 111, 118, 120, 125; plot to overthrow, 119; and postal rate protest, 77; Winnipeg *Tribune*, 116. *See also* Laurier, Wilfrid
Lemieux, Rudolphe, 148
Lethbridge *Herald*, 35-6, 65-6, 85-6, 88, 89
Lethbridge *News*, 35, 42, 88
libel, 11, 40, 53
Liberal party, 110; and A.J. Magurn, 112; bribery by, 123; and Clifford Sifton, 45; coverage in *Globe*, 112; and CPR, 138, 141; hydro issue, 153; influence of,

44; and Joseph Atkinson, 119; and launch of French-language daily, 35; Manitoba *Free Press*, 45, 129, 139; Montreal *Herald*, 80, 138; newspaper interests of, 108, 119, 140; newspaper networks, 110-11, 125; organs of, 73, 86, 117, 135, 148-9; in Montreal, 81; Ottawa papers, 45, 118, 123; Prime Minister Laurier, 113, plot to overthrow, 119; pro-war position, 119; and Robert Jaffray, 46; smear campaign against, 142; syndicate of, 137; Toronto *Evening Star*, 43; Toronto *Star*, 114, 119, 122; Tory takeover in Saint John, 109; and William Dennis, 120; Winnipeg *Free Press*, 140; Winnipeg *Tribune*, 116
Liebling, A.J., 161
Lindsay, T., 152, 154
linotype, 25, 26, 36, 158; economy of, 58, 59-60, 71, 156; and CPA, 40-1; Mergenthaler, 82. *See also* production, typesetting
liquor advertisements, 62-3, 74, 79, 80
literacy, 39
literature section, 17
"living profit," 70, 93
Livingstone, Jim, 41-2
London *Advertiser*, 10, 34; collusion by, 150; competitive market of, 82; controlled by T.H. Purdom, 37-8, 133; purchased by Joseph Atkinson, 91; street railway, 153
London (England), CAP established in, 101

London *Free Press*, 34; competitive market of, 82; position on nationalization, 153; protesting postal rates, 77; running comic strip, 20; Southam interest in, 90
London *News*, 34, 82
London (Ontario): newspaper market, 23, 24, 82; served by Toronto, 71-2. *See also* separate newspaper entries
Luxton, W.F., 139
Lynch, James M., 102
Lyon, Stewart, 15-16, 48-9, 50, 150

McBride government (BC), 110
McConnell, J.R., 68
McConnell, J.W., 154, 155
McConnell family, 8
McCuish, R.G., 118
Macdonald, John A.: and CPR, 138, 139; and patronage, 106-7, 109, 115-16; Toronto *Empire*, 122
McGibbon, D. Lorne, 81, 133, 154-5
McInnis, J.K., 85
McIntyre, Duncan, 144
McKane, John, 109, 133
Mackay, J.F., 47; editorial ethics of, 64; and front-page news, 18; *Globe* business manager, 11, 48, 71
Mackenzie, William, 130, 131; financial interests, 133, 149; owner of Toronto Railway Company, 151; public ownership issue, 154; and Toronto *Star*, 135, 146-7. *See also* Mackenzie-Mann interests
Mackenzie, William Lyon, 11

Mackenzie-Mann interests, 119, 129, 130, 140, 142
McKim, Anson, 68, 94. See also Anson McKim and Co.
McKim's Newspaper Directory, 116
McKittrick, J.J., 151
Macklin, E.H., 37, 46, 55, 60
Maclean, H.J., 97
Maclean, J.B., 65, 148
Maclean, W.F. "Billy," 7-8, 31, 107, 149, 150; business interests, 127, 151; Toronto *World* under, 44, 134, and advertising as news, 64, Sunday streetcars controversy, 151
MacNab, Allan, 138
MacNutt, L.C., 111
Magee, Charles, 36
Magurn, Arnott J., 46, 50, 149; Liberal ties of, 110-11, 112
Mail Job Printing Company, 143
mail-order advertising, 70, 72, 75
The Making of a Great Newspaper (Toronto *Star* movie), 30
The Making of a Metropolitan Newspaper (Calgary *Herald* movie), 30
Malone, E.T., 133
Manchester Guardian, 11
Manitoba *Free Press* (later Winnipeg *Free Press*), 4, 33, 135; advertisements, 49, 60; circulation, 55, 56, 57, 71; Clifford Sifton, 37, 45, 46; collusion by, 96-7; and CPR, 139-40, 144, 149; editor A.J. Magurn, 112; editorial positions, 15, 66, 119; editor John W. Dafoe, 15, 131;

financial state of, 30, 34, 37, 133; and government, 110; market of, 25, 83; news column, 115; and patronage, 109-10; and pricefixing, 95, 96-7; Prime Minister Laurier, 113; railways, 139; tax issue, 123-4; technological innovations, 26; *Telegram*, 129; *Tribune*, 91; vested interests and, 148-9; and William Van Horne, 146
Mann, Donald, 154. See also Mackenzie-Mann interests
Massey, Walter, 108
Mather, John, 149
Matheson, A.J., 10-11
Medicine Hat *News*, 67
medicines, patent, 62, 63
Meighen, Arthur, 119
mergers. See chains, concentration,
Miller, Orlo, 18
Moncton *Times*, 109
Monetary Times, 155
Montreal: advertising in; Anson McKim and Co., 68, display, 59; commercialization of press, 10; illustrated books, 55; newspaper market, 23-4, 24-5, 31, 53, 56, 76-82; convention in, 55; second-class postal rate, 74; and sensationalism, 19; and Southams, 65, 89; tramway issue, 154-5; unions, 49. See also separate newspaper entries
Montreal *Evening News*, 81-2, 100
Montreal *Gazette*, 4, 34; advertising, 49; Bank of Montreal, 150; bookkeeper Hugh Graham,

43; comic strips, 20; Conservative organ, 120-1; and CPR, 143, 146, 150; Hugh Allan, 159; and Kingston market, 76; managing director E.F. Slack, 117; quality newspaper, 19; and railways, 138; R.S. White, 51; technological innovations, 26
Montreal *Herald*, 77-81; advertising, 59; afternoon publication, 25, 78, 79; assistant editor Joseph Atkinson, 43; Boer War coverage, 28; circulation, 53, 56-7, 99; civic boosterism, 66; and CPR, 138, 143, 149; D. Lorne McGibbon, 133, 154-5; Hugh Graham, 154-5; and Kingston market, 76; merger with *Telegram*, 81; party ties, 44; patronage, 110, 121, 125; profitability, 34; publisher J.S. Brierley, 14; real estate market, 33; rivalling *Star*, 78-9; sale of, 31; sensationalism, 19
Montreal *Herald-Telegram*, 81
Montreal *Mail*, 76, 77, 81-2, 82, 87, 88, 133; CPR and, 143
Montreal *News*, 77, 81, 82, 87
Montreal *Standard*, 81
Montreal *Star*, 5, 29, 32, 77-81; Boer War coverage, 16-17, 28, 124; CAP, 101; circulation, 25, 52, 53, 56, 72; "clubbing" or "dumping," 72-3; and CP, 100; and CPR, 146; dollar daily, 76; editorial page, 15; emulated in Halifax,

120; Hugh Graham, 43, 111, 142; news column, 116; patronage, 108; "penny press," 157; pioneer of popular press, 16, 17; politics of, 50, 119, Conservative, 113, 114, 116; profitability of, 30, 34, 85, 92, and paper, 27; technological innovations, 26; tramways issue, 154–5
Montreal *Telegraph*, 76, 133
Montreal Tramways Company, 154–5
Montreal *Witness*, 27, 34, 45, 77, 79–81; censoring ads, 63; circulation, 72; demise of, 92; dollar daily, 78; and *Herald*, 79; Hugh Graham, 154; John Dougall, 7
Moosomin *Spectator*, 128
Morden *Chronicle*, 84
Morgan's advertisements, 59
Mortimer Printing Company, 121
Moylan, James, 109
Mulock, William, 74; and *Globe*, 113; leading inquiry, 152; and postal rates, 12, 103; and Toronto *Star*, 108, 122
Murdoch, Rupert, 89

National Association of Managers of Newspaper Circulation, 55
National Cycle and Automobile Co., 128
nationalization of utilities, 152–5
Nelson, John, 44
networking, 127–9
news agencies, 31; AP, 100, 101, 130, 144–6; CP, 82, 99–102, 104, 122–3, 159; WAP, 99–100, 145; wire services, 21, 99–102; railway, 144–6, CNR

Telegraph, 145, CPR Tel, 100, CP Telegraph, 145
newsboys: home delivery, 63
Newspaperdom, 18
newsprint. *See* paper
New York *Journal*, 21
Niagara Falls *Record*, 87
Niagara Falls *Review*, 87
Nichol, Walter C., 7–8, 43, 117–18, 135; business interests, 36, 133; connections, 126, 159; and patronage appointments, 111; Vancouver *Province*, 32, 127
Nicholls, Frederic: financial interests, 133, 149; Sunday streetcars, 151; Toronto *Star* takeover, 37, 146–7
North American (Philadelphia), 27
Nor'Wester, 126

oligopoly, 93, 101. *See also* amalgamations, chains, newspaper
Oliver, Frank, 107
omnibus newspaper, 17
Ontario Hydro, 153, 154
Orange Sentinel, 100
O'Reilly, P., 60
Osler, E.B., 109, 133
Ottawa: alderman P.D. Ross, 128; bribery, 152; comics, 20; Liberal press bureau, 111; newsman mayor, 108; newspaper market, 23, 24, 61, 76, 87; Southam penetration of, 160, newspaper premises, 33, organized labour, 102, public ownership, 153–4, publishers' pacts, 94–5. *See also* separate newspaper entries
Ottawa, Arnprior, and Parry Sound Railway, 72
Ottawa *Citizen*, 34, 150;

advertising, 63; and bribery, 123, 152; circulation, 56, 57; and CPR, 142–4; editorial positions, 116–17, 120, 154, Conservative, 126; features, 28–9; labour costs, 27; postal rates, 77; publishers' pact, 94–5; real estate profits, 33; sale of, 31; Southam newspaper, 32, 64–5, 89–90, 91, 118
Ottawa *Free Press*, 33; absorbed by *Journal*, 85, 87, 91, 94; A.J. Magurn and Liberal press network, 110; circulation, 53; editorial positions, 118, 154; financial state of, 34, 35; patronage, 110, 125, bribery, 152; P.D. Ross, 45; publishers' pact, 94; takeover by utility, 147
Ottawa *Journal*: advertising, 60, 62; business emphasis, 48; circulation, 56; comics, 20; editorial positions, 116, 153–4, Conservative, 116, 126; features, 29; financial state of, 34, 36; merger with *Free Press*, 85, 87, 91, 94; patronage, 108; P.D. Ross, 13, 45, 127–8; promotion department, 61; publishers' pact, 94; structure, 47; technological innovations, 26; vested interests, 150
Ottawa Typographical Union, 102
Ottawa Valley Press Association, 97–8

paper: cost of, 27, 85, 86, 94, 102–3; decrease in, 25; and dollar dailies, 71; and dumping, 73;

Index

papermakers' combine, 103, 104; shortage of, 77, 119; Southam chain and, 90; supply controlled by Hugh Graham, 82
Pardoe, Avern, 30
parliamentary debates, 15
"partyism," 8, 37, 114, 122
patent medicines, advertising of, 62, 63
Patrie, La (Montreal), 32, 34
patronage, 106–24; appointments, 111–12, 123, 125; information, 111. *See also* bribery
Pattullo, Andrew, 82
Pearson, B.F., 108, 126; acquiring Maritime newspapers, 37; Inter-Colonial railway, 142; interests of, 133, 134; tramways issue, 155
Pellatt, Henry, 149, 150, 154
Pelletier, L.P., 77
"penny press," 157
Pense, E.J.B., 32, 94, 104, 115
"people's press," 125
Perley, George, 36
Perth *Expositor*, 10–11
Petrolia *Advertiser*, 64
Philadelphia *North American*, 27
photographs, 17, 157; in Boer War coverage, 28; colour, 26–7; in weekly supplements, 29. *See also* engraving processes, illustrations
populism, 134–5; "civic populism," 10, 152
Port Arthur, 85
Port Hope *Times*, 43
postal rate, 12, 70, 94, 98, 102; CPA and, 40, 103; and "dumping," 73, 74–5; Montreal *Star*, 76–7

postal service, rail, 71–2
Prairie News, 18
press, freedom. *See* freedom of press
press, printing. *See* printing press
press agencies. *See* news agencies
Press Bureau, Liberal party, 110
Presse, La (Montreal), 34, 142
press galleries, 113
pressmen, organized, 102
Preston, W.H., 111
pricefixing: of advertising rates, 97–9; and CP, 159; and CPA, 104, 159; of subscription rates, 93–7, 99
printer: as editor, publisher, 88, 126, 132
printing contracts, 88, 143–4; patronage, 109–10, 120
printing press, 25–7, 36, 78, 79–80; Cox duplex, 82; engraving processes, 27, 28, 59, 156; rotary-web, 158. *See also* production
production: costs, 71, 85, 103; graphic reproduction, 25; stereotyping, 25, 36, 82; technology and, 25–7, 158; and unionization, 30. *See also* linotype, printing press, typesetting
Progressive party, 148
promotional gimmicks, 29–30, 55–6, 78–9. *See also* circulation
promotion department, 61
Protestant newspaper, 63, 79
public interest: role of press, 10–11
public ownership, 152–5
"public utility," press as, 11

publisher: business connections of, 132–4; control of editors, 50; populist appeals of, 134
Pulitzer, Joseph, 17–18, 26
Purdom, T.H., 37–8, 133
Purdom family, 153

Quebec City: newspaper market, 23, 27
Quebec City *Telegraph*, 132

Railway Commission, 145–6, 153
railways: and business/political coalitions, 125; and circulation, 70, 71–2, 77, 78; electric (radials), 154; influence of, 159; interests of, 130; lines, 72, 82, 140, 141, 142, 148; penetration of newspaper business, 137–44, 149; street railways, 153–5; Sunday streetcars, 147, 151–2; telegraph services of, 144–6. *See also* Canadian Pacific Railway, Grand Trunk Pacific Railway
RCMP, patronage appointment to, 112
real estate market, 33–4, 150–1
Regina *Leader*, 61, 109, 128
Regina *Province*, 85
Regina *Standard*, 85
Reid, William, 133
religion: agnosticism, 74; and comic strips, 20; Protestant newspaper, 63, 79
reporters. *See* journalists
Richardson, R.L., 107, 116, 140
Riley, R.T., 129
Riordon family, 123, 133; Toronto *Empire*, 126;

Mail, 37, 119; *News*, 37, 71
Robert, E.A., 154, 155
Roberts, Leslie, 81
Robertson, John Ross, 7–8, 31, 32, 45, 127, 135, 159; business interests of, 132; and CAP, 78, 101; CP, 100; MP, 107; newspaper as business, 12, 43; organized labour, 102; Ottawa *Journal*, 128; political independence of, 115, 116; public ownership issue, 154; second-class postal rate, 74; self-made man, 44; Toronto *Star* Liberal organ, 114; Toronto *Telegram*, 29
Roblin, R.P., 129
Rockefeller, John D., 73
Rogers, Robert, 107, 130
Ross, George, 108
Ross, James, 151
Ross, P.D., 35; business interests, 133, 149, 150; business side of newspaper, 36, 43; collusion among publishers, 99; Conservative, 126; independent spirit, 45; member of élite, 135; Ottawa *Free Press*, 91, merger with *Journal*, 87; Ottawa *Journal*, 20, 26, 60, 87, 127–8; political connections, 159; positions, 13, 94, 154; publisher- entrepreneur, 7–8; reporter, 127; self-made man, 44
Rossie, Melville, 150
Rossland *Miner*, 86
Royal Commission on Newspapers (Kent Commission), 3, 160
rural newspaper markets, 70–2
Russell, David, 133, 142

St Catharines *Standard*, 61
St Catharines *Star*, 85
Saint John: newspaper market, 23–4
Saint John *Globe*, 114
Saint John *Standard*, 109
Saint John *Star*, 87, 133
Saint John *Sun*, 109, 133
Saint John *Telegram*, 109, 142
Saint John *Telegraph*, 133
Saint John *Times*, 109, 133, 142
St Thomas, Ontario, 53, 86, 88, 91–2
St Thomas *Evening Journal*, 53
St Thomas *Times-Journal*, 86
Salada Tea advertisements, 58
salaries, 47–8, 85, 94. See also labour
Sanford, Senator, 128, 137
Sarnia, Ontario, 86
Saskatoon *Phoenix*, 109
Saturday Night, 16, 151
scandal news, 16, 19
schools, separate, 123
"scientific management," 6, 39–40, 44, 156
Scott, C.P., 11
Scott, W.D., 108
Scripps newspaper chain, 88
Senate, patronage appointments to, 111, 123, 125
Senate Special Committee on the Mass Media (Davey Committee), 3, 160
sensationalism, 5, 7, 10, 14–15, 39, 78–9; increased, 11, 16, 19–20; in US press, 18
separate schools issue, 123
Sheppard, E.E., 16, 146, 151–2
Sherbrooke *Record*, 76
shopping festivals, 61

Siegfried, André, 107
Sifton, Clifford, 7–8, 108; cabinet minister, 107; investments, 133; and J.S. Willison, 122; and J.W. Dafoe, 50; knighted, 111; Liberal party, 110–11, 112; Manitoba *Free Press*, 37, 46, 109, 135, 139; patronage, 126; policy-making role, 45; political agenda, 148–9; political connections, 159; self-made man, 44; shift to news, 115; single-tax issue, 123–4; Winnipeg *Free Press*, 15, 140, 149
Sifton family, 8, 91
Simpson's advertisements, 59
Skelton, O.D., 125
Slack, E.F., 49, 117, 146
Smith, D., 41
Smith, Donald, 139, 140
Smith, E. Norman, 35, 53, 91, 118
Smith, Frank, 133, 137
Smith, Goldwin, 11–12
smoking issue, 79
Social Darwinism, 135
Soleil, Le, 27
Somerset, W.B., 129
Somerset, W.J., 46, 55
Somerville, R.S., 48
Soper, Warren Y., 147, 154
South African war. See Boer War
Southam, Bill, 144
Southam, Fred, 64–5, 95–6, 144
Southam, Harry, 37, 89; focus on entertainment, 123; Hamilton *Spectator*, 63; Ottawa *Citizen*, 28–9, 32, 63; pricefixing, 95; publishers' agreements, 94
Southam, Richard, 120
Southam, William, 88–9,

221 Index

127, 159; editorial ethics, 65; Hamilton *Spectator*, 50, 116; hydro issue, 153
Southam, Wilson, 37, 89, 91; and CPR, 143–4; focus on entertainment, 123; Ottawa *Citizen*, 28–9, 32; patronage printing contracts, 120–1
Southam Corporation, 161
Southam Press (chain), 7–8, 132–3, 135, 159; branches, 37; bribery in form of advertising, 152; Calgary *Herald*, 35, 83, 95, 128; Canada's first chain, 88–9, 160; circulation, 54, 56; *Citizen*, 31, 94; Conservative party, 113, 119; CPR, 143; editorial ethics, 64–5; Edmonton *Journal*, 42, 137; merger of Ottawa *Journal* and *Free Press*, 87; political independence, 116–17; political positions within, 118; president P.S. Fisher, 138; pricefixing, 99; printing contracts, 143–4; *Province*, 127; real estate market, 33–4, 151; vested interests, 151; *Whig-Standard*, 161; Winnipeg *Tribune*, 97
Southam Printing, 120
Spanish-American War, 28
Sparks, N.S., 36
special editions, 67
sports news, 10, 17, 28, 49, 79, 157. *See also* entertainment coverage, features
Standard Oil, 73
Star Weekly, 29
stereotyping plants, 25, 36, 82

Stewart, J.J., 133
Stewart, J.W., 133
St John, Molyneaux, 139
Stratford *Beacon*, 126
Stratford *Herald*, 73, 84
Stratford newspaper market, 86
Strathcona, Lord, 108
street railway: interests in, 147; and nationalization, 153–5; Sunday streetcars, 147, 151–2
strikes, 102
subscriptions, 55–7, 83; home delivery, 63; out-of-town, 70–4, 75, 77; patronage, 108, 110, 125; rates for, 94, 104, and pricefixing, 93, 95–6, 97; wars, 78–9. *See also* circulation
Sunday streetcars controversy, 147, 151–2
Sun Life Insurance, 45
Sutherland, Robb, 99
Sydney *Reporter*, 108–9
syndicates: Boer War coverage and, 28; of businessmen and politicians, 38; lumbermen's, 150; party, 137; public ownership issue, 152; publishers', 126, 128; Southam, 90

T. Eaton Company: advertising by, 59, 60, 75; controlling Toronto *Star*, 148; and ethics of *Globe*, 64
tariffs: anti-tariff issue, 79
Tarte brothers, 32
Taschereau Commission, 103
tax issue, 123–4
Taylor, Frederick, 40
Taylor, L.D., 46
Taylorism, 40
telegraphic news services. *See* news agencies, railways

telephones: Bell Telephone, 64; Boer War coverage, 28; nationalization of, 152. *See also* utilities
temperance, 79, 80. *See also* liquor advertisements
Templeman, William, 107
theatre advertising, 63, 79. *See also* drama section, entertainment coverage
Thompson, John, 111
tobacco issue, 79
Toronto: advertising market in, 58, 62, 63–4, 88; circulation, 52, 75, dollar dailies, 76, out-of-town, 71–2; commercialization of press, 10; dailies joining CPA, 103; display ads, 59; failure of *News*, 21; merger of *Mail* and *Empire*, 24; newsman mayor, 108; newspaper market, 4–5, 23–4, 31, 34, 44, 54, 56; organized labour, 102; pricefixing, 97; public ownership issue, 154; second-class postal rate, 74; sensationalism, 19; Southam printing, 89; unionization, 30, 49. *See also* separate newspaper entries
Toronto *Empire*, 8, 119, 133; collusion by, 99; Conservative organ, 38, 122, 137; merger with *Mail*, 15, 24, 85, 122, 126; promotional products, 55
Toronto *Evening Star*, 43
Toronto *Globe*, 4–5, 13–14, 32, 48–9, 50, 119, 135; advertising, 49–50, 58, 63, Eaton's, 60; A.J. Magurn, 110; Boer War coverage, 28; business

manager J.F. Mackay, 11, 47, 48; circulation, 56, 71–2; CPR, 138, 140–1; CP Telegraph, 145; editorial, 15–16, 64, 118–19, 124; editor John Cameron, 19; F.A. Acland, 46; financial interests, 133; front-page news, 18; George Brown, 7; George Cox, 37, 108, 126, 133, 142, 159; government pressure, 113; influence of business office, 48; and Kingston, 76; labour, 102; Liberal party, 44, 110, 112, 113, 114, 122, 137, 138, patronage contracts, 121; market expansion, 25; Montreal *Star* correspondents, 78; news column, 116; photographs, 27; profitability, 34; promotional products, 55; quality newspaper, 19; reporter Joseph Atkinson, 43; Robert Jaffray, 37, 108, 123, 126, 159; scooped by Conservative papers, 111; special editions, 67; Sunday streetcars, 151; and Tories, 44; vested interests, 148, 149, 150

Toronto Hydro, 154

Toronto Institute for the Blind, 112

Toronto *Mail*: Anson McKim and Co., 68; Boer War coverage, 28; collusion by, 99; Conservative party, 111; editorial, 15–16; merger with *Empire*, 24, 85, 122, 126; photographs, 27; political independence of, 119, 122; promotional products, 55;

Riordon family, 37

Toronto *Mail and Empire*, 31, 34; comics, 20; editor Arthur Wallis, 123; and Kingston, 76; labour, 27; pro-war, 118–19; reporter W. Sanford Evans, 128; W.J. Darby, 55

Toronto *News*, 31–2, 34, 46, 148, 149; Boer War coverage, 28; cartoons, 26; circulation, 53, 57, 71–2; "clubbing" or "dumping," 72–3; collusion by, 97, 99, 150; Conservative party, 113, 135; demise of, 21–2, 87, 88, 92, 149; editorial, 15, 50, 118–19; financial interests, 133; first dollar daily, 71; *Globe*, 114; Grand Trunk Pacific, 142; Joseph Flavelle, 13, 31, 37, 147; and Kingston, 76; linotype, 26; populist, 134; promoting, 55; Riordon family, 37; Stratford *Herald*, 73; technological innovations, 25–6; Tory takeover, 109; unionization, 30

Toronto Press Club, 13

Toronto Railway Company, 151

Toronto *Star*, 15, 32, 33, 34, 36–7, 47, 92, 149; advertising, 27, 52, 57, 60; Boer War coverage, 28; circulation, 53, 56, 102; collusion by, 97; commercialization, 12; controlling interests, 148; "dumping" by, 72–3; editorial, 118–19, 153, 154; E.E. Sheppard, 146–7; entertainment news, 21; financial interests, 133; Frederic

Nicholl, 37; George Cox, 133, 142; independent, 117; industrial edition, 67; inverted pyramid style, 21; Joseph Atkinson, 14, 20, 43–4, 45, 122; and Kingston, 76; labour, 102; Liberal party, 108, 114, 119; market expansion, 25; modern style, 20; news column, 116; patronage, 110; populist, 134; promoting Ontario, 67; promotional gimmicks, 30, 55–6; sale of, 31; sensationalist, 19; Sunday streetcars, 151–2

Toronto *Star Weekly*, 29

Toronto *Sunday World*, 29, 151

Toronto *Telegram*, 29, 32, 34, 47; Boer War coverage, 28; CAP, 101; cartoon, 26; Charles Clarke, 21; circulation, 53; CP practices, 100–1; editorial, 15; emulated in Halifax, 120; John Ross Robertson, 12, 45, 74; and Kingston, 76; labour, 102; news column, 116; patronage, 108; "penny press," 157; pioneer of popular press, 16, 17; politically independent, 116; public ownership, 154; real estate interests, 150; structure, 47–8

Toronto Typographical Union, 102

Toronto *World*, 34; ad as editorial, 63, 64; cartoons, 26; circulation, 71–2; collusion by, 97; Conservative party, 111; demise of, 44, 87; editorial, 15; exposé on vested interests, 149;

and Kingston, 76; nationalization of telephones, 152; party ties, 116; pioneer of popular press, 16, 17; Sunday streetcars, 151; *Sunday World* edition, 29, 151; W.F. Maclean, 133, 151

Tory party. *See* Conservative party

trade journals, 18

transportation interests, 159. *See also* railways

Tupper, Charles, 12, 74, 108–9, 114

typesetting, 25; introduction of linotype, 26, 158; unionization in, 30, 49, 102. *See also* linotype, production

Union government, 88, 118–19, 123, 160

unionization, 30; of journalists, 49, 127; of pressmen, 102; of typographers, 49. *See also* labour

United Kingdom. *See* Great Britain

United States: ABC, 54; anti-trust legislation, 101; Canadian newspapers resembling American, 17–18; concentration of ownership, 3, 88

utilities, 147; nationalization of, 152–5, and influencing of press, 152, 159. *See also* hydroelectricity

Vancouver: newsman mayor, 108; newspaper market, 5, 23–4, 53, 87; Southams, 89, 160. *See also* separate newspaper entries

Vancouver *Evening Journal*, 87

Vancouver *News-Advertiser*, 33, 44, 87, 100, 110

Vancouver *Province*, 34–5; circulation, 53, 54; political independence of, 117; sensationalist, 19; Southams, 32; sued by *World*, 53; Walter Nichol, 36, 127

Vancouver *Sun*, 87, 100, 109, 133

Vancouver *Times*, 87

Vancouver *World*, 32; L.D. Taylor, 46; real estate market, 33; rivalling *Province*, 19, 53; R.S. Somerville, 48

Van Horne, William, 133, 138–9, 140–1, 146

Vernon *News*, 67

Victoria *Colonist*, 110, 133, 145

wages, 47–8, 85, 94. *See also* labour

Walker, Edmund, 131

Wallis, Arthur, 123

war: conscription debate, 88, 114. *See also* Boer War, Spanish-American War, World War I

Waterloo, Ontario, 32

Watson, W.J., 64

weeklies, country: practice of "dumping" and, 72–5

West, promotion of, 66

Western Associated Press (WAP), 99–100, 145

Western Canadian Press Association, 98

Western Publishers' Association, 99

White, R.S., 20, 51, 107

White, Thomas, 4

White family, 8, 138

Whitney, James, 149, 150

Whyte, William, 131

Willison, John S., 14, 31–2, 50, 111, 112; circulation figures, 53, 54, 99; Clifford Sifton, 46; collusion by, 99; Conservative party, 112, 113, 135; CPR, 138, 140–1; editorial control over, 50; *Globe*, 44; knighted, 111; Liberal interference, 122; observations, 13, 36, 147; position on Boer War, 124; and *Telegram*, 150; Toronto *News*, 53, 114, 148; editor, 21; unbiased column, 116

Windsor newspaper market, 24

Windsor *Record*, 86

Winnipeg: newsman mayor, 108; newspaper market, 23, 24, 83, 84; Southam penetration of, 160; opening of Eaton's, 60; publishers' pacts in, 96–7; W. Sanford Evans, 130–1. *See also* Manitoba *Free Press*, separate newspaper entries

Winnipeg *Call*, 139

Winnipeg College of Music, 130

Winnipeg *Sun*, 139, 144

Winnipeg *Telegram*, 34, 37, 110; circulation, 57; demise of, 85, 87; Mackenzie-Mann interest in, 140; provincial patronage and, 110; and Southams, 91; subscription pact, 97; W. Sanford Evans, 128–30; William Mackenzie, 133

Winnipeg *Telegraph*, 83, 115

Winnipeg *Tribune*, 34, 48, 116; civic boosterism, 66; CPR and *Free Press*, *Sun*, 144; Eaton's, 60; rivalling *Free Press*, 83, 139–40; Southams, 91; subscription pact, 97

wire services. *See* news agencies
Wodell, John, 50
women's features, 10, 17, 39, 157; and advertising, 29, 60; extra staffs, 28; second-class postal rate, 77. *See also* entertainment coverage, features, sports coverage
Women Teachers Association, 20
Wood, Alfred, 147
Wood, Josiah, 133
Woods, J.H., 36, 42–3; Calgary *Herald*, 29, 83–4, 89, 95, 113, 118, 138; Conservative party, 113; Edmonton *Journal*, 137; networking, 128; pricefixing agreements, 95; railways, 138, 144; resisting political pressure, 119; and Southams, 65; World War I, 85
Woodstock *Express*, 82
Woodstock newspaper market, 86
Woodstock *Sentinel-Review*, 82
Woodstock *Times*, 82
workers. *See* labour
World (Pulitzer), 18
World War I, 5, 85, 119, 123, 160

yellow journalism, 18–20
"The Yellow Kid" comic strip, 20
Young, John J., 128